Brittany with Kids

Jane Anderson

[illegible]son

Introduction

Imagine nature created the world's finest adventure playground and handily stuck it on the northwest corner of France. That's Brittany. Both familiar and pleasingly alien in one go, it has all the vital ingredients for the kind of holiday kids will remember forever.

As Cornwall is to England, so Brittany is to France, though usually without the tourist tat. Go to a beach here and it's mostly nature in the raw. As well as the beaches (there's a whopping 2800 km of coastline to explore), there are child-orientated sailing schools, treetop adventures, Arthurian legends, fairy-tale castles, awesome standing stones, chic islands, giant lighthouses, a plethora of animal parks and aquariums and pretty villages locked in the past.

Strong in cultural identity, Brittany is often thought of as a country in its own right. It is both the end of the earth (the literal meaning of Finistère) and the beginning – the perfect start for little overseas explorers.

Globetrotting travel writer and photographer **Jane Anderson** (janeandersontravel.com) believes travel is one of the greatest gifts you can give a child and is honoured to be able to report on her experiences.

Pointe du Raz.

Franck
Elisa
Elise
Françoise
Françoise
Elodie
Elodie
Fred
Emeline
Emeline

About the book

Brittany with Kids is like a crêpe au beurre, full of good things and designed to energize. It's all about exploring this incredibly rich piece of France, and getting the best out of it for yourself and your children. There's lots of cool stuff to browse, and it's ideal for slipping into a coat pocket or glovebox for on-the-spot holiday reference. On this page you'll find useful background information on getting the most out of the book, plus some important safety advice.

Beach safety

The 'FLAGS' code by the RNLI (rnli.org.uk) is a handy checklist for staying safe at the beach:

F Find the red and yellow flags and swim between them.
L Look at the safety signs.
A Ask a lifeguard for advice.
G Get a friend to swim with you.
S Stick your hand in the air and shout for help if you get into difficulty.

Green seaweed

Brittany has seen an abnormal growth of green seaweed in a few bays over the last 30 years, linked to the increase of nutrients in the water from agricultural and urban sources. When large quantities decompose they can give off toxic gases and must be avoided. To reduce any risk involving green seaweed:

- Do not step on heaps of dried seaweed that have a whitish crust.
- Move away quickly if you detect a strong smell of rotten eggs and avoid muddy areas and the mouths of rivers and streams.
- Call 112 (European emergency number) in the event of any problem or sickness.

Blue Flag awards

These are given for one season only and are subject to change. At the time of writing, there were 20 Blue Flag beaches and seven Blue Flag marinas in Brittany (blueflag.org).

Weather, tides and cliff paths

- Consult bbc.co.uk/weather for five-day forecasts for main towns such as Roscoff, Brest or Quimper.
- Check the website tide.frbateaux.net for tidal predictions.
- Tide tables give information on local tidal range, which varies with the phases of the moon.
- Remember tides occur twice a day.
- Be careful not to get cut off by the tide when walking along the shore. Set off when the tide is on its way out and keep an eye on it.
- Make sure children playing on the beach are not in danger of the tide or waves.
- If you're going surfing, a useful website is surf-forecast.com.
- Cliffs and dunes are ecologically sensitive areas, and it is important to keep to the paths in these areas to avoid further erosion.
- Care must be taken with young children at all times on cliff paths.

Symbol key

Beaches

- Blue Flag award
- Café/bar/restaurant
- Beach shop
- Deckchairs
- Beach huts
- Water sports
- Amusement arcades
- Lifeguards on patrol (summer)
- No dogs in summer (Jun-Sep)
- Toilets nearby
- Car park nearby
- Warning! Strong currents

Campsites

- Tents
- Caravans
- Shop
- Playground
- Picnic area
- Disabled facilities
- Dogs welcome
- Beach within walking distance
- Electric hook-up
- Family bathroom
- Baby care area
- Bike hire
- Café/takeaway van
- Campfires permitted

It is up to parents to individually assess whether the information given in *Brittany with Kids* is suitable or appropriate for their children. While the author and publisher have made every effort to ensure accuracy with subjects such as activities, accommodation and food, they cannot be held responsible for any loss, injury or illness resulting from advice or information given in this book.

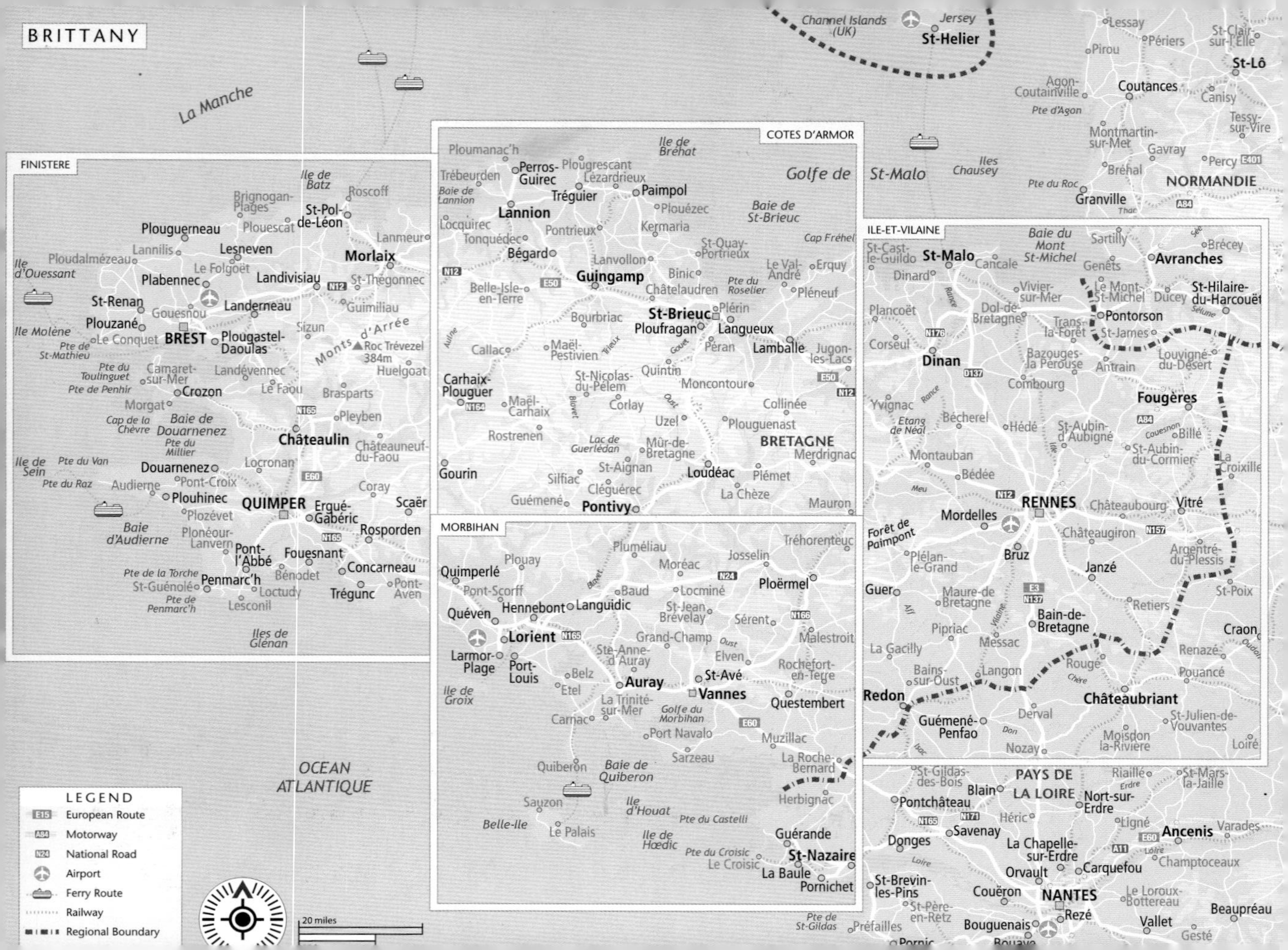

BRITTANY
FINISTERE
COTES D'ARMOR
MORBIHAN
ILE-ET-VILAINE
NORMANDIE
BRETAGNE
PAYS DE LA LOIRE
La Manche
Golfe de St-Malo
OCEAN ATLANTIQUE
Channel Islands (UK)
Jersey
St-Helier
BREST
QUIMPER
Morlaix
Châteaulin
Douarnenez
Landerneau
Landivisiau
St-Pol-de-Léon
Roscoff
Concarneau
Lannion
Guingamp
St-Brieuc
Paimpol
Tréguier
Perros-Guirec
Lamballe
Loudéac
Pontivy
Carhaix-Plouguer
Gourin
Lorient
Auray
Vannes
Ploërmel
Quimperlé
St-Nazaire
La Baule
Guérande
RENNES
St-Malo
Dinan
Fougères
Vitré
Redon
Châteaubriant
Avranches
Granville
Coutances
St-Lô
NANTES
Ancenis
Monts d'Arrée
Roc Trévezel 384m
Baie de Douarnenez
Baie d'Audierne
Baie de St-Brieuc
Baie de Quiberon
Golfe du Morbihan
Belle-Ile
Ile de Groix
Ile d'Ouessant
Ile de Sein
Ile de Batz
Ile de Bréhat
Iles de Glénan
Iles Chausey
Baie du Mont St-Michel
LEGEND
European Route
Motorway
National Road
Airport
Ferry Route
Railway
Regional Boundary
20 miles

Contents

Adventure parks & labyrinths

Breizh Park Finistère 114
Cobac Parc Ille-et-Vilaine 38
Enigmaparc Ille-et-Vilaine 42
Labyrinthe Végétal Paimpol Côtes d'Armor 81
La Récré des 3 Curés Finistère 114
Le Labyrinthe de Pont-Aven et sa Mini Ferme Finistère 119
Parc d'Attractions Odet Loisirs Finistère 114
Parc de Loisirs Bel Air Finistère 114
Peninsula Le Labyrinthe Finistère 121
Popcorn Labyrinthe Morbihan 165

Amazing one-offs

Addes storytelling in the forest, Finistère 122
Centre de Découverte du Son (Sound Discovery Centre) Côtes d'Armor 80
La Cité de la Voile (Eric Tabarly Sailing Museum) Morbihan 166
Le Village Gaulois Côtes d'Armor 76
Locronan Finistère 111
Maison des Minéraux Finistère 129
Musée de Préhistoire Morbihan 160
Musée du Loup (Wolf Museum) Finistère 130
Musée du Poète Ferrailleur (Scrap Metal Poet) Morbihan 161
Vélo Rail Ille-et-Vilaine 43

Animal & bug attractions

Branféré Park Morbihan 158
Chèvrerie du Désert Ille-et-Vilaine 40
Domaine de Menez Meur Finistère 128
Insectarium Morbihan 159
L'Abeille Vivante et la Cité des Fourmis (Living Bee and City of Ants) Morbihan 162
Le Domaine de la Bourbansais Ille-et-Vilaine 39
Parc Animalier du Quinquis Finistère 121
Parc Ornithologique de Bretagne Ille-et-Vilaine 45
Pont Scorff Zoo Morbihan 160
Zooparc de Trégomeur Côtes d'Armor 76

Aquariums & sea attractions

Aquarium du Golf Morbihan 169
Aquarium Marin de Trégastel Côtes d'Armor 76
Aquashow, Audierne Finistère 114
Ferme Marine Ille-et-Vilaine 42
Grand Aquarium de St-Malo Ille-et-Vilaine 51
Marinarium, Concarneau Ille-et-Vilaine 126
Musée de l'Amiral, Pouldreuzic Finistère 119
Musée de la Pêche, Concarneau Finistère 124
Océanopolis Finistère 116
Port Musée Finistère 114

Breathtaking beaches

Arzon Morbihan 154
Baie des Trépassés Finistère 106
Carantec Peninsula Finistère 107
Les Sables Blancs Morbihan 154
Plage de Kérel, Belle-Ile-en-Mer Morbihan 176
Pléneuf-St-Val-André Côtes d'Armor 73
Pointe de la Torche Finistère 109
St-Cast Côtes d'Armor 73
St-Lunaire Ille-et-Vilaine 33
Trez Bellec Finistère 109

Childhood rites of a Breton holiday

Discover the legends of King Arthur
Drink Breton Cola
Eat crêpes and galettes
Go sand-karting
Sail your first boat
Scale a rampart
Speak your first French words – out loud
Spot a lighthouse or two
Stay in a gîte
Wear a stripy Breton T-shirt

Fab & free

Find Merlin's Tomb in the Forest of Brocéliande, Ille-et-Vilaine 55
Go back in time and see the standing stones at Carnac, Morbihan 152
Hold a snail at the Snail Farm, Finistère 105
Picnic in the Parc du Thabor in Rennes, Ille-et-Vilaine 30
Spot a pink rabbit on the Pink Granite Coast, Côtes d'Armor 70
Take a tour of a Breton biscuit factory, Finistère 104

Take in the view at Pointe du Raz, Finistère 104
Track some mammals along the Nantes–Brest Canal 153
Visit the National Botanical Conservatory, Finistère 104
Walk the ramparts at St-Malo or Concarneau 47 & 124

History lessons

Château de Fougères Ille-et-Vilaine 37
Château de Josselin Morbihan 158
Château-Musée de Dinan Côtes d'Armor 84
Cité des Télécoms Côtes d'Armor 80
Ecomusée de St-Dégan Morbihan 162
Fort la Latte Côtes d'Armor 77
Maison des Johnnies Finistère 119
Musée de Bretagne Ille-et-Vilaine 39
Musée de la Résistance Morbihan 164
Musée de l'Ecole Rurale Finistère 132

Rainy day options

Centre de l'Imaginaire Arthurien Ille-et-Vilaine 55
Musée des Poupées (Dolls Museum) Morbihan 158
Maison de la Baie, Hillion Côtes d'Armor 81
Maison du Costume Breton Morbihan 163
Manoir de l'Automobile Ille-et-Vilaine 44
Musée de la Fraise (Strawberry Museum) Finistère 119
Musée de l'Electricité Côtes d'Armor 82
Musée des Beaux Arts Finistère 120
Musée des Phares et Balises Finistère 133
Planétarium de Bretagne Côtes d'Armor 83

Treetop fun

Arbreizh Adventure Finistère 113
Breizh Park Finistère 114
Camors Adventure Forest Camors Adventure Forest 157
Domaine du Roc Morbihan 180
Forêt Adrénaline Ille-et-Vilaine 36
Forêt Adrénaline Morbihan 157
Parc des Grand Chênes Ille-et-Vilaine 39
Parcabout, Ile de Groix Morbihan 14
Parcours Aventure le Poisson Volant Morbihan 157
Vallée de Pratmeur Morbihan 182

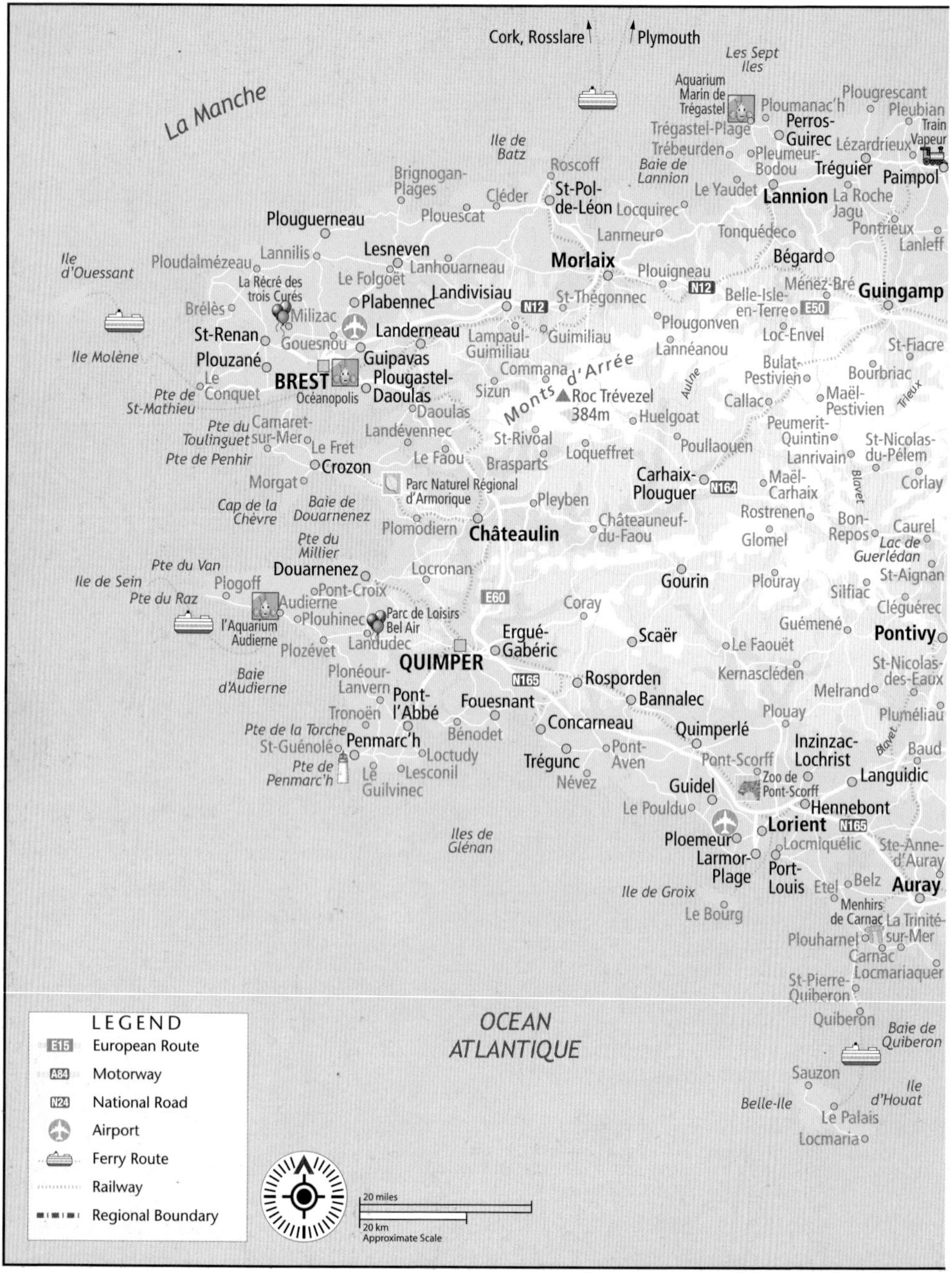
Cork, Rosslare
Plymouth
La Manche
Les Sept Iles
Aquarium Marin de Trégastel
Ploumanac'h
Plougrescant
Pleubian
Perros-Guirec
Train Vapeur
Trégastel-Plage
Trébeurden
Pleumeur-Bodou
Lézardrieux
Tréguier
Paimpol
Ile de Batz
Roscoff
Baie de Lannion
Brignogan-Plages
St-Pol-de-Léon
Le Yaudet
Lannion
La Roche Jagu
Cléder
Plouescat
Locquirec
Plouguerneau
Lanmeur
Tonquédec
Pontrieux
Lanleff
Ile d'Ouessant
Ploudalmézeau
Lannilis
Lesneven
Morlaix
Bégard
Lanhouarneau
Plouigneau
La Récré des trois Curés
Le Folgoët
N12
Ménez-Bré
Guingamp
Landivisiau
Brélès
Plabennec
St-Thégonnec
Belle-Isle-en-Terre
E50
Milizac
Plougonven
St-Renan
Landerneau
Lampaul-Guimiliau
Guimiliau
Loc-Envel
Ile Molène
Gouesnou
Lannéanou
St-Fiacre
Plouzané
Guipavas
Commana
Monts d'Arrée
Bulat-Pestivien
Bourbriac
BREST
Plougastel-Daoulas
Le Conquet
Océanopolis
Sizun
Roc Trévezel 384m
Aulne
Callac
Maël-Pestivien
Trieux
Pte de St-Mathieu
Daoulas
Huelgoat
Peumerit-Quintin
Pte du Toulinguet
Camaret-sur-Mer
Landévennec
St-Rivoal
Poullaouen
St-Nicolas-du-Pélem
Le Fret
Loqueffret
Lanrivain
Pte de Penhir
Le Faou
Brasparts
Crozon
Carhaix-Plouguer
Maël-Carhaix
Corlay
N164
Blavet
Morgat
Parc Naturel Régional d'Armorique
Cap de la Chèvre
Baie de Douarnenez
Pleyben
Rostrenen
Bon-Repos
Caurel
Plomodiern
Châteaulin
Châteauneuf-du-Faou
Lac de Guerlédan
Glomel
Pte du Millier
Pte du Van
Douarnenez
Locronan
St-Aignan
Ile de Sein
Plogoff
Pont-Croix
Gourin
Plouray
Silfiac
Pte du Raz
Audierne
E60
Coray
Cléguérec
l'Aquarium Audierne
Plouhinec
Parc de Loisirs Bel Air
Guémené
Pontivy
Ergué-Gabéric
Scaër
Landudec
Le Faouët
Plozévet
QUIMPER
St-Nicolas-des-Eaux
Baie d'Audierne
Plonéour-Lanvern
N165
Kernascléden
Rosporden
Melrand
Pont-l'Abbé
Fouesnant
Bannalec
Tronoën
Plouay
Pluméliau
Concarneau
Pte de la Torche
Quimperlé
Bénodet
Inzinzac-Lochrist
St-Guénolé
Penmarc'h
Pont-Aven
Blavet
Baud
Loctudy
Trégunc
Pont-Scorff
Pte de Penmarc'h
Le Guilvinec
Lesconil
Zoo de Pont-Scorff
Languidic
Névez
Guidel
Hennebont
Le Pouldu
Lorient
N165
Iles de Glénan
Ploemeur
Locmiquélic
Ste-Anne-d'Auray
Larmor-Plage
Port-Louis
Belz
Auray
Ile de Groix
Etel
Menhirs de Carnac
Le Bourg
La Trinité-sur-Mer
Plouharnel
Carnac
Locmariaquer
St-Pierre-Quiberon
OCEAN ATLANTIQUE
Quiberon
Baie de Quiberon
Sauzon
Ile d'Houat
Belle-Ile
Le Palais
Locmaria
LEGEND
E15 European Route
A84 Motorway
N24 National Road
Airport
Ferry Route
Railway
Regional Boundary
20 miles
20 km
Approximate Scale

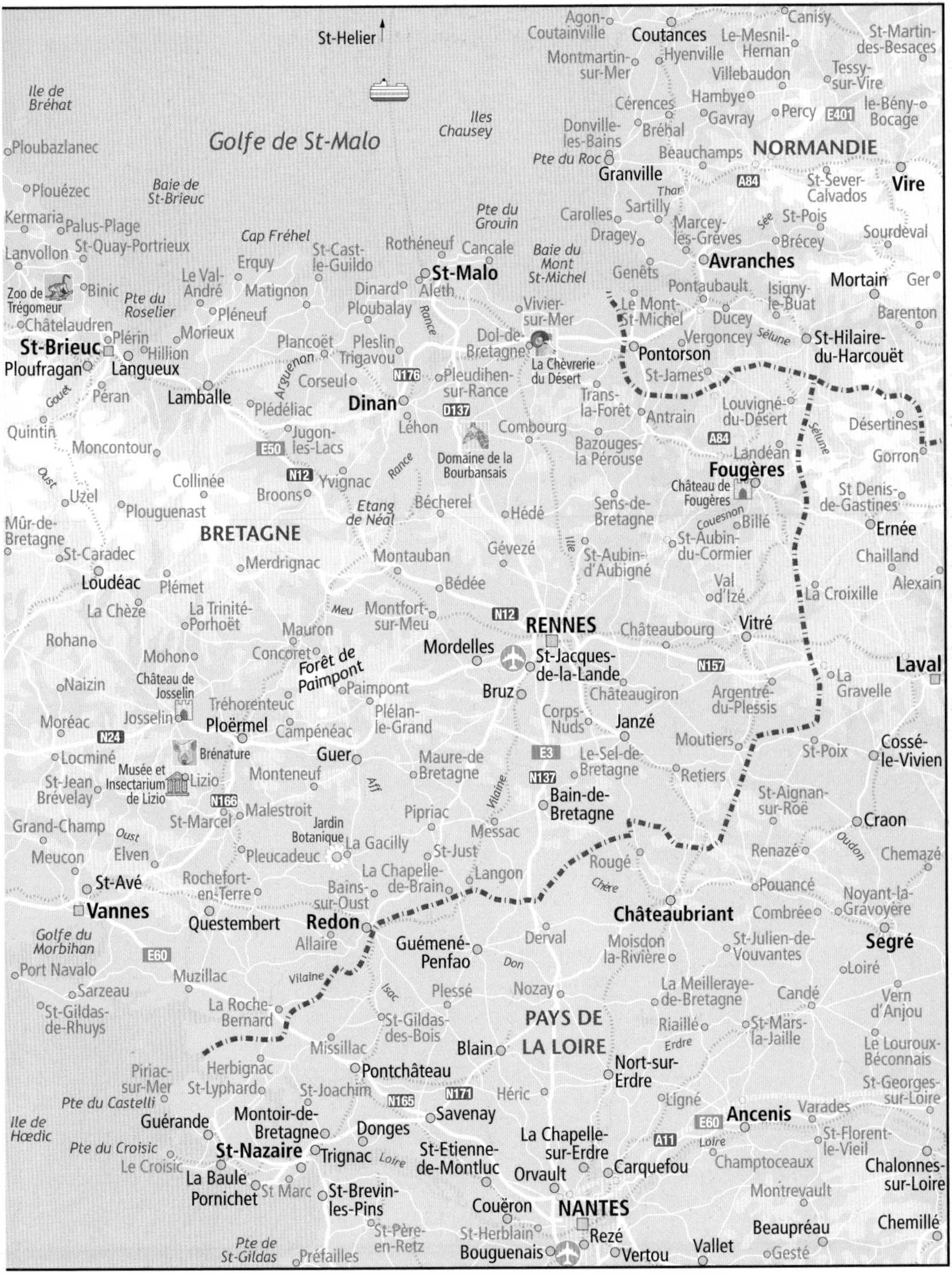

St-Helier
Agon-Coutainville
Coutances
Canisy
Le-Mesnil-Hernan
St-Martin-des-Besaces
Montmartin-sur-Mer
Hyenville
Villebaudon
Tessy-sur-Vire
Ile de Bréhat
Iles Chausey
Cérences
Hambye
Gavray
Percy
E401
le-Bény-Bocage
Golfe de St-Malo
Donville-les-Bains
Bréhal
Ploubazlanec
Pte du Roc
Beauchamps
NORMANDIE
Granville
A84
St-Sever-Calvados
Vire
Plouézec
Baie de St-Brieuc
Thar
Pte du Grouin
Carolles
Sartilly
Kermaria
Palus-Plage
Marcey-les-Grèves
Sée
St-Pois
Sourdeval
Cap Fréhel
Dragey
Brécey
Lanvollon
St-Quay-Portrieux
St-Cast-le-Guildo
Rothéneuf
Cancale
Baie du Mont St-Michel
Genêts
Avranches
Erquy
Le Val-André
Matignon
Dinard
St-Malo
Aleth
Pontaubault
Isigny-le-Buat
Mortain
Ger
Zoo de Trégomeur
Binic
Pte du Roselier
Pléneuf
Ploubalay
Rance
Vivier-sur-Mer
Le Mont-St-Michel
Ducey
Barenton
Châtelaudren
Plérin
Morieux
Plancoët
Pleslin
Dol-de-Bretagne
Vergoncey
Sélune
St-Hilaire-du-Harcouët
St-Brieuc
Hillion
Trigavou
La Chèvrerie du Désert
Pontorson
Ploufragan
Langueux
Arguenon
Corseul
N176
Pleudihen-sur-Rance
St-James
Gouet
Péran
Lamballe
Plédéliac
Dinan
D137
Trans-la-Forêt
Antrain
Louvigné-du-Désert
Désertines
Quintin
Jugon-les-Lacs
Léhon
Combourg
Bazouges-la Pérouse
A84
Landéan
Gorron
Moncontour
E50
Domaine de la Bourbansais
Fougères
Oust
N12
Yvignac
Rance
Château de Fougères
St Denis-de-Gastines
Uzel
Collinée
Broons
Etang de Néal
Bécherel
Hédé
Sens-de-Bretagne
Couesnon
Billé
Ernée
Mûr-de-Bretagne
Plouguenast
BRETAGNE
Ille
St-Aubin-du-Cormier
St-Caradec
Merdrignac
Montauban
Gévezé
St-Aubin-d'Aubigné
Chailland
Loudéac
Plémet
Bédée
Val d'Izé
La Croixille
Alexain
La Chèze
La Trinité-Porhoët
Meu
Montfort-sur-Meu
N12
RENNES
Châteaubourg
Vitré
Rohan
Mauron
Mordelles
St-Jacques-de-la-Lande
N157
Laval
Mohon
Concoret
Forêt de Paimpont
La Gravelle
Naizin
Château de Josselin
Paimpont
Bruz
Châteaugiron
Argentré-du-Plessis
Tréhorenteuc
Plélan-le-Grand
Corps-Nuds
Janzé
Moréac
Josselin
Ploërmel
Campénéac
Moutiers
Cossé-le-Vivien
N24
Brénature
Guer
E3
Le-Sel-de-Bretagne
St-Poix
Locminé
Maure-de-Bretagne
Musée et Insectarium de Lizio
Lizio
Monteneuf
N137
Retiers
St-Jean-Brévelay
Aff
Vilaine
Bain-de-Bretagne
St-Aignan-sur-Roë
N166
Malestroit
Pipriac
Craon
Grand-Champ
St-Marcel
Jardin Botanique
Messac
Oust
La Gacilly
St-Just
Renazé
Oudon
Meucon
Elven
Pleucadeuc
Rougé
Chemazé
La Chapelle-de-Brain
St-Avé
Rochefort-en-Terre
Bains-sur-Oust
Langon
Pouancé
Chère
Noyant-la-Gravoyère
Vannes
Châteaubriant
Combrée
Questembert
Redon
Derval
Golfe du Morbihan
Allaire
Guémené-Penfao
Moisdon la-Rivière
St-Julien-de-Vouvantes
Segré
E60
Don
Port Navalo
Muzillac
Vilaine
Loiré
Isac
Nozay
Sarzeau
Plessé
La Meilleraye-de-Bretagne
Candé
La Roche-Bernard
Vern d'Anjou
St-Gildas-de-Rhuys
St-Gildas-des-Bois
PAYS DE LA LOIRE
Riaillé
St-Mars-la-Jaille
Missillac
Blain
Erdre
Le Louroux-Béconnais
Piriac-sur-Mer
Herbignac
Pontchâteau
Nort-sur-Erdre
St-Lyphard
St-Joachim
St-Georges-sur-Loire
Pte du Castelli
N165
N171
Héric
Ligné
Ile de Hœdic
Guérande
Montoir-de-Bretagne
Savenay
E60
Ancenis
Varades
Donges
La Chapelle-sur-Erdre
St-Florent-le-Vieil
Pte du Croisic
St-Nazaire
Trignac
St-Etienne-de-Montluc
A11
Loire
Le Croisic
Loire
Carquefou
Champtoceaux
Chalonnes-sur-Loire
La Baule
Orvault
Pornichet
St Marc
St-Brevin-les-Pins
Montrevault
Couëron
NANTES
Chemillé
Pte de St-Gildas
St-Père-en-Retz
St-Herblain
Rezé
Beaupréau
Préfailles
Bouguenais
Vertou
Vallet
Gesté

Family favourites

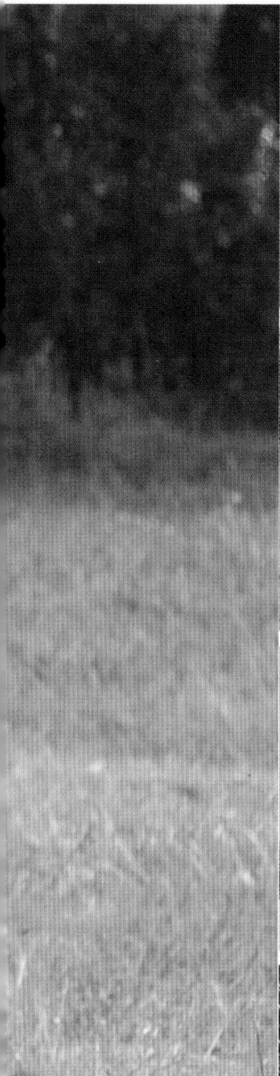

14 Parcabout

16 Cycling holidays

18 Auberge des VoyaJoueurs

20 Char à Bancs Ferme-Auberge

Parcabout

Tell your kids they're going to be sleeping in a 'nest' in a tree on a tiny Breton island and the excitement levels will be palpable. Parcabout is quite simply the maddest and most enjoyable way to spend a night in Brittany. Located on Ile de Groix off the south coast of Morbihan (take the ferry from Lorient), Parcabout is essentially how life would be if we lived in the trees. It's both an adventure playground and a place to sleep. Several thousand square metres of netting have been strung among Californian golden jubilee pine. There are walkways, vast hammocks and massive trampolines, allowing children and adults alike to scramble and bounce around this suspended woody wonderland.

The maroon-and-white 'nests' or pods, which look like huge balloons snagged in the branches, are waterproof spherical tents designed by Chien Noir (Black Dog). With a large round mattress filling the 3 m diameter, two pillows, a duvet and a smart blue cover, they wouldn't look out of place in a design hotel. Each nest is large enough for two adults and two small children. There's no chance of anyone falling out of the nest, as they all have extensive netting to prevent this. You have to be strong enough to climb up a netting tunnel to get to your nest, which may be more of an issue for adults than kids, and it's not recommended for anyone prone to sleepwalking. Some nests are closer to the ground than others (4-8 m), so take your pick and wake up literally with the birds.

On the ground there are washing and changing facilities and a lovely rustic café called The Lobster. An acoustic band called Aperozik often plays here in the early evening in the summer months.

56590 Ile de Groix, T02 97 86 57 61, parcabout.fr. Jul-Sep and school holidays daily 1000-1900. Off-season Wed, Sat and Sun. Occasional night openings. Nests cost €69 for two people. Breakfast is €8 per person. If you come for the day, €19 adult, €14 teens (12-17), €11 child (4-11) and €6 child (under 4), family rate -10%.

Cycling holidays

Kids can't get enough of cycling and the sense of freedom it offers, whether they're toddlers strapped in the pull-along behind dad's bike or racing along independently, hands-free. Brittany is made for cycling holidays, especially since the development of *Voies Vertes* (Green Ways), paths that follow the routes of old railways, towpaths and forest trails, and are open only to non-motorized transport, making them really safe for families.

There are currently 840 km of *Voies Vertes*, following eight routes, which families can dip in and out of, depending on how much they want to cycle. Much of the accommodation on or near the routes provides bicycle storage, basic repairs, equipment and laundry rooms. A map of the B&Bs, campsites and hotels is available on the Randobreizh website (randobreizh.com). There are also several bicycle hire companies along the *Voies Vertes*, so you can hire your bike when and where you like.

Alternatively, leave the organization of your trip to someone else. The family-run business Breton Bikes, started by Kate and Geoff Husband 20 years ago, organizes cycling-camping tours, following specially devised child-friendly cycling routes and stopping off at pre-booked camping sites along the way. The company can provide every conceivable piece of equipment for children who want to cycle (not just the bikes) and supplies all equipment at the campsites, right down to knives and forks. If you don't want to camp, there is a gîte for fixed-centre tours, or you can opt for hotel-based tours.

Breton Bikes, T02 96 24 86 72, bretonbikes.com
Camping (Jun-late Aug) adult £195-260/week, child (10-17) £190/week, child (4-9) £95/week and under 3s £60/week. Bikes and all equipment provided. Hotels or gîtes (year round) adult £440-495/week, child (10-17) £395/week, child £295/week and under 3s £195/week, including breakfast.
Voies Vertes, T02 99 36 15 15, randobreizh.com.

Auberge des VoyaJoueurs

If your kids are nuts about board games, puzzles and any kind of mind-benders, they will love the originality of Auberge des VoyaJoueurs. This groundbreaking new eco-hotel brings together 400 games from all four corners of the world. It is situated south of the Forest of Paimpont, near the mystical forest of Merlin and King Arthur (see page 52), overlooking the wonderfully named Chaperon Rouge (Little Red Riding Hood) lake.

Games from Africa, the Americas, Asia, Europe and Oceania can be played alone or in teams. There are cards to deal, dice to roll, marbles to shoot, pins to bowl, tops to spin, words to find and pawns to move. The world games rooms and the game library will keep you entertained for hours or you can head outdoors to play giant Connect 4 or chess. If you tire of games, there are plenty of magical walks you can take from the auberge.

This place is all about letting your mind dream whilst also engaging in fun tasks. The philosophy behind it is about sustainable development, and the building consumes seven times less energy than most modern buildings of the same size. All 10 rooms are at ground level and there are eight twin rooms and two family rooms for up to four people. Three of the rooms are designed for disabled guests. The duvets and pillows are made of bamboo fibres and there are private bathrooms with natural lighting. Breakfasts are hearty and healthy to set you up for a day of gaming and evening meals offer traditional and world cuisine.

If you're bringing a baby, you can reserve all the necessary equipment, which makes coming by train all the more viable. There's a shuttle from Rennes, Vannes and Redon train stations.

Rue du Chaperon Rouge, 56380 Monteneuf, T02 97 93 22 18, auberge-des-voyajoueurs.com. €89/night for a family room. Extra bed €15. Baby cot no extra charge. Open year round, except first 3 weeks of Jan.

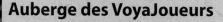

Char à Bancs Ferme-Auberge

Char à Bancs, a 10-minute drive inland from Binic, is one of those really special places that you rarely come across. Its success lies in the hard graft and imagination of the aptly named Lamour family, who have embraced ecotourism by bringing an old farm back to life as a magical and ultra-stylish place in which families can enjoy rural Breton life. And the amazing thing is it won't break the bank. At the heart of it all is La Maison des Lamour with five B&B rooms all decorated in sophisticated rural chic, an exciting blend of old and ultra-modern.

There are four stunning self-catering cottages. No 1 was the bakehouse of the 15th-century farm and has a fitted kitchen, sitting room, washroom, television, private terrace and vegetable garden. On a level with the garden is a double bedroom and up in the mezzanine is a bedroom with two single beds. Everything has been thought of, from barbecue to baby equipment. Cottage No 2, once the outhouse of the farm, has been beautifully transformed, and No 3 was the forge. No 4, the main part of the farm, is by far the largest, with three ample bedrooms, perfect for big families or family and friends.

There's a fabulous restaurant called the Farm Inn, famous for its *potée de Plélo*, a delicious meat and vegetable stew cooked for four hours in a huge caldron in the chimney. The Lamours also make their own farm cider and rhubarb jam.

Outside there's a large wooden fort in which kids can let their legs and imaginations run wild, along with a little hill crisscrossed with tunnels to climb through, a slide and swings, a wooden horse, a field full of ponies to pet and ride in summer, and a river where you can hire a pedalo.

Moulin de la Ville Geffroy, 22170 Plélo, T02 96 74 13 63, aucharabanc.com. B&B rooms €74-100/night for 2. Additional guests €15. Gîtes Nos 1-3 €410-550/week. Gîte No 4 €1600/week. Farm Inn restaurant open July & Aug Wed-Mon, Sep-Jun weekends only, closed Jan. For other farm stays see Bienvenue à la Ferme (Welcome to the farm), bienvenue-a-la-ferme.com/en.

Dig for glory
Make the perfect sandcastle

1 Location is crucial. Site your castle near a stream so it's easy to divert water into the moat. Also, make sure the sand is neither too dry nor too sticky.

2 A moat without a boat is no fun at all. Create a harbour on one side of your castle, using a piece of driftwood as a gate. Periodic dredging will be required.

3 Using a spade, carve steps and terraces on the flanks of the castle. Add pebbles and shells for windows and seagull feathers for medieval banners.

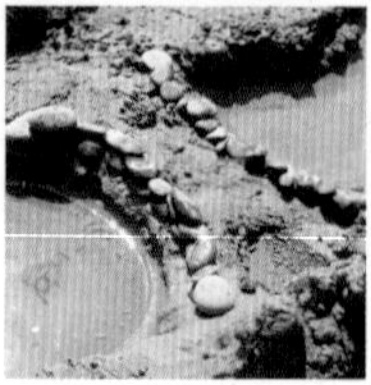

4 Don't overlook your outer defences. At least one tide-restraining wall will be required outside your moat. This should feature crenellations or 'dribble sand' towers.

5 Main access should always be via a bridge with pebble parapets (or a drawbridge using flat driftwood). Cobbles make ideal stepping stones across the moat.

6 Special features can include jetties to outlying towers and lighthouses, or tunnels scooped by hand through sturdy bastions of the main castle.

Sensational sandcastles
T02 97 53 67 64,
sensation-bretagne.com
Take sandcastle-building to a new level at Le Breizh Sable Tour (the Breizh Sand Sculpture Tournament), which takes place in some seaside towns in July and August. You can join a free workshop run by sand sculptor Laurent Dagron and learn the secrets of his

Pirate for the day

St-Malo, Dinard and Roscoff were once famous pirate lairs, and the Sentier des Douaniers (Customs Trail coastal path), now used for hiking, played a vital role in stopping smuggling along the coast. Take your earring and hook along for some re-enactments – go into any tourist shop for piratical props, from eye patches to cutlasses. Yo-ho-ho and a bottle of Briezh Cola!

Kids' stuff

Calling all Asterix fans

Go into any bookshop in Brittany and you'll come across the crazy adventures of Asterix, which first appeared in the Pilote comic in 1959. Brittany is where the feisty little Gaul and his companion Obelix fought the invading Romans in 50 BC, or so the story goes. There's long been debate about the location of the village in which the heroes hang out. Cap d'Erquy on the Emerald Coast bears similarities, but don't bother looking for the 'real one': Village Gaulois near Pleumeur-Bodou is a reconstruction of a Gaulish village for Asterix fans. levillagegaulois.free.fr (see page 76).

Five things to spot

- **A Breton in a beret**
- **A lighthouse**
- **A black and white Breton flag**
- **A bottle of Briezh Cola**
- **A crêperie**

success. On the final day there's a big competition. It's part of 'Sensation Bretagne', an event run by 19 popular coastal resorts in July and August. All sorts of free events take place, including beach clubs, games and films.

On the trail of Merlin

A fan of the hit TV series *Merlin*? Then set off for the Forêt de Paimpont, where, legend has it, Merlin was bewitched by Viviane, who brought up Lancelot. There are miles of paths to explore, but beware the Valley of No Return…(see page 23).

Good reads

These books have great illustrations, and might help you learn a little French:

- *Découvre en Bretagne* series by Christophe Boncens including *Une petite Bretonne!*
- *Ma Première légende de Bretagne* series by Christophe Boncens including *La Sirène et le Pêcheur.*

Seashore safari

Brittany's vast coastline is a boon for rock-pooling fans. Set off on your own, equipped with a good guidebook such as *The Seashore*, Usborne Spotter's Guides. Wear shoes with a good grip, take care to disturb animals and plants as little as possible, particularly when looking under rocks, and leave creatures where you find them. Top spots include Plage du Guesclin (page 32), Plage St-Gilles (page 106), Camaret (page 107), and St-Columban (page 154).

Remember to check tide times to ensure you do not become trapped by the rising tide.

Neolithic lingo

Cairn piles of stones surrounding a tomb.
Cromlech a circle of standing stones.
Dolmen a megalithic burial monument made of large stone slabs.
Enceinte standing stones forming a circle or quadrilateral.
Menhir a tall, upright stone, isolated or in alignments.
Tumulus a large tomb built of piled-up stones or earth.

Boredom busters

Buzz words
Pick a word, then turn on the radio or play a story CD and try to be the first to shout 'buzz' when the word is mentioned.

Car bingo
Give players a sheet of paper and ask them to write down 25 different numbers between one and 99. The person in the front passenger seat calls out the last one or two digits from the licence plates of passing cars. The winner is the first to cross off all their numbers and shout 'Bingo!'

Following on
Take turns to name famous people, countries or towns, each beginning with the last letter of the previous name.

Licence to thrill
Make up phrases based on the letters of licence plates. For example 234 IFS 00 could be 'Ice-cream for Sally', 'Ian fancies Susan' or 'I feel sick!'

The Minister's Cat
Players describe the cat with adjectives (able, acrobatic, etc) beginning with specified letters, losing a life if they have to move to a new letter.

Motorway snap
One player picks a colour and model of car. The next person to see a car that matches shouts snap and scores one point.

Everyday is pancake day

Many Bretons eat several crêpes at a sitting. If you visit a Breton home, be prepared to start with a plain buttered dark pancake, move on to a few savoury ones, then get stuck into the sweet ones with jam and fruit. Don't count, just eat!

Here is a recipe for crêpes to make at home:

110 g plain flour
pinch of salt
300 ml milk
1 egg
15 g melted butter
sunflower oil

Mix the plain flour and salt in a large bowl. Create a well in the centre and add the egg plus half of the milk. Use a wooden spoon to stir into a thick, lump-free batter. Beat in the rest of the milk and the melted butter. If you have a blender, you can whizz all this together. Heat a non-stick frying pan on medium heat and grease lightly with oil. Pour around 3 tbsp of batter into the pan to coat the base. Cook for just over a minute until golden brown. Then comes the best bit – tossing the pancake. Cook for another minute. Serve with sugar and lemon or any other sweet ingredient.

SPECIALITE DE DEUIL

Ille-et-Vilaine

Contents

Le Café du Coin d'en Bas, St-Malo.

CRÊPERIE
GRILL
La Motte
Picquet
LA
MOTTE PICQUET

You must

❶ Eat galettes in Rennes.

❷ Follow the trail of Merlin in the Forêt de Paimpont.

❸ Ride in the Nautibus submarine at the Grand Aquarium in St-Malo.

❹ Zip line at Big Oak Park.

❺ Pat a four-legged friend at the Desert Goat Farm.

❻ Ride Le Train Marin across the Bay of Mont St-Michel.

❼ Swing in the Surcourf pirate ship at Cobac Parc.

Otherwise known as Haute Bretagne (High Brittany), Ille-et-Vilaine may have the smallest coastline of the four departments, but wow does it pack a punch with the mighty Bay of Mont St-Michel and the ancient ramparts of St-Malo greeting ferries from Britain. Inland lies King Arthur's forest, the historic Breton capital of Rennes and so much more.

The most easterly, the most landlocked and some would say the least Breton department holds some of the greatest gems for families. Scale the ramparts for free in the summer months in **St-Malo** and discover a town full of pirate history before heading out to the Grand Aquarium. Just a quick hop across the water is **Dinard**, one of the first places to attract British families to Brittany. There's even a plaque on the Promenade de la Lune (also called the Promenade des Anglais) commemorating the arrival of the first British residents in 1836. A British film festival is held here in October (see page 35).

Dinard has plenty of fantastic beaches. Other seaside towns include **St-Lunaire**, **St-Briac-sur-Mer**, **St-Coulomb** and **Cancale**, all geared up for visiting families with free entertainment and sandcastle-building contests in summer. An exploration of the immense **Bay of Mont St-Michel** is a must, not least to see the amazing oysters and mussels.

The great Rance estuary is a playground for families, especially at **St-Suliac**, where the Club Nautique de Rennes gets kids on the water in Optimists, catamarans and kayaks or trying their hand at windsurfing.

Head further inland and there's much to attract families, from cute animals at the Desert Goat Farm near **Dol-de-Bretagne** to amusement rides at Cobac Parc in **Lanhelin** and the nearby Domaine de la Bourbansais in **Pleugueneuc**, with its Siberian tigers, lions and lemurs, all more than a little out of place in this rural Breton setting. Further east, towards the department border, are the fairy-tale castles of **Fougères**. Go west to follow the trail of King Arthur in the **Forest of Paimpont**, one of Europe's most beautiful natural woods and steeped in Arthurian legends.

A trip to **Rennes** combines the best of old and new Brittany with its lively yet ancient streets and wonderful attractions, including the Science Centre and Brittany Museum. It's a chance to sample some of the best galettes and crêpes in Brittany and down a Briezh Cola!

Exploring the ancient streets of Rennes.

Out & about Ille-et-Vilaine

Fun & free

Abseil the ramparts

Every Wednesday during July and August from 1600-2200, St Malo's Garden in the moat at the foot of St-Malo's mighty ramparts turns into an activity zone for kids aged four and over, with traditional Breton games, circus skills and more. On particular days during the high season over-sevens can abseil the ramparts. All activities are free. Check with the tourist office (T02 99 81 20 59, saint-malo-tourisme.com) for exact timings.

Go Geocatching

Discover the highlights of Haute Bretagne in a modern-day treasure hunt by car, using 'geocatching', GPS references (if you don't have your own GPS navigation system, you can hire one from the tourist offices in St-Malo, Rennes, Brocéliande and Redon) to seek out more than 20 hidden treasures

(tresorsdehautebretagne.fr). Some trails are based on fairy tales and legends, others on historical buildings or writers such as Victor Hugo and Chateaubriand.

Browse the books

For the French version of Hay-on-Wye, head to Bécherel, a town devoted to secondhand bookshops. Kids will have fun rummaging around in Librairie Guriziem (rue de la Chanvrerie, T02 99 66 87 09), which stocks children's books, from Tin Tin to Noddy, and has a lovely *salon de thé* where you can chill out with a cuppa while the kids are provided with paper and crayons. Sleepy Bécherel comes alive with a book fair on the first Sunday of each month, and at its Easter book festival and August book night, when all the book shops stay open late into the night and hold special readings. Contact the tourist office (T02 99 66 75 23, becherel.com) for more details.

Picnic in the Parc

The Parc du Thabor in the centre of Rennes (place St-Melaine) is much used by locals, students and visitors. It was laid out in the 19th century by Denis Bulher in the grounds of the former abbey. Picnic in the shade of mature trees or among the formal French-style gardens with their regular beds, fountains and statues. Kids will like the topiary animals, carousel, outdoor table football, botanical gardens and orangery. Don't miss the **Jardin des Catherinettes** with its fountains, grottos and islands.

Get creative

The sometimes anarchic (in a good way) **Quartiers d'Eté festival** (T02 99 36 81 08, crij-bretagne.com), held in Parc des Gayeulles in east Rennes over three days in July, is full of youthful folk doing creative and energetic things for your free entertainment. There's music, from hip hop to slam, open-air cinema, crazy sports like mountain-bike polo, a graffiti wall to express your inner Banksy, pony rides, juggling and jewellery-making. In other words, something for everyone.

Meander along the Route de Vilaine

This lovely drive between Redon and Rennes uses quiet roads and passes many scenic spots. You could easily while away a day following the trail (look for the brown signs). If you feel like a riverside walk or picnic not far from Redon, the little quay at **Brain-sur-Vilaine** provides an idyllic location.

Run riot in Dinard

If you want a change from the beach in Dinard, head to the park. Parc de Port-Breton in Dinard (av de la Libération, T02 99 46 74 64, daily 0800-1830) has a couple of children's play

Route de Vilaine.

areas, a sports field, a rose garden, a water feature, lovely sea views, trees to climb, a pets corner with around 60 animals and birds including llamas, wallabies, deer and donkeys, plus a walkway in the shape of the tree-based Celtic zodiac from which the Druids deduced personality traits.

After a fun afternoon in the park, head to La Promenade du Clair de Lune. Every evening from July to mid-September this wonderful walkway along the seafront lights up and musicians create a convivial ambience with free entertainment.

Do the dance

During July and August in Pays de Redon, Thursday (2100-2300) is dancing night – Breton style. You can join in the fun and learn some basic steps, as local dance groups give a free introduction. Venue details from the tourist office (T02 99 71 06 04, tourisme-pays-redon.com).

Join the chestnut harvest

In Redon, the whole month of October is a celebration, loosely based on the chestnut harvest. It's a massive event embracing food tastings, culinary and musical competitions (using Breton instruments) and children's entertainment. Many of the activities are free.

Celebrate Bastille Day

Join in the local celebrations and firework displays that take place in most towns on 14 July, Bastille Day. The coast is a good place to catch the action, or head for Rennes (T02 99 28 55 55, ville-rennes.fr), which stages a large celebration on the Plaine de Baud.

Find the Fairy Rock

Visit La Roche aux Fées (Rock of the Fairies), one of the best-preserved dolmens in Europe. Situated in the commune of Essé, 30 km southeast of Rennes, this 5000-year-old passage grave is made up of around 40 blocks of purple shale, each weighing several tons. Legend has it that fairies built it overnight to prove their existence and that loving couples who count the same number of stones are guaranteed everlasting happiness. This type of passage grave was common during the third millennium BC.

Marvel at a massive menhir

The Champ Dolent menhir (35120 Dol-de-Bretagne) is the biggest menhir in the area at nearly 10 m tall and 8.7 m wide. Legend has it that two brothers and their armies fought against each other and the massacre was so famous that the blood of the warriors turned into a river, causing the wheel of a mill downstream to start turning. A hand from heaven separated the warriors and a rock fell from the sky and smashed into the earth. Since that time the menhir has sunk by one inch every century. The story goes that the world will end on the day that the Champ Dolent rock is completely underground.

Best beaches

Anse du Guesclin

A beach with a view! The Fort du Guesclin lies at the eastern end of this wild, concave beach at St-Coulomb. A great place for messing about with buckets and spades or putting your fishing net to use in the rock pools. Just 200 m offshore you'll find wild oysters on the rocks! There's a little customs officers' hut for spying out smugglers on the Pointe des Grands Nez (Big Noses Point), at the other end of the beach.

Cancale – Plage de Port Mer

A few kilometres north of the oyster capital Cancale, this family beach is well sheltered from prevailing winds by the Pointe du Grouin. It has lots of facilities, including an excellent sailing school and a kids' club in summer, and there's a good choice of refreshments at hand.

Dinard

Dinard retains the architecture and atmosphere of its origins as a 19th-century resort favoured by the British. The famous Promenade du Clair de Lune is also known as the Promenade des Anglais. Enjoy a floodlit stroll among the flowers and musicians on a summer evening. Director Eric Rhomer used the Plage de L'Ecluse in several of his works. It's a neat stretch of sand between rocky points, with a seawater pool and lots of organized activities to occupy kids in summer, such as sandcastle competitions at the Mickey Club.

Plage de Cherrueix

This beach in the Bay of Mont-St-Michel is the first beach inside the Breton border. There's such a long tidal reach here that swimming isn't always possible, but the vast expanses of exposed sand make it a very popular venue for sand-yachting – the

Grand Bé island off St-Malo.

2012 World Championship is to be held here. Explore the bay in comfort on the little Train Marin, leaving from Cherrueix.

St-Briac

This seaside commune is a popular family choice with many sandy beaches to choose from. The dune-backed **Plage de Port Hue** holds a Pavillon Bleu mark for the quality of its water, or try the picturesque **Plage de la Salinette**, lined by wooden beach huts and offering glimpses of the chunky Château du Nessay through the trees.

St-Malo

The vast Grande Plage lies just northeast of the famous walled city, providing a traditional day out on the sands. For a more atmospheric experience than the **Grande Plage**, try the small sand and rock **Plage de Bon Secours** below St-Malo's walls. Access to the Intra-Muros for a bite to eat is easy, and there's a great seawater pool with diving board – the only bit visible at high tide! At low tide you can stroll across to the island of **Grand Bé**, where writer Chateaubriand is buried.

St-Lunaire

If it's a Blue Flag beach you're after, you'll be spoilt for choice at St-Lunaire, with four on offer. Most popular are the **Plage de Longchamp**, a great surfing strand, and **La Grande Plage**, close to the tourist office, where you can hire bikes in summer. There are lots of things to do, with mini-golf and tennis nearby, the Yacht Club for equipment hire, and a kids' beach club in summer. The rocky finger of the **Pointe du Décollé**, a fab viewpoint, separates the two beaches.

Action stations

Horse riding
La Foucheraie – Centre de Loisirs Equestres

La Foucheraie, 35190 Cardroc, T02 99 45 82 55, ranch-de-la-foucheraie.com.

Horse-riding excursions for an hour, a day, a weekend or a week. Set off and discover the Paimpont Forest, the megalithic sights of St-Just or the Emerald Coast. Two- to four-day treks are available for youngsters from the age of eight.

Poney-club de St-Malo

2 chemin du Vau Garni, 35400 St-Malo, T02 99 19 08 61, poneyclub-stmalo.com.

This friendly riding school near the Rance tidal barrage welcomes everyone from age three, with beginners' classes from age five. Come for a one-off lesson or a series of courses. As well as riding there are pony games and Sunday treks along the banks of the Rance.

Karting
Karting de St-Malo

Les Nielles, 35350 St-Meloir des Ondes, T02 99 89 16 88, karting-saint-malo.fr. Jul and Aug daily 1000-2000, rest of the year weekends 1000-nightfall, weekdays (except Tue) 1200-nightfall. €15 adult, €12 child (6-12).

Outdoor karting offering high-speed fun for adults and children over five.

Kayaking
Base Nautique de Lannion

11 bd Louis Guilloux, 22300 Lannion, T02 96 37 43 90.

Gildas Miossec and his team offer kayaking and rafting throughout the year. They provide one-off lessons, equipment hire and courses (during school holidays). Various kayak trips are available: hike along the Pink Granite Coast or paddle down the Léguer river. In summer, a multi-board training course is organized.

Sailing

There are around 16 sailing schools in Ille-et-Vilaine. Point Passion Plage offers a Pass'Sensations book of tickets that can be used at any of their member sailing schools: €92 for 25 tickets, €170 for 50 tickets and €316 for 100 tickets. An hour's catamaran use costs €46 or six tickets. For more details, see pointplage.fr.

Club Nautique de Rennes

Club Nautique de Rennes, quai de la Rance, 35430 St-Suliac, T02 99 58 48 80, http://cn.rennes.pagesperso-orange.fr.

In the Rance estuary, not far from St-Malo, this centre runs a wide range of activities throughout the year, including classes in sailing (Optimists and catamarans), windsurfing and sea kayaking, and also offers equipment hire and discovery trips. Children learn to sail aboard the Minigal – a wooden craft the size of an Optimist and specifically for children.

Point Passion Plage de Cancale – Port Mer Sailing School

Plage de Port Mer, 35260 Cancale, T02 99 89 90 22, pointplage.fr.

A member of Point Passion Plage, Port Mer in Cancale enjoys a sheltered location and is ideal for learning how to sail from an early age. From May to September it provides windsurfing, dinghy and catamaran lessons. If the idea of combining a family activity with a gastronomic cruise appeals, go for the lunch excursion aboard a Loguivy lugger, an authentic old sailing vessel. If you want thrills, head out to sea aboard a 7-m trimaran, a replica of a Formula One yacht.

Point Passion Plage de St-Lunaire

Yacht Club de St-Lunaire, bd de la Mer, 35800 St-Briac sur Mer, T02 99 46 30 04, pointplage.fr.

From April to October, you can hire a boat, take to the sea for the first time or take lessons from the Yacht Club on the main beach in St-Lunaire. The fleet includes dinghies, catamarans, windsurfing boards and open two-seater kayaks. In summer, Point Passion Plage also offers kayaking, surfing, paddle boarding and trampolining on Longchamp beach.

Rain check

Cinema

The British Film Festival in Dinard in October has been going for more than 20 years. Dozens of films are shown at five different venues for €5.50 a performance (or €60 for a carte pass that covers everything). T02 99 88 19 04, festivaldufilm-dinard.fr.

- **Cinéma Arvor,** 29 rue Antrain, 35700 Rennes, T02 99 38 78 04.
- **Cinéma Aurore,** 19 bd de Laval, 35500 Vitré, T02 99 75 07 29.
- **Cinéma Duguesclin Cancale,** 5 Impasse Saint-Méen, 35260 Cancale, T09 77 74 84 98.
- **Cinéma Le Colombier**, place du Colombier, 35000 Rennes, T08 36 68 03 07.
- **Cinéma Gaumont**, esplanade Charles de Gaulles, Rennes, T02 99 31 53 22.
- **Ciné TNB**, rue Saint-Hélier, 3500 Rennes, T08 36 68 00 39.
- **Le Club**, Forum Gare 35300 Fougères, T02 99 99 01 79.
- **Le Vauban**, 10 bd Tour d'Auvergne, 35400 St Malo, T02 99 56 45 81.
- **Vers le Large**, 4 Route Dinan, 22100 Dinan, T02 96 39 13 83.
- **Les Alizés**, 2 bd Albert 1er, 35800 Dinard, T08 92 68 69 26.

Indoor soft play

- **Les P'tits Pirates à St Malo**, 22 rue Croix Désilles, 35400 St-Malo, T02 99 81 13 67, lesptitspirates.wifeo.com. Pirate-themed soft play for two- to 12-year-olds, with trampolines and karting.

Indoor swimming pools

- **Aquatide**, bd du Maine, 35370 Argentré-du-Plessis, T02 23 55 09 63.
- **Centre Aquatique Dolibulle**, rue de l'Abbaye, 35120 Dol-de-Bretagne, T02 99 80 71 75, piscine-dolibulle.com.
- **Espace Aquatique Océlia**, route d'Iffendic, 35160 Montfort-sur-Meu, T02 99 09 05 05.
- **Piscine de la Conterie**, 2 rue Léo Lagrange, 35131 Chartres-de-Bretagne, T02 99 77 47 99.
- **Piscine du Bocage**, route d'Argentré-du-Plessis, 35500 Vitré, T02 23 55 16 20.
- **Piscine Olympique**, rue Georges Clémenceau, 35400 St-Malo, T2 99 81 61 98.
- **Piscine Sports Loisirs**, 2 esplanade de l'Hôtel de Ville, 35510 Cesson-Sévigné, T02 99 83 52 10.

Karting

- **Dinard Karting**, 21 rue de la Ville es Mesnier, 35800 Dinard, T02 99 46 55 47, dinard-karting.com.
- **Karting Cap Malo**, Zac Cap Malo, 35520 Melesse, T02 99 13 31 33, kartingderennes.fr.
- **Karting de St-Malo**, Les Nielles, 35350 St-Méloir-des-Ondes, T02 99 89 16 88, karting-saint-malo.fr.

Bon Secours beach, St-Malo.

Wishbone Club Dinard
Plage de l'Ecluse, 35800 Dinard, T02 99 88 15 20, wishbone-club-dinard.com.
Offers classes for all ages (from age 5) in windsurfing, sailing, catamarans and kayaking.

Walking
Forêt de Fougères
This has many kilometres of walking, cycling and riding trails. Activity programmes (for a day or a week) can be organized at La Ferme de Chênedet (chenedet-loisirs.com) in the heart of the forest. There's also a lake for canoeing or kayaking.

Forêt de Paimpont
There are many circuits both easy and strenuous in the Fôret de Paimpont. The Valley of No Return may have an ominous name, but the scenery is superb.

Woodland adventure
Forêt Adrénaline
Oxylane Village, ZAC du Pluvignon, 35830 Betton, T02 90 84 00 20, foretadrenaline.com. Spring and autumn Wed, Sat and Sun and school holidays 1400-1900, Jul and Aug daily 1000-1930. €19 adult, €15 child (9-13), €10 (5-8), €5 (2-4).
A bit like Go Ape! in the UK, this is a family-friendly tree-top assault course involving zip wires, tree climbing, rope bridges and Tarzan nets. There are four courses, aimed at different ages, including one for very young children (from the age of 2). Briefings can be done in English. There is another Fôret Adrénaline in Morbihan (see page 157).

Horizon Sport et Nature
5 rue du Douet Fourché, 35120 Dol-de-Bretagne, T08 73 83 48 07, horizonsportnature.net.
Offers everything from climbing and mountain biking to orienteering and archery for both children and adults. Aims to stretch and challenge participants.

Big days out

Baie du Mont St-Michel
Any child confronted with a view of the iconic island abbey of Mont St-Michel must wonder where they've landed. Set in the vast Baie du Mont St-Michel, against an ever-changing big sky, it brings to mind a Gothic-style version of Disney's Cinderella Castle.

This rocky tidal island has been a monastic stronghold since the eighth century and remains a site of pilgrimage for many, but for most families it's a man-made marvel that's a fascinating place to explore, with ancient streets, a delicate cloister almost overhanging the sea, a crypt supported by massive pillars and an inspiring Romanesque abbey church. Here the solidity of faith stands on the shifting sands of the bay. It's actually set just across the border in Normandy, but much of the phenomenal Baie du Mont St-Michel, a World Heritage Site, lies in Brittany.

This is a bay that holds many delights for families, though they are always beholden to the weather and extreme tidal variations. This means you should only walk out across the bay with an experienced guide from the specialist Maison de la Baie visitor centre (Vivier-sur-Mer, maison-baie.com, year round). It offers walks and tractor-pulled rides out onto the bay to find out about the tides and marine life, as well as the production of oysters and *moules de bouchot* (mussels grown on posts), which are famous here. Tours are in French but some of the guides will also give English explanations – ask in advance. There's also the **Banc des Hermelles**, an extraordinary reef built by sea-worms.

One of the best options, for kids and adults alike, is **Le Train Marin** (Gare St-Michel, Centre Bourg, 21 rue du Lion d'Or, 35120 Cherrueix, T02 99 48 84 88, decouvrirlabaie.com, €12 adult, €8 child (4-11), a yellow tractor-drawn trailer. As well as exploring the mighty bay, you'll learn how dredging for shrimps is done – with audience participation. Don't forget your wellies and book in advance.

Château de Fougères
Ville de Fougères, 35301, T02 99 99 79 59, chateau-fougeres.com. Jul and Aug daily 1000-1900, May, Jun, Sep daily 1000-1300, 1400-1900, Oct-Apr 1000-1230, 1400-1730, closed Jan and Mon out of school holidays. €7.50 adult, €4.50 child, under 6s free, family pass €19.50. Audio tour in English available.

One of the biggest forts in Europe, this château fits exactly the image we have of a fairy-tale castle with its pointy towers, crenulations and beautiful moat. What's more, it makes a special effort to entertain and interest kids. There's a special route for children (aged 7-12) in the Mélusine tower, named after the fairy said to have been responsible for many medieval buildings. Kids are guided by fairy cousins of Mélusine, namely Mélusa, a female fairy who loves history and talks about the big events and the remarkable characters in the castle's history, and Mélusin, an elf boy who is passionate about military architecture and knows everything about the structure of the castle. Kids are given the task of solving 10 enigmas.

Alligator Bay

If you're heading into Normandy to see Mont St-Michel and want an extra draw for the kids, visit Alligator Bay (62 route du Mont St-Michel, 50170 Beauvoir, T02 33 68 11 18, alligator-bay.com, Apr-Sep 1000-1900, Oct-Mar 1400-1800, Dec and Jan weekends only, €11.50 adults, €7.50 child 4-12), which has the largest number of alligators in Europe, a dragons' maze stocked with boas and iguanas, plus a tortoise farm. Alternatively, the phenomenal GR34 hiking path that follows Brittany's coast starts here on the Breton-Norman border, first passing in front of the chapel of Ste Anne beside Cherrueix, a great place for sand-yachting.

Gothic skies at Baie du Mont St-Michel.

Cobac Parc

Axe Rennes/St-Malo, D75, 35720 Lanhelin, T02 99 73 80 16, cobac-parc.com. Apr to mid-Sep, Jun, early Jul, late Aug daily 1100-1800 (except Mon in Jun), mid-Jul to mid-Aug 1030-1830, mid-Sep to Mar Wed, Sat and Sun 1100-1800. €16 adult, €13.50 child (3-11), 2-day ticket €29 adult, €24 child. Free parking.

With 12 ha of woodland and 30 different activities for children and adults, this is the only amusement park in this part of Brittany. It has a relaxed feel, with nothing very sophisticated, but that adds to the charm and kids love it. Several rides evoke St-Malo's piratical past. They include a Surcourf pirate ship, which swings from side to side as if pitching through heavy seas, and the Tour du Gué, resembling a boat mast, on which gondolas swivel to and fro. One of the top rides in the park is the Corsaire roller coaster.

But there are also gentler rides for young children, including a little train, a traditional merry-go-round and a fun steeplechase ride. There's a rope bridge across the lake, pedalos, go-karts, mini-golf, bouncy castles and trampolines. Bring your swimsuits, as there's a heated aquapark (Jun-Aug), with slides and a shallow pool for little ones (for boys and men, a very strict swimming trunks/ Speedos rule applies, so no baggy shorts). If you don't want to bring a picnic, there are cafés, including Cobby self-service and Rapido Pasta and Pizza, plus ice cream, pancake and waffle stalls. Meals cost from around €6.90 to €10.90.

La Cancalaise

La Halle à Marée, 35260 Cancale, T02 99 89 77 87, lacancalaise.org. Call for sailing times. From €24 adult, €12 child (6-14).

Feel the wind in your sails with a voyage around the Baie du St-Michel on board the majestic *La Cancalaise*, an antique fishing vessel. Traditional sailing techniques are demonstrated.

Cobac Parc.

Half-day trips are long enough for kids and this isn't one for tiny tots. Remember to take your own drinks and snacks along.

Le Domaine de la Bourbansais

35720 Pleugueneuc, T02 99 69 40 07, labourbansais.com. Apr-Sep daily 1000-1900, Oct-Mar 1330-1730 (school holidays 1000-1800). €16.50 adult, €12.50 child (3-12), including all activities, zoo shows, feeding times and garden games. Guided tours of the château €3.

This zoo, in its leafy setting, has more than 400 animals and 60 different species, including Siberian tigers, giraffes, gibbons, lions and wolves. The Madagascan lemurs, introduced in 2010, have proved a big hit with visitors, who are allowed to approach them. New to the zoo in 2011 is 'Griffon Vultures, Lords of the Sky!', offering five daily shows and a feeding session with biologists. There is also a twice-daily falconry show with 50 falcons, plus playgrounds, a restaurant, café and souvenir shop. The château and its French-style gardens can be visited on a guided tour.

Les Champs Libres à Rennes

10 Cours des Alliés, 35000 Rennes. T02 23 40 66 00, leschampslibres.com. Tue 1200-2100, Wed-Fri 1200-1900, Sat and Sun 1400-1900. To visit the Brittany Museum, the Science Centre or the temporary exhibition in the Anna Conti Room €4 adult, €3 child. For all exhibitions €7 adult, €5 under 26, under 8s free.

This vast futuristic building contains the **Musée de Bretagne** (Brittany Museum), Espace des Sciences (Science Centre) and the public library, the latter in a central glass wedge that rises above the galleries. Inside is a sometimes confusing world of circuitous paths, empty spaces and hi-tech exhibits, but it's a good option on a rainy day. The Musée de Bretagne recounts Brittany's history and culture from prehistoric times (listen to Breton being spoken), while Espace des Sciences has an interesting permanent section upstairs on the geology of Brittany, with rock samples and magnifying glasses provided. A booklet in various languages is provided for the Laboratoire de Merlin, a separate section where children (and adults) can carry out experiments. But best of all is the Planetarium on the top level. Don't miss a trip to the shop for some great educational souvenirs, and there's a lovely café with a terrace.

Ligne Baie

lignebaie.fr, 1-day pass €10 adult, €5 child, 2-day pass €18 adult, €9 child.

Ligne Baie is a super-scenic train ride from St-Malo to Mont St-Michel and on to Granville in Normandy. There's free bike loan from some stations and organized activities such as oyster-tasting, exhibitions and on-board entertainment.

Visit Parc des Grands Chênes

Why? If you like the idea of scaling treetops, navigating wood and rope bridges high above the ground, swinging from harnesses, scrambling through barrels and whizzing across aerial zip lines, all in a beautiful Breton oak forest, Big Oak Park is the place for you. Children can vent their superhero fantasies in this wonderful adventure playground. There's also sailing available in a fleet of miniature boats. Bring your own picnic and snacks, or try the Restaurant Le Moulin de la Forêt. Don't forget to dress for the occasion with sturdy footwear and covered elbows and knees for little ones.

Where? Forêt de Villecartier, Bazouges, 35560 La Pérouse, T06 88 72 73 40, parcdesgrandschenes.fr.

How? Apr-Jun and Sep-Nov weekends except Sat morning, Jul and Aug daily 0930-1900. Courses for over 5s, over 8s and adult courses from 10 years (minimum height 1.4 m). €25 adult, €15 young person (10-13), €10 child (5-9).

Don't miss Chèvrerie du Désert

Chèvrerie du Désert (Desert Goat Farm) is what *Brittany with Kids* is all about. Authentic local attractions built on hard work and genuine expertise that totally entrance kids.

Everything about this goat farm is low key, from the pretty home-made goats' cheeses in the farm shop (some of the best in Brittany) to the beautiful desert goats that seem so effortlessly well cared for and content. Run by Roselyne and Claude (who speaks English, should you have any questions), there are no gimmicks, rides or souvenirs, just a farm with animals that kids can interact with, from gobbling turkeys to bobbing rabbits. First up are the exotic birds, such as zebra finches and ornamental poultry. Then come the incredible 'Dogues de Bordeaux', the amazing-looking Bordeaux mastiffs – thankfully in their cages.

Follow the twisting paths, passing water fountains and little grottos, to a pretty field shaded by a massive oak tree. It's here that young kids can pet young kids. These dwarf goats are incredibly cute and friendly. Children can go into the field and explore their shelter. It's all very relaxed with no crowds, even in high summer.

Other fields have miniature ponies in the style of Thelwell, an ostrich or two, some friendly Poitou donkeys to pat, Jersey

cows and Ouessant sheep. Inside the immaculate barns you'll find the adult desert goats in all their glory. Again, children can watch them, pet them and perhaps help sort their feed. There are also Vietnamese pot-bellied pigs with the cutest piglets you're ever likely to see, and you can watch the goats being milked at 1730. There are also free quiz sheets for seven- to 12-year-olds.

Grab a bite

The farm has a lovely shop selling fresh goats' cheeses of different vintages – the longer they're kept the stronger they get. Roselyne and Claude use all kinds of flavourings, such as herbs and pepper. There's a great café with tables outside under the shade of an apple tree where you can enjoy a *crêpe sucré* (€2.10) or special goats' cheese dishes.

Essential information

Le Désert, 35540 Plerguer, 8 km west of Dol-de-Bretagne off D676. T02 99 58 92 14, chateaubriand.com/Partenaires/chevrerie-du-desert.htm. Apr-Jun and Sep Mon and Wed-Sat 1430-1830, Sun and public holidays 1100-1830, Jul and Aug daily 1100-1830. €5 adult, €4 child.

More family favourites

Ecomusée du Pays de Rennes

Ferme de la Bintinais, route de Châtillon-sur-Seiche, 35200 Rennes, T02 99 51 38 15, ecomusee-rennes-metropole.fr. Apr-Sep Tue-Fri 0900-1800, Sat 1400-1800, Sun 1400-1900, Oct-Mar Tue-Fri 0900-1200, 1400-1800, Sat 1400-1800, Sun 1400-1900. €4.60 adult, €2.30 child (6-14).

In a beautifully restored farm, this museum traces five centuries of developments in farming: everyday life, farm work, working environment and agriculture. Reconstruction of the farm rooms, objects, machines and furniture bear witness to this evolution, and there are documentary films and interactive games. In order to get the most out of the farm, including the 15-ha agricultural area with gardens and orchards, allow 1½ hours for your visit. In the grounds, you'll find Breton breeds, orchards and gardens.

Enigmaparc

ZA du Bois de Teillay, Quartier du Haut Bois, 35150 Janzé, T02 99 47 07 65, enigmaparc.fr. Call or check website for opening hours which vary throughout the year. €12.50 adult, €9.50 child (5-11), under 5s free.

This theme park comprising 11 'worlds' transports you back in time and to other lands. Delve into ancient Egypt, the 1930s, the Middle Ages, or cross the world to Asia or Africa, solving riddles and games of skill along the way and using your best powers of deduction. Kids quickly get the hang of things and it's enjoyable for adults too, whether they're exploring an Egyptian tomb, taking photos on safari in South Africa, solving optical illusions or finding their way out of a maze.

Etincelles Aquatiques

Etang de la Forge, 35640 Martigné-Ferchaud, T02 99 47 83 83, etincelles-aquatiques.org). Early Aug. Book online €14 adult, €6 child (5-15), under 5s free.

An evening treat for older kids who like a spectacle (shows don't start until 2215 when it's dark), this is an open-air show of music, dance and fireworks in a stunning lakeside setting. The stories feature local mythical or historical figures such as the fairies from the nearby Roche aux Fées (see page 31). Come before the show for a traditional supper of galettes and crêpes and don't forget to bring cushions and warm clothes. Book well in advance.

La Ferme Marine

L'Aurore, 35260 Cancale, T02 99 89 69 99, ferme-marine.com. Jul to mid-Sep daily 1400 in English, mid-Feb to Jun Mon-Fri and mid-Sep to mid-Oct at 1500 in French. €7 adult, €3.70 child, €19.30 family.

This oyster farm offers guided tours to see how oysters are grown and processed in Cancale's scenic oyster beds. Also contains a fabulous seashell exhibition and has a surprisingly sophisticated shop with great jewellery for mums and girls.

L'Atelier Manoli Musée et Jardin de Sculpture

9 rue de Suet, 35780 La Richardais, T02 99 88 55 53, manoli.org. Jul and Aug daily 1030-1230, 1500-1900, Apr-Jun, Sep and Oct plus school holidays and weekends 1500-1900. €4.50 adult, €4 student, under 10s free.

For a kiddie-accessible burst of Breton art, head to the museum and sculpture garden dedicated to Pierre Manoli. This is where he lived and worked and kids will love exploring the house and garden with its menagerie of strange creatures.

L'Atelier-Musée de l'Horlogerie Ancienne

37 rue Nationale, 35300 Fougères, T02 99 99 40 98. Call for opening times. €4.50 adult, €2.50 child (10-17).

This quirky little museum is devoted to timepieces of all shapes and sizes. There's a workshop where you can see a watchmaker practising his craft.

Maison Nature et Mégalithes

10 allées des Cerisiers, 35550 St-Just, T02 99 72 69 25, landes-de-cojoux.com. Daily Jul and Aug 1000-1230, 1400-1800, May, Jun, Sep and Oct Wed and Sun 1400-1730, Mar, Apr and Nov Sun 1400-1730. €3 adult, under 15s free.

The relationship between man and nature from Neolithic times

Hit or miss?

Vélo Rail

Médréac train station, 45 km northwest of Rennes on D220. T02 99 07 30 48. Jun-Sep daily 1000-1800, Apr, May, Oct and public holidays 1400-1800. Departures on the hour; rest of the year by appointment. From €8 pair adult, €2 child.

Does two bikes welded together on an old rail track sound like a good idea to you? Only in France would this two-person contraption actually catch on. With a choice of two circuits, one covering 6 km and taking about an hour, the other covering 14 km and taking around two hours, this makes a scenic day out, passing though the Néal Valley, the forest of Montauban and some megalithic remains. You can stop for a picnic along the way. Under 8s ride in a sort of hammock swung between the parents' bikes; older kids get special mini bikes of their own, also ridden in pairs. People of reduced mobility can ride a special motorized wagon, and there's a road train with a rural tunes soundtrack for everyone. Could it be any more kitsch?

Boat trips

Corsaire Company
Gare Maritime de la Bourse, 35400 St-Malo, T08 25 13 81 00, compagniecorsaire.com. 1 hr to full day. Call for prices.
Boat trips along the coast, leaving from St-Malo, Dinard or Dinan. One of the best ways to discover the Emerald Coast.

Croisières Chateaubriand
Gare Maritime du Barrage de la Rance, 35780 La Richardais, T02 99 46 44 40, chateaubriand.com. Year round. Reservations recommended. 1½-hr cruise €16 adult, 3-hr cruise €25 adult, under 12s free. Lunch cruises €70 adult, €20 child (under 12).
The glorious Rance estuary that divides St-Malo from Dinard is the setting for this family-friendly cruise. Take in islands, hidden coves, old watermills and fishing villages, as well as marine life such as cormorants and seals. The lunch and dinner cruises have special menus for under 12s, featuring steak, chocolate cake and a lollipop.

right up to modern day is explored with guided tours of Les Landes de Cojoux, Brittany's second largest megalithic site, located to the west of the village of St-Just. If you don't want to take the guided tour, you can follow a 7-km round trail, described on an information leaflet available at the centre. It's a nice walk through ancient moorland, with the added interest of the stones. If you decide to take a picnic, there's a boulangerie in the village where you can pick up supplies.

Manoir de l'Automobile

4 rue de la Cour Neuve, 35550 Loheac, T02 99 34 02 32, manoir-automobile.fr. Daily except Mon 1000-1300, 1400-1900, Jul and Aug daily 1000-1900. €8.50 adult, €7 child (10-16).
Bring out the boy racer in your kids with this vast museum devoted to cars, cars and more cars. There are around 400 vehicles, from old bangers to Formula One racers plus a few thousand scale models. There's a racetrack next door for karting and quad biking.

Musée de la Batellerie de l'Ouest (Inland Waterways Museum)

12 quai Jean Bart, 35600 Redon, T02-99 72 30 95. Mid-Jun to mid-Sep daily 1000-1200, 1500-1800, out of season Sat, Sun, Mon, Wed 1400-1800, closed Nov-Mar. €2 adult, €1 child.
Set on the quayside, this museum offers an interesting insight into the heritage of the inland waterways of Brittany and the lost way of life of canal folk. There's an evocative film (English version) to set the scene, and afterwards you can browse a collection of old photographs and artefacts, including La Bricole, the harness used by men (or sometimes women) to pull their boat when they had no horse. Kids who like a challenge will love the automated model that gives you the chance to bring a boat through a miniature lock.

Musée des Beaux-Arts de Rennes

20 quai Emile Zola, 35000 Rennes, T02 23 62 17 45, mbar.org. Call for opening times. €4.20, under 18s free.
Okay, this is a heavy-duty art gallery, so perhaps one for older kids only, but it is a fabulous collection with artworks ranging from ancient Egypt to the present day, including contemporary Breton artists. For kids who speak French, on Wednesdays there are workshops on changing themes, such as Fantastic Animals, The Sky and Hats. The tourist office in Rennes (ville-rennes.fr) runs guided tours of the gallery by arrangement. If you want a quick look around without your toddler, there is a crèche at certain times. Call for details.

Musée Louison Bobet

5 rue de Gael, 35290 St-Méen-le-Grand, T02 99 09 67 86. Jul-Sep daily 1400-1700, rest of the year closed Tue. €3 adult, €2 child.
This quirky Breton museum celebrates the life and cycling of local hero Louison Bobet who

won three consecutive Tours de France (1953-1955). The old-fashioned kit and bikes are a history lesson all in themselves.

Musée des Transmissions – Espace Ferrié

Av de la Boulais, 35512 Cesson-Sévigne, T02 99 84 32 87, espaceferrie.fr. Call for opening times. €3 adult, children free.

This modern museum manages to spark curiosity in the origins of modern-day communications technology that children now treat as the norm – "What, you didn't have the internet, computers and mobiles when you were at school, Dad?" There are many fascinating objects, from ancient telephones to a German 'Enigma' decoding machine, used in the Second World War. Many inventions originally intended for the battlefield end up in our homes, including radar and the internet.

Parc Ornithologique de Bretagne

53 bd Pasteur, 35170 Bruz, T02 99 52 68 57, parc-ornithologique.com. Apr-Sep 1400-1900, Jul and Aug 1000-1200, 1400-1900, Oct to mid-Nov and mid-Feb to Mar Sun 1400-1800. €6.50 adult, €3.90 child (3-12).

Our feathered friends are here in abundance. This is a great place to show your kids just how diverse the bird world is with everything from Siberian geese to Australian black swans. All the old favourites are here from colourful parrots and peacocks to more unusual pompom headed ducks. Aviaries are in a wooded park, making this a pleasant stroll.

Let's go to...

St-Malo

St-Malo is a living and breathing adventure playground, ringed with ancient ramparts and steeped in pirate legends. It has Toy Town trains and carousels, as well as surprisingly good beaches and magical islands.

If you are in Brittany only for a weekend, St-Malo is a great place to head. It combines a historic centre with a vibrant modern character, and has plenty to entertain families, including a superb beach (see page 33).

Where to park

St-Malo is one of those rare parts of Brittany that suffers from traffic congestion, so it's best to arrive early to park. Inside the walled city is possible out of peak season (€1.50/hr) but it's easier to use an external car park, such as the Cale de Dinan or to park near the tourist office in esplanade St-Vincent. In July and August free buses run between the Parking Paul Féval and the Intra-Muros. The ferry port is within easy walking distance of the Intra-Muros and the train station is about 850 m away.

The city has a strong identity. Its own flag flies proudly from the castle, and it stages one of France's best rock music festivals. The port retains its importance in the fishing industry and is a base of Brittany Ferries. St-Malo's citizens are known for their strong, independent spirit, summed up by the famous motto, 'Ni français, ni breton, malouin suis' (I'm not French nor Breton, I'm Malouin).

The magnificent city walls are a reconstruction, painstakingly restored after devastating bombing in the Second World War. The old city within these walls is called Intra-Muros and known locally as *Le Rocher* (the rock).

Get your bearings

The tourist office (esplanade St-Vincent, T02 99 81 20 59, saint-malo-tourisme.com) supplies free maps that point out places of interest, including a 'Hidden St-Malo' map with walking tours and attractions, all in English. You can also pick up a young explorers' guide (€1) for seven- to 12-year olds, encouraging them to discover the pirate history of the town in a playful way through clues and riddles, with plenty of surprises along the way. It's also worth getting a Pass Malo (€1), giving discounts on attractions and accommodation throughout the region.

Getting around

If you want to get around using green power, call a **Cyclomouv** tricycle taxi (T06 60 53 51 02, cyclomouv.com). They run on electricity and cost €1 plus €1 per kilometre per person (child under 5 free with adult).

Brittany Ferries has teamed up with **Locvelec** (109 bd Chateaubriand, T02 99 40 80 32), an electric bicycle hire company that offers 10% off hire prices to customers with a Brittany Ferries travel document. Bikes cost from €6 per hour up to €45 per weekend. Child seats, trailers and bags are also available for hire.

Tour the ramparts

The rampart walk is less than 2 km and a great way to orientate yourself (if you have a buggy, you'll have to carry it up and down loads of steps, but there are no problems once you're up top). Kids might like to arm themselves with a pirate patch and toy sword to recreate the swashbuckling days of St-Malo's past; there are plenty of little shops selling such items. One of the best times to do the rampart walk is in the evening when you can watch the sun setting over the water.

Walk clockwise from the **Porte St-Vincent**, with the port basins below, crossing the oldest gate, **Grand'Porte**, and then swing right past the statue of corsair Dougay-Trouin, admiring the typical 18th-century façades of the buildings, and the resort of Dinard across the water (a regular ferry connects the towns). Turning east at the little tower of St-Philippe, you'll see the statue of Jacques Cartier ahead, outside the **seawater swimming pool**. When the tide is high, the top of the diving board rises out of the sea like a strange monster.

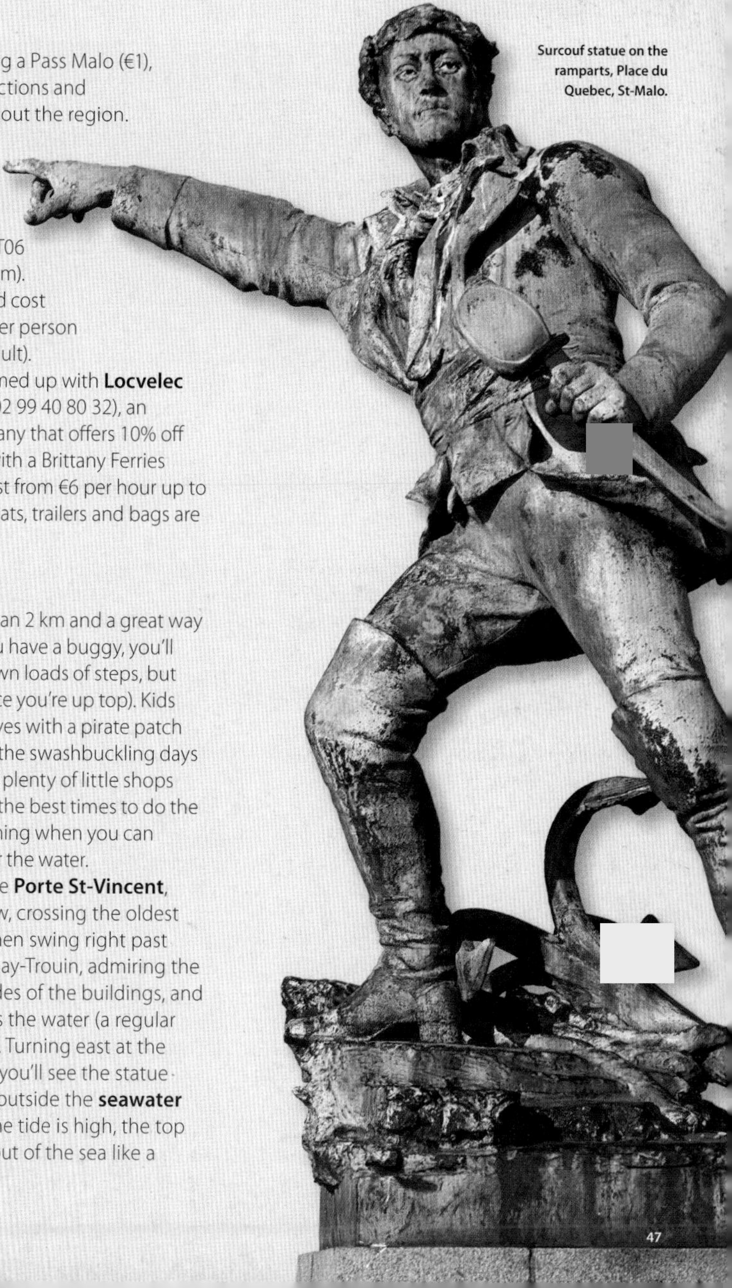

Surcouf statue on the ramparts, Place du Quebec, St-Malo.

Let's go to... St-Malo

Protection from the ramparts.

Bon Secours beach.

This is the place to view the offshore islands, especially **Grand Bé**, the burial place of Chateaubriand (see below). At low tide it can be reached on foot using a cobbled path. If you decide to visit Grand Bé, be sure to keep one eye on the tide because the path becomes quickly submerged. Alternatively, remain at your vantage point on the ramparts, where fun can be had watching a small flotilla of boats assemble, ready to help any stranded tourists as the tide rolls in. **Petit Bé** with its fort is behind.

Robert Surcouf's statue commands his own terrace, reached by a wooden footbridge, before the **Bidouan Tower**, which you can climb for the views. Turning to the eastern side, you'll see the **Fort National**, also walkable, depending on the tides, before you. This largely 17th-century military stronghold and one-time execution site, with a drawbridge jail and powder magazine, offers English-speaking guides and marvellous views back over St-Malo. The walk finishes by the **castle** and **museum** (Apr-Sep daily 1000-1200 and 1400-1800). Exhibitions chart the city's history through to the Second World War, the devastation and reconstruction of the city, and reveal the famous people associated with St-Malo, from the intrepid explorer Jacques Cartier (1491-1557), colonizer of Canada, and François-René de Chateaubriand, the founder of Romanticism in French literature.

Go shopping

Shops worth seeking out include **La Marelle** (16 rue Cordiers, Intra-Muros, T02 99 40 94 79, la-marelle-jouets-saint-malo.com), an atmospheric toyshop that is sure to catch any child's eye. Many of the toys are evocative of the area, including wooden pirate ships, Asterix figures, Moomins and Tintin.

La Droguerie de Marine (66 rue Georges Clemenceau, St-Servan-sur-Mer, T02 99 81 60 39) is an old-style marine hardware shop with classic products such as Marseille soap, brushes, paints, varnishes, knives and storm matches. There are lots of delightful objects that will appeal to children, such as Pop Pop boats, little tin craft that move when you place a candle in them. There are also nautical books in English and local delicacies.

Another interesting nautical shop is **Gauthier Marines** (2 rue Porcon de la Barbinais, T02 99 40 91 81, gauthiermarines.com) selling model ships, globes, lanterns and so on.

Plenty of shops sell *Produits Régionaux*, from traditional bowls with names on to tins of butter biscuits. There are also some smart boutiques like **Marouch** on rue Ste-Barbe for mums to explore. Also worth a look is **La Boutique Sentimentale** (3 place du Poids du Roy, T02 23 18 35 85), selling stylish and attractive Fair Trade products. There are lovely clothes for adults and kids, cushions, crockery, soft toys and colouring pencils.

Music & events

St-Malo is renowned for one of France's top rock events, **La Route du Rock**, which takes place here each August (laroutedurock.com).

Etonnants Voyageurs, a wide-ranging celebration of travel writing, draws a huge international crowd of armchair travellers and adventurers each May in a very convivial atmosphere (etonnants-voyageurs.com).

Le Petit Train de St-Malo

Jump aboard Le Petit Train de St-Malo (35400 St-Malo, T02 99 40 49 49, lepetittrain-saintmalo.com; €5.50 adult, €4 under 10s) for a fun, 30-minute tour of the 'privateer town' with commentary in French and English (evening tours until 2030 Jul and Aug). It departs from Porte St-Vincent at the foot of the castle. Near the starting point for the Little Train, between the tourist office and the old walls, don't miss a ride on the old-fashioned **carousel**. There may be bigger, flashier aquariums, such as the one just outside the city (see page 51), but kids will love the **Petit Aquarium** (place Vauban, T02 99 56 94 77) set into the ramparts. If you just want a great place for kids to let off steam while mum and dad have a sit down, head for the playground at **Place des Frères Lamennais**.

There are many **historical buildings** in St-Malo, including, St Vincent Cathedral and the ship owner's mansions (all are shown on tourist maps from the tourist board, see page 46). If you visit just one of these, make it **Maison Internationale des Poètes et des Ecrivains** (5 rue du Pélicot, T02 99 40 28 77, mipe.asso.fr), the only half-timbered house dating from before 1661, when a devastating fire swept through the town.

Activities

St-Malo is a major centre for sailing and yachting and a superb place for your kids to catch the bug. Start by contacting **St-Malo Station Nautique** (Maison du Sport, place Georges Coudray, Paramé, T02 99 56 18 88, nautisme-saint-malo.fr) for information on sailing schools, sand yachting, kayaking, kite-surfing, diving and more. Alternatively St-Malo Surf School (2 av de la Hoguette, T02 99 40 07 47, surfschool.org) offers lessons for three- to 13-year-olds as well as adults.

If the kids fancy trying their hand at fishing while in St-Malo, **Oliver Berry Guide de Pêche** (16 rue Auguste Hovius, T06 62 79 19 67, guidepechesaintmalo.com) runs a fishing school for kids aged six to 14. On a Wednesday in July and August, older children can have a go at abseiling down the ramparts (see page 30).

Grab a bite

Bar du Soleil

Plage Bon Secours, T02 99 40 85 32.

On the prom, this is a great beach café with plastic tables and chairs outside. Watch the locals play boules while you tuck into cheap and hearty dishes after a busy morning on the beach.

Crêperie Chantal

2 place aux Herbes, T02 99 40 93 97. Apr-Sep 1130-2230, Oct-Feb 1130-1500, 1830-2130, closed Mon (except school holidays).

If you want to get away from the madding crowd, try the oldest crêperie in St-Malo, dating back to 1955, in this quiet spot. The two-level dining area, with an upstairs kitchen, is bright and cheerful, the service is swift, and the crêpes are excellent.

Let's go to... St-Malo

La Bouche en Folie

14 rue de Boyer, T06-72 49 08 89. Daily 1200-1400, 1900-2200, closed Mon and Tue out of season.

This is a lovely restaurant with a genial atmosphere, in a quiet street. The menu is creative, with an innovative slant on well-known dishes, such as risotto of red mullet with mushrooms, and *crème brûlée* with pear and ginger. A real treat for mums and dads, and offers a great-value three-course menu for €15.

La Brigantine

13 rue de Dinan, T02 99 56 82 82. Jul-Sep daily 1200-2200, rest of year closed Tue and Wed.

It's easy to miss the narrow façade of this crêperie – look for the wooden ship plaque – and it has an unassuming interior, but its excellent crêpes, made from organic *blé noir* flour, are popular with locals and visitors.

La P'tite Rôtisserie Restaurant

6 rue de la Corne de Cerf, T02 99 40 21 92, laptiterotisserie.com.

Come for a family treat in this modern baroque restaurant. If the weather is warm, sit outside. Tables have Play-Doh for kids. Cancale oysters cost €8 for six or there's beef tenderloin with mushrooms for €17.50. The €10 kids' menu includes chicken and chips and dessert.

Le Bistro de Jean

6 rue de la Corne de Cerf, T02 99 40 98 68, 1200-1400, 1900-2230, closed Wed and Sun, Sat lunch.

A typical French eating experience awaits in this bistro adorned by ancient sporting equipment. There's no menu, just a blackboard or two with regular dishes and the day's specials.

Le Café du Coin d'en Bas

3 rue St-Barbe, T02 99 56 41 90, cafes-historiques.com.

This quirky den looks like a salty old bar that has been stuffed full of curios, from Spanish dolls to accordions, stuck everywhere from the ceiling to the bar pumps. Kids love the spooky details.

Stay the night

See Sleeping, page 56.

Ferry ride

Take a trip on one of the *vedettes* (little ferries) to the nearby resort of Dinard, the town of Dinan, Cap Fréhel and the island of Cézembre, or even to the Channel Islands. The tourist office can supply information.

Around St-Malo

Grand Aquarium de St-Malo
Av du Général Patton, 35402 St-Malo, T02 99 21 19 00, aquarium-st-malo.com. Apr-Jun and Sep 1000-1900, first half of Jul and last half of Aug 0930-2000, second half of Jul and first half of Aug 0930-2200, Oct-Mar 1000-1800 (check for dates closed in Nov and Jan). €15.50 adult, €9.50 child (4-14), under 4s free, family 10% discount. Night in the Shark's Ring €400 for three people, €100 per extra adult and €80 per extra child (6-14).

With over 10,000 creatures, this aquarium will have you hook, line and sinker. A dark entrance sets the scene for marine explorations of the past. The first tank has tiny fluorescent 'Moon' jellyfish, followed by a tank of rays that show off their alien-like underbellies as they glide by. And so it begins. There's plenty to delight: cylinder anemones, giant crabs, huge pollack, menacing barracuda...

There are eight themed rooms, covering cold water environments to tropical seas. Most exhibits are labeled in English. Don't miss the Shark's Ring, a circular tank with you at the centre, with 360° views of 3-m long sharks gliding by, accompanied by four marine turtles and a giant grouper.

Little ones will love the extensive touch pools where ray, turbot and dogfish can be gently handled. Scallops and starfish also inhabit this tactile area, which focuses on Breton sea life.

Leading off from the touch pool is the Nautibus submarine which simulates diving deep under the oceans. Zones of turbulence and mysterious wrecks add to the excitement. This attraction is popular so be prepared to queue in quite claustrophobic conditions.

If you book in advance, it's possible to stay overnight with the sharks, learning all kinds of fascinating facts – that they have up to 80,000 teeth in their life, eat over three tonnes of food a year and can perceive a heart palpitation at 500 m distance. Scary! The night also includes a guided tour of the whole aquarium, including its technical wing, and you can watch the sharks being fed.

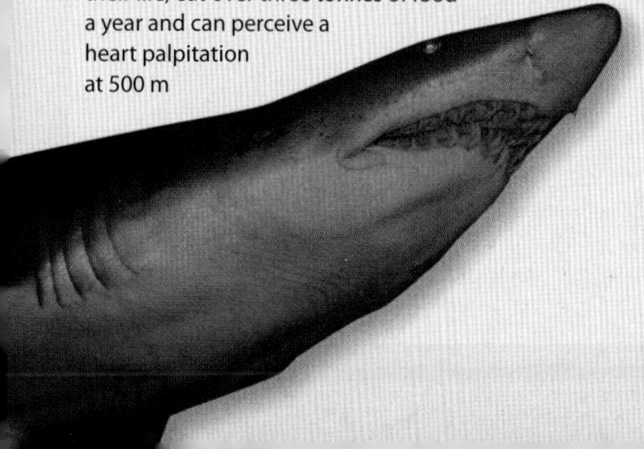

The aquarium's Le Terre et Bleu Café serves sandwiches from €4.60, pasta with cheese from €6.80 and vanilla yogurts from €2.30.

Labyrinthe du Corsaire (The Pirates' Maze)
Route de Quelmer La Passagère, 35400 St-Malo, T02 99 81 17 23, labyrintheducorsaire.com. Early Jul-Aug 1030-1900, €7.50 adult and child over 3.

On the Rance Estuary just south of St-Malo, this extensive corn maze has four different routes and is great entertainment for kids. There are plenty of other puzzles aside from the maze, along with a small farm and bouncy castles, including a huge galleon and a treasure box.

Le Clos-Poulet

Le Clos-Poulet, the countryside around St-Malo, contains many fine corsairs' houses called *malouinières*. The tourist office in St-Malo can supply leaflets with a driving or cycling tour of some of the best. The Manoir de Limoëlou (musee-jacques-cartier.com, Jul-Aug daily 1000-1130, 1430-1800, Sep-Jun Mon-Sat, €4), was the house of Jacques Cartier, who discovered Canada. It is now a museum documenting his achievements.

Pointe du Grouin and Cancale

Take the coast-road (D201) towards Cancale via Pointe du Grouin for great sea views across to the Channel Islands. Binoculars will be useful for watching shags and oystercatchers on the Ile des Landes bird reserve. The magical mound of Mont St-Michel lies to the east, and the hump of Mont-Dol inland.

Rochers Sculptés, Rothéneuf
Daily 0900-1900, closed 1200-1400 in winter. €3 adult, under 12s free.

These sculpted rocks are a true curiosity. Carved over 25 years by a reclusive priest, Abbé Fouré, they represent the Rothéneuf clan of pirates and adventurers, who mostly came to a sticky end at the time of the French Revolution. Dozens of individuals and creatures are shown in strange postures of life or death, like the man lying with an arm around his dog, a sea-monster, a cow, and a cruel husband. The location alone is worth a visit.

Forêt de Paimpont

(the Forest of Brocéliande)

Brocéliande is the mythical name for the Forêt de Paimpont, located about 30 km west of Rennes and also known as the Forest of King Arthur. The remains of Argoat, a vast forest covering the centre of the Breton peninsula during the Middle Ages, it is the source of many Celtic legends, especially Arthurian ones.

Even if your kids aren't into King Arthur and the Knights of the Round Table – and most are thanks to the BBC's highly successful series *Merlin* – the Forêt de Paimpont is a beautiful place to explore with plenty of things to see and do.

For those of you who need a little refresher on the tales of King Arthur, or thought they were all set in Cornwall or Wales, here goes. According to one version of the legend, King Arthur summoned the Knights of the Round Table to find the Holy Grail, hidden in the Brittany woods. It was here that the wizard Merlin, friend and advisor to the young Arthur, met and fell in love with Viviane, the Lady of the Lake. Merlin loved Viviane so much that he built her a crystal citadel under the pool reflecting the Château de Comper at Concoret (see page 55). Taking advantage of Merlin's infatuation, Viviane persuaded him to teach her his spells. Using this magic, she restored his youth at the Fontaine de Jouvence and then imprisoned him in perpetuity in nine magic circles, as solid as rock.

The modern Arthur industry taps into the love of magic in all of us, and indeed the power of the legend has created its own particular reality here. Several springs, rocks and standing stones in the forest are linked to Merlin myths. Not being able to reach them by car (most are accessed by well-worn footpaths) adds to the sense of quest and fulfilment, which kids are sure to appreciate.

Paimpont

One of the main centres for exploring the forest, Paimpont is an attractive village best known for its 13th-century lakeside abbey, which holds summer exhibitions and concerts, and has picnic areas and

Tourist offices

Montfort-sur-Meu, 4 place du Tribunal, 35160 Montfort-sur-Meu, T02 99 09 06 50.
Paimpont, 5 esplanade de Brocéliande, 35380 Paimpoint, T02 99 07 84 23.
Tréhorenteuc, 1 place Abbé Gillard, 56430 Tréhorenteuc, T02 97 93 05 12, broceliande.valsansretour.com.

walks by the lake. Don't miss a stroll down Paimpont's high street with its stone cottages. The shops are devoted to all things magic. **Au Pays de Merlin** (28 rue du Général de Gaulle, T02 99 07 80 23, closed Mon and Tue out of main season) stocks everything for aspiring knights, magicians, witches and Arthurian souvenir hunters, and also hires out bikes. Kids in need of an Arthurian haircut can visit The Enchanted Scissors.

Chêne à Guillotin

It's worth a little drive to see this remarkable oak tree, said to be over 1000 years old and still flourishing. With a 9.6-m circumference, it lies near Vaubosard, southwest of Concoret.

A Pass Brocéliande, giving reduced entry fees at a number of attractions, is available from tourist offices.

Les Jardins de Brocéliande

Route des Mesnils, 35310 Breal-sous-Montfort, T02 99 60 08 04, jardinsdebroceliande.fr. Apr-Oct Tue-Sat 1330-1800, Jul and Aug daily 1100-1900. €6.50 adult, €3 child (6-18), under 6s free, €15 family.

One of France's prize gardens, with sumptuous beds, themed, landscaped and wild areas plus an orchard, Les Jardins de Brocéliande hold family events and have two themed trails. Discover the gardens barefoot on 'Awake your feet', a 1-km trail with different textures underfoot – sand, rock, wood, water and shells – and surprises along the way; 'Put on your senses' takes you on a 200-m trail while blindfolded. Fabulous for kids.

Montfort-sur-Meu

This medieval town has a great Ecomuseum. Set in a striking 14th-century tower, **Ecomusée du Pays de Montfort** (2 rue du Château, 35160 Montfort-sur-Meu, T02 99 09 31 81, ecomuseepaysmontfort.free.fr, Apr-Sep daily, Oct-Mar Mon-Thu, closed

White stag with a golden necklace in the church of Tréhorenteuc.

lunchtime), harks back to a pre-industrial time when kids played with toys made from natural materials. Catch a toy-making workshop or a temporary exhibition. For something more 21st-century, the tourist office (see page 53) offers guided tours by SatNav. A fun way to explore the historic Pays de Montfort area, the system works via a PDA (personal digital assistant) that fits in the palm of your hand. Information clips, quizzes and archive images are automatically programmed to appear at specific points. It's somewhere between a modern-day treasure hunt and an interactive guided tour.

Tréhorenteuc

This small village, with a year-round friendly tourist office (see page 53), is the starting point for walks in the Val Sans Retour (see page 55). The tourist office offers guided, narrated walks all year round, so long as you book in advance. The delightful 17th-century church was given a revamp in the 1950s by Abbé Gillard, who developed the theme of the Arthurian legends and the Holy Grail in the decor of the church. There are paintings of the Round Table, a frieze of the White Stag and a window showing the Holy Grail. It all works surprisingly well.

Sleeping

For a highly individual place to stay, book a few nights at Auberge des VoyaJoueurs (see page 18). See also pages 56, 58 and 61.

The forest is mostly private, so walking away from popular sites is not advised during the hunting season (Oct-Mar).

Merlin magic

The Fôret of Paimpont is dotted with sites linked to the Arthurian legends. To locate them, pick up a map from the tourist office in Paimpont or Tréhorenteuc.

Château de Comper/Centre de l'Imaginaire Arthurien
Château de Comper en Brocéliande, 56430 Concoret, T02 97 22 79 96, centre-arthurien-broceliande.com. Apr-Jun, Sep-Oct 1000-1730, closed Tue and Wed, Jul and Aug 1000-1900, closed Wed. €5.50 adult, €4.50 child (8-18), under 8s free.
The best place to start hunting for Arthurian legends is the turreted Château de Comper near Concoret, housing the Centre de l'Imaginaire Arthurien, which stages exhibitions, events and themed walks on the Arthurian legends. The lake next to the castle is where the Viviane, also known as the Lady of the Lake, lived in a crystal palace built by Merlin the magician.

Fans of *Excalibur* and the *Sword in the Stone* will have a field day here. Extravagantly costumed tableaux (shame about the wigs) bring the legends to life, with illustrated panels filling in the gaps. There are many artistic interpretations of Merlin and fairies, and a space with crayons where children can colour in their own knights and dragons. The emphasis is on the complex character of Merlin, and his combination of wise counsel and sorcery. His relationship with Viviane gets lots of attention, and you can have a good look for the Lady of the Lake from the windows. Once you have a ticket, you can also walk in the park with its lakeside and woodland trails.

Val sans Retour (Valley of No Return)
The highlight of a visit to the Forest of Brocéliande, this valley is the perfect setting for a walk. It is here that the sorceress Morgan le Fay, half-sister of King Arthur, is said to have imprisoned unfaithful youths. To visit the Valley of No Return, leave Tréhorenteuc (see above) in the direction of Campéneac, and park in the most distant of the parking areas just outside the village. From here it is an easy 300-m stroll up to the Miroir aux Fées (Fairies' Mirror), a spookily quiet and glassy lake. Beside it is the 'Golden Tree', a remarkable sculpture that was created as a symbol of the forest's powers of regeneration after fires in 1990. Wander on up into the valley, where the stream water runs red. Older children may enjoy the climb up onto the ridge overlooking the lake (bear left beyond it) with great wide views, or you can return to the parking area on a shorter circuit by following the path up past the Golden Tree.

Merlin's Tomb and the Fontaine de Jouvence
At the other end of the forest from the Valley of No Return are the slight remains of a megalith, long ruined by treasure-seekers, known as Merlin's tomb. It is little more than two stones and a holly tree, but recognizable by the votive offerings left by modern pagans. The footpath leads on for a few hundred metres to the Fountain of Youth, a circular enclosure of stones around a rather sluggish spring where Merlin's youth was restored by Viviane.

Fontaine de Barenton
The beautiful trail of a little over a kilometre leading up to the *fontaine* starts from a car park in the hamlet of Folles Pensées or Mad Thoughts: whether the spring water gave you these or cured you of them is uncertain. This idyllic location was where Merlin met Viviane and fell in love.

Merlin's tomb.

Pick of the pitches

Camping de Barenton

Folle Pensées, 35380 Paimpont, T02 97 22 68 87, souriez.com. pagesperso-orange.fr/barenton.htm. Year round.

If you really want to get away from it all and make the most of the enchanted forest, this is the place to do it. It's a great location and good for walkers. There are caravans (frescoed with scenes from King Arthur) to rent and a *gîte d'étape* (a stop-over for hikers) providing 22 places.

Camping Municipal de la Cité d'Alet

Allée Gaston Buy, 35400 St-Malo, T02 99 81 60 91, ville-saint-malo.fr. €17.75 car and caravan, €13.40 car and tent.

This municipal site is cheap and cheerful with a few outstanding features, namely a ruined 18th-century fort and a German blockhouse from the Second World War now containing a little museum on St-Malo's occupation and liberation. There's a kids' play area and mini-golf, and three shower blocks between 300 places. It's a short drive from the ferry port at St-Malo and near the beach, with lovely views over the Rance estuary and plenty of water sports to hand.

Chênedet Loisirs

Ferme de Chênedet, route forestière de la Villeboeuf, 35133 Landéan, T02 99 97 35 46, chenedet-loisirs.com. Year round.

Rent a yurt with a pretty painted door at this activity centre deep in the forest of Fougères, or camp by the lake. The yurts are set in a group, quite close together. There's horse riding here and ponies for little ones.

Domaine de Tremelin

Lac de Tremelin, 35750 Iffendic, T02 99 09 73 79, domaine-de-tremelin.fr. Gîtes open year round, €150/2 nights. Camping Apr-Oct €4-5/person.

This wooded lake setting is an idyllic spot for families. As well as 20 basic gîtes for six to eight people and 100 campsite pitches, it has an adventure playground and a clean supervised beach. Other facilities include pedaloes, electric boats, play areas, mini-golf, a little train, quads, motorbikes, tree ladders and swinging circuits, a trampoline, horse riding, bike hire, tennis, canoeing and windsurfing lessons. There's a lso a pleasant restaurant.

Domaine du Logis

35190 La Chapelle aux Filzméens, T02 99 45 25 45, domainedulogis. com. Apr-Nov. €8-14 pitch, €4-4.50 adult, €2.50 child (2-12); 4-person mobile home €300-600/week.

WC

For a campsite with lots of character and high standards, Domaine du Logis is a great option. Set in the grounds of a turreted castle are 180 pitches for tents, caravans and campervans, along with good mobile homes to rent where you can hire baby equipment such as a highchair, cot and bath. The highlight of this site is the beautiful swimming pool and toddler pool surrounded by old stone buildings with a café and plenty of places to sunbathe – parents can relax as it's a safe environment. There are some nice wooden climbing frames and a quiet library in which kids can wind down. Activities include a bouncy castle, trampoline, volleyball, basketball, badminton, football, crazy golf, giant chess, table tennis and table football. From May to September the site offers fishing and kayaking plus hikes and cycle rides. There's also a BMX track and a fitness room for parents. A kids' club for six- to 12-year-olds runs on weekday mornings in July and August.

Le Vieux Chêne

Baguer-pican, 35120 Dol-de-Bretagne, T02 99 48 09 55, camping-vieuxchene.fr. Apr-Sep €10.50-23/pitch for 1 person, €4.50-6 extra adult, 2-bedroom cottage for 4 €2.50-3.90 child (4-12); €271-275/6 nights.

Located in the Mont-St-Michel bay area, this is a great location. There are 199 pitches for tents, caravans or campervans, as well as cottage-style mobile homes and chalets to rent. There's a heated pool (May to mid-Sep) with slides, two toddler pools, playgrounds, crazy golf, table tennis, billiards and a video games room. There's lake fishing for carp or perch. During summer holidays there's a kids' club from 1000-1200 (Sun-Fri), and plenty of evening fun with mussels-and-chips parties, bingo, karaoke and live music.

Farm favourites

Gîtes de la Ferme de Kersillac

Kersillac, 35290 Gael, T02 99 07 76 48, broceliande.giteskersillac.com. €250-458/week.

These two pretty stone cottages sleeping up to six reflect their setting with murals of fairies and forest scenes. Families are free to look around this tranquil dairy farm.

Domaine de la Briquerie

Les Champs de Roz

8 Grande Rue, Roz Landrieux, 35120 Dol-de-Bretagne, T02 99 48 25 19. €45/night for 2, €15 extra person.

This old farmhouse near Dol-de-Bretagne is part of the *Bienvenue à la ferme* scheme, and Mme Mainsard is a very welcoming host. There are five rooms, including a family room and a mini-apartment with kitchenette on the ground floor. Look forward to a delicious breakfast with freshly made crêpes and *craquelins* (crackers), a local speciality.

Best of the rest

Château du Pin

Prés de Montfort, 35750 Iffendic, T02 99 09 34 05, chateaudupin-bretagne.com. €110-130/family suite, €380-520/week self-catering in Le Logis (sleeps 4).

This stylish, upmarket château hotel would be in the 'Splashing out' category, but for its well-priced self-catering option called Le Logis, which has a living room, kitchen facilities and two bedrooms. There's everything you need for a self-catering stay from washing machine to your own private garden. The château has two family suites, Victor Hugo and George Sand, both beautifully decorated. Nice touches include flowers, handmade quilts, storybooks and teddy bears.

Domaine de la Briquerie

Rose Cottage (3 bedrooms) and Vine Cottage (2 bedrooms). 35660 Langon, T+44(0)845 489 0140, babyfriendlyboltholes.co.uk. €370-€950/week, €60/night (minimum 3 nights).

These recently renovated detached stone cottages nestling in the grounds of a former 19th-century hunting lodge on the banks of the River Vilaine have everything you need for children – true to the Baby Friendly Boltholes philosophy. There's direct access to a long-distance cycle path, and the detached cottages share a heated outdoor pool, handy kids' play area and pretty gardens. Chef Hélène offers a parent-friendly evening meal delivery service several nights a week.

Ferme de la Vieuville
35260 Cancale, T02 23 15 19 30, fermedelavieuville.fr. €50-72/night B&B, €315-840/week.
A stylish but cosy B&B with self-catering facilities and three lovely family gîtes sleeping between four and six, this converted 18th-century farmhouse is a great option for families. Exposed stone walls and clever lighting make everything that bit more chic than your average rustic hideaway. This is great value for money, even more so when you discover the heated pool with its barn-like roof and lovely chill out area. It's just a five-minute walk to Cancale, yet this place is off the beaten track and peaceful.

Hôtel Le Nautilus
9 rue de la Corne de Cerf, 35400 St-Malo, T02 99 40 42 27, lenautilus.com. €74-82/double room with child's bed, €84-92/family room for 4 (2 adjoining rooms or 1 room with double bed and bunkbeds).
A popular and very friendly hotel near the busy heart of the Intra-Muros. It's a colourful place in all ways: nice bedrooms over several floors (lift) with bright furnishings and en-suite showers, and lively artwork adorning the little breakfast room and bar, which have a nautical theme. Good value for money in a central location.

Hôtel San Pedro
1 rue Ste-Anne, 35400 St-Malo, T02 99 40 88 57, sanpedro-hotel.com. Mid-Mar to late Nov, €58-71/double.
Mireille Morice's personality has much to do with the success of the San Pedro. Everything is on a small scale here, which adds to the exceptional charm and style of this appealing hotel. Bonuses are a sea view on the top floor and special breakfast treats. It's located in a quiet part of the Intra-Muros, and the ramparts and swimming pool are on the doorstep. Highly recommended.

La Clef du Four
La Touche Pichard, 35720 Plesder, T02 23 22 01 35, laclefdufour.com. Family suite €90 with breakfast. Price per night decreases the longer you stay.
This B&B in a handsome stone house is a value-for-money find. Of the five rooms, one is a family room with space for five. Whilst the decor is nothing special, guests have use of a kitchenette and there's a covered pool and a garden with slides, mini tractors and trikes.

La Lanterne
110 rue de la Pinterie, 35300 Fougères, T02 99 99 58 80. €48/double.
This *gîte urbain*, a few paces from the château and the medieval quarter, has been renovated with style and imagination. The four attractive bedrooms have exposed stone walls, chic modern decoration and colourful shower rooms. The kitchen, where breakfast is served, is available for guests to use if they wish, and there's a garden area too.

La Maison du Graal
21b rue du Général de Gaulle, 35380 Paimpont, T02 99 07 83 82, lamaisondugraal.net.
Ideally placed for the lake and abbey in Paimpont, this B&B in the main street has two rooms of good size with parquet floors, wrought-iron beds and private bathrooms, plus the sort of decorative details that fit the atmosphere of the Brocéliande experience. Romantics should opt for 'Merlin & Viviane'. Best for older children who don't mind sleeping separately from their parents.

La Pensée
35 rue de la Grève, 35800 St-Lunaire, T02 99 46 03 82, la-pensee.fr. €95-105/self-catering for 4.
The great thing about this pretty B&B and self-catering apartment is its proximity to the beautiful Grande Plage at St-Lunaire. Wood

decor, mosaics and old furniture plus private gardens or verandas make this a pleasing choice.

Le Grénier d'Ernestine

Les Basses Barres, 35310 Bréal-sous-Monfort, T02 99 60 34 03, grenier-ernestine.com. From €72 for family room.

It's clear from this laidback B&B that the owners have a large family and aren't a bit phased by kids tearing around the place. There are five cosy rooms sleeping between three and six, with old dolls, teddies and toy cars dotted around. There's a mini farm with donkeys, ponies, horses and goats.

Le Village Mahana

La Vallée Piet, 35730 Pleurtuit, T02 99 88 73 21, gites-mahana.com. €280-680/week.

This attractive and super family-friendly group of five gîtes (sleeping 2-7) named after the islands of French Polynesia make a great base just a couple of kilometres inland from Dinard and St-Lunaire. There's a lovely outdoor pool fenced off for safety, and loungers for sunbathing. There's a kids' play area with a lovely wooden Wendy House, slide, swings and table tennis. Owner Mahana will babysit on request.

Résidence Reine Marine

65/67 av Président John Fitzgerald Kennedy, 35400 St-Malo, T02 99 40 75 00, residence-reinemarine.com. 1-bedroom south-facing apartment for 4 €72-€205/night, €360-1025/week.

This classy family accommodation is right by the beach and has panoramic views of the bay of St-Malo. There are 67 luxurious self-catering apartments that sleep up to six. Best of all it's part of the Thermes Marins de St-Malo empire, which means guests have access to the thalassotherapy centre, Aquatonic pool, spa and St-Malo golf club. Apartments are modern and spacious with fresh furnishings in nautical blue and white. Guests can use the children's club at its sister establishment, Le Grand Hôtel des Thermes (€22 per half-day). There are also windsurfing, sand-yachting and catamaran sessions and courses. During July and August there's a beach club for three- to 10-year-olds in front of the Grand Hôtel.

Splashing out

Château de la Motte Beaumanoir

35720 Pleugueneuc-Plesder, T02 23 22 05 00, la-motte-beaumanoir.com. €170-205/double, €280-340/family suite for up to 5.

If you've always wanted to stay in a French château, this could be your dream hotel. The real beauty for families is what lies outdoors, for there's a forest to explore, a heated pool, tennis courts, bikes for hire and boats on the lake. Mums and dads will appreciate the spa, the billiards and the golf. There are two lovely family rooms to choose from.

Place du Champ Jacquet, Rennes.

Grand Hôtel Barrière

46 av George V, BP 70143, 35801 Dinard, T02 99 88 26 26, lucienbarriere.com. €140-220 double.

A member of Leading Hotels of the World, the grande dame of Dinard is the real deal when it comes to splashing out. Although it's posh, it has got looking after families down to a fine art with Club Diwi & Co for four- to 12- year-olds, an indoor pool, interconnecting rooms and kids' menus.

Le Relais de Brocéliande

5 rue des Forges, 35380 Paimpont, T02 99 07 84 94, relais-de-broceliande.fr. €69-98 for a double room plus a child under 12, €84-113 family room for 4.

If you're splashing out, this Logis de France is a good choice, situated near the lake and abbey in Paimpont. Rooms in the older building or garden annexe are spacious, comfortable and well equipped. Family rooms are available. Welcoming staff and a good restaurant too.

Les Gîtes Marins at Maisons de Bricourt

62 rue des Rimains, 35260 Cancale, T02 99 89 64 76, maisons-de-bricourt.com. €2318/week for 4.

Stunning seaside cottages which look like something out of *Elle Decoration*. Designed for two to eight people, the cottages combine modern comforts with a simple, refined decor. Each cottage is set up around a main room that serves as the kitchen, dining room and living room. The comfortable rooms have their own toilet or spacious bathroom. Guests can pick their own vegetables and herbs for cooking, and every morning a basket of fruits, dairy products, bread and brioches is delivered to your door. Parents should visit La Maison de Gwenn for a foot massage (la-maison-de-gwenn.com) on the same complex; the whole family can dine at the Château Richeaux Restaurant and go for ice creams at Grain de Vanille.

Cool & quirky

Le Boat

T+44 (0)844 463 3594, leboat.com. A boat sleeping 4 from £1610/week.

If you want a week or two on a self-driven river or canal cruiser, Le Boat is a great place to start. The vessels are easy to steer and require no experience, and you can hire bikes so that you can stop off and explore. To cover the distances requires no more than four to five hours' cruising a day, but you need to factor in 20 minutes to get through each lock. The Best of Brittany Cruise is a two-week cruise beginning in Messac and taking in Redon, Josselin, Nantes and back to Messac.

Chambres
d'hôtes

Eating Ille-et-Vilaine

Quick & simple

Au Goût des Hôtes

8 rue Rallier du Baty, 35000 Rennes, T02 99 79 20 36. Mon-Sat 1200-1400, 1930-2300, Sun (Jul and Aug) 1200-1400, 1930-2300.

The best in a string of restaurants on a popular eating square. Typical bistro-style fare – chicken crumble, bream *en croute* – with some good combinations of flavours and textures. The lunchtime set menu at €15 for three courses is very good value. There's an attractive upstairs room, too, and an outdoor terrace.

L'Abri Cotier

39 rue des Douves, 35600 Redon, T02 99 71 13 42. Thu-Tue1200-1400, 1900-2200.

A very welcoming eaterie with nautical decor. The Tricot Menu at under €20 is excellent value with a buffet of starters (meat, fish, salad) and a wide selection of mains. Pork in cider sauce is delicious, and the pistachio, strawberry and salted caramel dessert works well. Serves straightforward good food at excellent prices.

Au Temps des Moines Crêperie

16 av du Chevalier Ponthu, 35380 Paimpont, T02 99 07 89 63. Wed-Sun 1200-1400, 1900-2200, irregular opening Nov-Apr.

This excellent crêperie in an old house has a pretty garden setting on the lakeside. Eat in the enclosed veranda or outside. The menu is simple, but the crêpes have some unusual savoury fillings – try the tomato and anchovy. Very good value.

Café Babylone

12 rue des Dames, 35000 Rennes, T02 99 85 82 99. Closed Sun.

This cheerful café is a handy breakfast or coffee stop right next to the cathedral. It has an outdoor terrace and operates as a bistro-type restaurant later in the day.

Crêperie L'Akène

10 rue du Jeu de Paume, 35600 Redon, T02 99 71 25 15, creperieakene.com. Thu-Tue 1200-1400, 1830-2200.

Attractive interior with frescoes of a Breton family eating their daily *soupe*. Try the thick local sausage and caramelized onions wrapped in a buckwheat blanket, or a dessert crêpe filled with rich sweet chestnut cream. A very good selection of Breton beers is available.

Crêperie des Portes Mordelaises

6 rue des Portes Mordelaises, 35000 Rennes, T02 99 30 57 40. Wed-Mon 1200-1400, 1900-2300.

This little crêperie has the perfect mix of historic and foodie appeal for both adults and kids. Situated on one of Rennes' oldest cobbled streets, across the road from the home of Anne de Bretagne, who married the king of France and thereby joined Brittany to the motherland in 1532. It is hard to miss with its bright orange exterior and kids' play kitchen outside. It is family owned, and staff go out of their way to make everyone feel welcome. All ingredients are organic. Mums and dads might try the delicious Anne de Bretagne galette, with leeks cooked in butter with smoked bacon, egg and cream, at €7.40. A kids' menu costs €6.90 for a savoury galette with two fillings, a sweet crêpe and a local cola or orange juice.

Crêperie Grill Le Raoul II

3 place Raoul II, 35300 Fougères, T02 99 99 31 97. Daily 1200-1430,1900-2230.

This is one of several eateries in the square overlooking the château, ideal if the family wants a cheap, filling meal to get up their strength for all those tower stairs. The menu is basic, with slightly stodgy crêpes, salads and tasty omelettes, grills (sausage, steak, chicken) and *moules frites*.

Grain de Vanille

12 place de la Victoire, 35260 Cancale, T02 99 89 64 76, maisons-de-bricourt.com. Daily.

Down a small road leading to the sea, the walls of Grain de Vanille previously housed a bread oven. This delightful tearoom indulges the Breton sweet tooth with buttery cakes, ice creams and sorbets. While parents might like a refreshing local cider, kids can sample the famed hot chocolate, with or without spices. Many sweets, including salted butter caramels, are made on the premises as are the jams and marmalades, which are delicious on the breads baked in the wood oven of Château Richeux.

La Gourmandise Crêperie

26 rue d'En-Bas, 35500 Vitré, T02 99 75 02 12. Tue eve-Sun 1200-1400, 1900-2200.

This little strip of a restaurant in the medieval town of Vitré has a huge fireplace that takes up much of one wall. The food here is incredibly good value – a daily special like veal escalope in a creamy mushroom sauce followed by crème brûlée costs just €8. Crêpes are substantial and tasty. The bill comes (with sweets) in a little wooden chest.

La Saint-Georges Crêperie

11 rue du Chapitre, 35000 Rennes, T02 99 38 87 04. Tue-Sat 1200-1400, 1900-2230.

Something original: a crêperie that is contemporary in appearance and has a sophisticated menu. The downstairs room is sober compared with the two funky options above – and don't miss the TV in the toilet! The crispy crêpes are good too: try George Harrison or maybe George Boy.

Le Daniel

19 rue Jules Simon, 35000 Rennes, T02 99 78 85 82. Closed Sun afternoon and Mon morning.

This pâtisserie by Les Halles, the indoor market, is a peaceful place for good tea or coffee, luscious cakes or a hearty quiche-and-salad lunch. Also has a range of chocolate to die for.

Le P'tit Bouchon

13 bis rue Chateaubriand, 35300 Fougères, T02 99 99 75 98. Mon-Sat 1200-1400, 1900-2200.

This is a lovely family-friendly place to eat, with Eric greeting the guests and Isabelle producing traditional dishes in the kitchen. The interior is all wood and stone, with charmingly eclectic decor, large bookcases and a fish-tank. The food is simply good – starters of hot salads and terrines and daily specials that might include roast pork with apple or rabbit in mustard sauce.

Le Surf

Plage de Longchamp, St-Lunaire, T06 80 26 08 58. Early-2200 (hours vary according to season and weather).
This snack bar at the western end of St-Lunaire's Plage de Longchamp is just a humble covered terrace with plastic tables and chairs along the sea wall, yet it serves Nutella and banana paninis, crêpes, steak and even whole lobster (which must be ordered a day in advance). Substantial seafood salads start from €12 and children's ham or frankfurters with chips from €3.50. There's ice cream or hot chocolate for afters.

Tivabro

13 place de Marchix, 35300 Fougères, T02 99 17 20 90. 1200-1400, 1900-2130, closed Mon (also Wed and Sun evening outside Jul and Aug).
The best crêperie in town (has *Crêperies gourmandes* mark) in a very fine half-timbered house in the medieval quarter. Galettes and crêpes are made from organic flour and locally sourced ingredients, and there's a wide choice of fillings. The ice creams are truly delicious.

Cancale oysters

At low tide tractors cross the sands to the oyster beds off Cancale's Port de la Houle. On a fine day it's nice to watch the action and the distant views of Mont St-Michel while enjoying a tray of oysters with a wedge of lemon from one of the stalls (€2.50 for six). Eat them on the steps down to the beach, tossing the shells back into the sea. If your kids' reaction is "yuk!", then stock up on picnic food from one of the many grocery shops along the front.

If you prefer to eat in, choose from the following in Cancale:

Au Pied d'Cheval You can buy fresh oysters and mussels to take out or eat in. Omelettes for the non-fish fanciers. Why 'horse's hoof'? It's the name of a large oyster.

Au Rocher de Cancale Charges €12.50 for nine oysters, up to €79 for a meal comprising oysters, a platter of *fruits de mer* and wine for two people.

La Maison Blanche Overlooking the oyster area, with a large heated terrace and every manner of shellfish and fresh catch of the day.

Au Vieux Safran A very popular traditional restaurant specializing in *fruits de mer* (€26), but with plenty of other options.

Le Surcouf You'll get an excellent rich fish soup here, and a *fricassée* of the sought-after Breton (blue) lobster for €48.

Posh nosh

Auberge du Chat-pitre

18 rue du Chapitre, 35000 Rennes, T02 99 30 36 36, auberge-du-chat-pitre.com. Mon-Sat 2000-2300.
Medieval restaurant in one of the most attractive houses on this ancient street. Costumed waiting staff, musical entertainment and robust dishes (ragoût of lamb with honey and almonds, gingered pork and sausage). Kids will love the dress-up and the quirky touches like the Puss in Boots puppet. You need to book.

La Pointe du Grouin Hôtel/ Restaurant

Pointe du Grouin, 35260 Cancale, T02 99 89 60 55, hotelpointedugrouin.com. Apr-Nov 1200-1400, 1900-2200, restaurant closed Tue (and Thu lunch outside Jul and Aug).
Eat delicious food with views of the Ile de Landes and Mont St-Michel in the distance. Any dish here is good, and accompanied by imaginative vegetable dishes. Good wine list. Set menus from €20 up to the *gastronomique* at €78.

Hôtel de la Vallée

6 av George V, 35800 Dinard, T02 99 46 94 00, hoteldelavallee.com. Daily.
An attractive waterside dining room with outdoor terrace make this a great location. There are no set menus, so on the pricey side, but the *carte* has a wide selection of shellfish, the house speciality, as well as other fish

and meat options. The truly yummy desserts might include chocolate fondant or rhubarb tiramisu. Worth it for a treat.

Local goodies

L'Epicier Breton

3 quai Thomas, 35260 Cancale. Daily 1000-1800.

An emporium of Breton products, especially beer, cider and whisky, biscuits and cakes, Quimper pottery, nice cider and – not surprisingly – oyster knives.

The Farm Shop, Chèvrerie du Désert

Le Désert, 35540 Plerguer, 8 km west of Dol-de-Bretagne off D676. T02 99 58 92 14, chateaubriand.com/Partenaires/chevrerie-du-desert.htm. Apr-Jun and Sep Mon and Wed-Sat 1430-1830, Sun and public holidays 1100-1830, Jul and Aug daily 1100-1830.

Wonderful home-made Breton goat's cheese, jams, honey, cider, apple juice, terrines and butter biscuits. There's a modest little café, too, with outside tables for galettes, cheese platters and goat's milk crêpes. See page 41.

Halles Centrales

Place Honoré Commeurec, 35000 Rennes. Mon-Sat 0700-1900, Sun 0930-1230).

Superb meat, cheese, fish and vegetables. On Saturday, don't miss Rennes' huge morning market in place des Lices, selling the best produce from the region.

Fresh from Baie du Mont St-Michel

Sheltered by the sea wall running along the Breton length of the bay, the land here is highly productive, and you'll find fresh vegetables and quality meat and dairy products in abundance. One of the old windmills that once dotted the bay, Moulin de la Saline at Cherrueix, contains La Maison des Produits du Terroir, which celebrates the bay's rich culinary traditions with interactive displays and demonstrations (La Saline, 35120 Cherrueix, T02 99 80 84 79, lamaisonduterroir.fr, Apr-Oct daily, closed lunchtime, €4 adult, €3 child, €11 family). A shop sells specialities of the region.

Cancale oyster farm.

Côtes d'Armor

Contents

Binic beach.

You must

❶ Spot a rock rabbit on the Pink Granite Coast.

❷ Become Tarzan at Vivons Perchés.

❸ Treat yourself to a stay at Petites Maisons dans la Prairie.

❹ Conquer La Pointe de Plouha.

❺ Take a surf workshop at Seven Islands Surf Club, Perros-Guirec.

❻ Catch a summer show at Fort La Latte.

❼ See how Asterix lived at Le Village Gaulois.

❽ Discover the origins of the iPhone at La Cité des Télécoms.

This may be the least populated of the four departments of Brittany, but in summer its coastal towns fill up with families lured by the promise of good old-fashioned bucket-and-spade action and the majestic Bay of St-Brie in which glittering sailing careers are launched by children as young as five.

It's not every day your child can spot Napoleon's hat, a witch or a tortoise taking shape in solid rosy rock, but that's the wonder of the **Pink Granite Coast**. This entrancing stretch of coastline is a great introduction to the magic of the northern coast and its interior known as Côtes d'Armor.

Perros-Guirec draws the crowds in summer to its three sandy beaches where you'll find everything from Théâtre Guignol (France's answer to Punch and Judy) to high-energy water sports and rock-pooling. Wherever you go along this fabulous coast of craggy cliffs you'll come across busy hangouts, including **Ploumanac'h**, **Paimpol**, **St-Quay**, **Binic** and **Erquy**. Don't miss the impressive Trieux steam train ride from Paimpol to **Pontrieux**. Just inland from Binic is the relatively new Zooparc de Trégomeur, with animals and plants from Asia and Madagascar introducing a tropical edge.

The wild coast around **Cap Fréhal** is a must-see, not least for the jaw-dropping sight of Fort La Latte, perching perilously on the sea cliffs. If you want to see puffins and perhaps the odd seal, catch a boat to the glorious **Sept Iles** and the picturesque **Ile Bréhat**.

Pleumeur-Bodou is a hub of family-friendly attractions. There's great forest fun to be had by swinging through the treetops at Vivons Perchés, and Gallic life is re-enacted with more than a touch of Asterix at Le Village Gaulois. You can then zoom forward a few thousand years to the Cité des Télécoms and Brittany Planetarium.

St-Brieuc, the only large town in Côtes d'Armor, is home to the Art Rock Festival every Whit weekend and to BMX challenges. This region has wonderful one-offs. Horse fans won't want to miss the National Haras (Stud) at **Lamballe** and no child should miss the enchanting sound park in **Cavan**.

Down south, on the border with Morbihan, lies **Lac de Guerlédan**, the largest lake in Brittany, offering extensive walking and cycling trails as well as kayak, pedalo, boat and water-ski hire from Beau Rivage on the north bank.

To the far east of Côtes d'Armor is the medieval town of **Dinan** near the wonderful **Rance estuary**. With its rampart walk and little tourist train that tootles around the half-timbered houses, this is a living history lesson and a great place to explore. Go in July for lots of free kiddie fun at the Festival des Remparts, one of the largest medieval festivals in Europe. At other times, head down to the port of Dinan, where you can hire a boat and simply mess about on the river.

The church at Lehon, near Dinan.

Out & about Côtes d'Armor

Fun & free

Shape up

Côte de Granit Rose is like a giant's seaside playground. The huge granite rocks have been transformed into weird and wonderful shapes by the force of tides and winds. Starting at Trestraou beach in Perros-Guirec, walk along the GR34 *sentier des douaniers* coastal path between Perros-Guirec and the port of Ploumanac'h, a stretch of coast dotted with sandy coves and clear rock pools, where kids can delight in spotting immense pink boulders resembling poured bottles of wine and tortoises. You'll encounter weather-beaten rocks, some as high as 20 m, including Napoleon's Hat, the Devil's Castle, a witch, a rabbit and many more. The round trip is 7 km and takes about two hours. Do the walk in the early morning or evening for the most dramatic light effects.

Get dancing

For a real taste of Breton culture attend either Bugale Breizh or the Festival de la St-Loup, both in Guingamp (dansebretonne.com). Bugale Breizh, on the first Sunday in July, includes a one-day festival celebrating the children of Brittany. It brings together many children's traditional dance groups, dressed in Breton costume, kicking off at 1400 with a procession to the Jardin Public. Kids can enjoy workshops and classes, including embroidery, puppet-making, cooking and traditional games. The Festival de la St-Loup takes place mid-July, and is a gathering of musicians and dancers from all over the Celtic world. There are paying concerts, with tickets available in advance from the tourist office (T02 96 73 89), but there are also free street processions and free classes in Breton dance. Guingamp is also a great place to bring the kids on Thursday from mid-July to early August, when puppet shows, singing, comedy and circus acts take place from 1500, and show theatre from 1800, in the place du Centre and Jardin Public.

Explore a hidden valley

For delightful walks, head out of Ploumanac'h into the Traouiero Valley, home to rare ferns, moss and aquatic plants, where footpaths take you past rocks and streams, shaded by large trees. The valley was once the haunt of smugglers.

Bag a beach

Perros-Guirec is one of Brittany's most popular family resorts,. On Thursdays in July and August, the 'Place aux Mômes' at the Palais des Congrès just behind Trestraou beach is a free family programme of burlesque circus, theatre, Guignol (Punch and Judy-style puppet show), acrobatic dance, poetry, singing, electro-pop concerts and more. Les Estivales is another summer programme of free activities,

Binic beach entertainment.

including beach volleyball, mountain biking, archery and health workshops. If you read French, ask the tourist office at 21 place de l'Hôtel de Ville (T02 96 23 21 15) for *Kid*, a free magazine with information on Perros-Guirec's beach clubs and the like, plus comic strips and quizzes.

Stay up late

In St-Brieuc on Thursday and Friday evening in July and August, 'Les Nocturnes' bring music and theatre to the streets. From punk and garage to clowns and puppets, there's something for everyone.

Step back in time

St-Brieuc's well laid-out Musée d'Art et d'Histoire (cours Francis Renard, rue des Lycéens Martyrs, Tue-Sat 0930-1145, 1330-1745, Sun 1330-1745) is free to visit. On three floors, the main themes of 19th-century life in the area are revealed, with maritime history and model boats at ground level, looms and spinning implements on the first floor, and furniture and costumes, including many *coiffes* (Breton lace headdresses) above. Temporary exhibitions cover a range of arts and crafts.

Have a blast in Binic

Known as the 'beauty spot of the Armorican coast', Binic is part of the Sensation Bretagne collective (sensation-bretagne.com/station-binic.php) with much to offer families. The festival 'Place aux Mômes' takes place in front of the beach on Tuesday in July and August. Children can get involved with puppetry, clowns, dance, juggling and music.

Follow in the footsteps

Said to be the highest in Brittany, the cliffs of Plouha and Gwin Zegal offer some of the best coastal walking in Côtes d'Armor, with the GR34 footpath running all the way up the Côte du Goëlo. Start from Palus Plage and walk north to Plage Bonaparte, passing many fine viewpoints such as La Pointe de Plouha (104 m), an up-and-down route of about 8 km. On the way, admire the harbour of Gwin Zegal, where boats are moored to the cut-off tree trunks planted in the sand with weighted roots. These gave rise to a legend that robbers were once tied to the trunks and left to the mercy of the tides. Plouha tourist office (T02 96 20 24 73) has a pack of leaflets detailing circular walks in the area.

Spot white horses

Just north of Trébeurden lies a protected area of freshwater marshland called the Marais du Quellen separated by dunes from Goas Treiz beach. Come here for nature walks, and to see the rare white Camargue horses. Trébeurden Tourist Office, T02 96 23 51 64, trebeurden.fr.

“”

We asked our two young boys what local activities they like best and they came up with a list of favourites, in no particular order:

- Beaches for every activity: rock-pooling, building sandcastles, bodyboarding or evening picnics.
- Bike rides around the car-free island of Bréhat.
- Walks in the Léguer valley, or on the rugged cliff tops with sea views along the coast.
- An afternoon at the 'sound park' in Cavan (see page 80).
- Getting dressed up as knights and trying on real armour at one of the many annual festivals.
- Flying down the zip wires and climbing the Tarzan vines at Vivons Perchés (see page 75).

Clara and Martin Cronin live in the Côtes d'Armor countryside with their two sons, Kit, aged nine, and Francis, six, and run three beautiful gîtes (gites-en-tregor.com), see page 92.

Best beaches

Binic

You'll find a warm welcome in the little port of Binic, which is rightly proud of its 'Famille Plus' accreditation. This guarantees the quality and quantity of activities and entertainment on offer in the summer months, with children very much in mind. In particular, kids can enjoy the sea-water pool at La Banche when the tide is out – the Bay of St-Brieuc has one of the longest ebbs in the world – or have a donkey ride. There are good evening events too.

Erquy

The very popular resort of Erquy, with its pretty harbour, is hemmed by a line of sandy beaches broken only by the jutting Cap d'Erquy, which has fabulous views over the Côte Emeraude. The huge Plage de Caroual has something for everyone, with lots of action for energetic types and a children's club on the sand in summer. If you want something less crowded, try the Plage du Portuais, a gorgeous little beach sheltered between rocky outcrops, accessible from the coastal path, north of the town centre.

Lancieux Plage de St-Cieux

There are steps down to this Blue Flag beach, well placed for facilities and with plenty of organized fun in summer. Join in with beach volleyball or enter a good-humoured competition to build the biggest sandcastle. The gentle slope of the bay and calm waters make this a good bathing option for very small children.

Palus Plage

On the Côte de Goëlo, this delightful beach is reached by a small road off the D786, winding through verdant countryside. A large pebble and sandy crescent, enclosed by green hills, is perfect for swimming or for exploring shore life at low tide. Kids can also enjoy the playground or an ice cream from the beachside bar in high season. If more substantial sustenance is required, there's a crêperie and family restaurant too. It also offers easy access to the coastal path, with stunning views of the Bay of St-Brieuc.

Perros-Guirec

On the Côte de Granit Rose at Perros Guirec, Plage de Trestraou on the northern shore is great for younger kids. There's a sailing club, the Jardin des Mers, in summer, and Club de Plage for children (aged 2-11) in July and August, offered by the half-day, full-day or week. Kids will make a beeline for the old-fashioned carousel (Easter-Sep) on the square near the beach. For beach gear and toys try L'Ile aux Jouets (T02 96 23 16 02) at 41 place de l'Hôtel de Ville near the tourist office.

Pléneuf-St-Val-André

There's a very jolly and familial atmosphere at this resort, and the beautiful clean white sand of the Grande Plage stretches for more than 2 km. It was created as a new bathing resort in the late 19th century, as the gracious villas bear witness. You can take an atmospheric stroll along the promenade for great views of the bay and the Ile de Verdelet, a bird reserve. The sailing centre is at the southern end of the beach, near the very picturesque Port de Dahouët, where you can take a boat to the Ile de Bréhat in summer.

St-Cast

This traditional family resort has seven sandy beaches around its promontory. The most central, La Grande Plage, is a glorious stretch of sand between two headlands, perfect for family lazing or swimming in the blue-green waters of the Emerald Coast. Shop for those essential buckets and spades or fishing nets in the shops lining the promenade. You won't be short of refreshment choices either. A short walk to the north leads to the port, and there's another long beach, Plage de Pen Guen, to the south.

Trébeurden

On this impressive rocky coastline, the Plage de Tresmeur is a wide sweep of fine white sand between two points. Beach huts and a promenade contribute to the holiday atmosphere, with lots for tiny tots to enjoy, and even a disco for the not-so-tiny. There's good walking on the old customs officers' coast path, with the pink granite formation of Le Castel offering great views over the beach. Can you make out the 'face' of Le Père, father of Trébeurden?

Trégastel

Trégastel has 12 beaches in all, including those around the Ile Renote (but beware of strong currents on the north side). Between the beaches the coast is craggy and packed with oddly shaped rock formations. The best, sheltered option is the central Grève Blanche, with its ugly line of beach huts, but beautiful sand and views. Two islets are accessible on foot at low tide, one the appealingly named Ile aux Lapins (Rabbit Island).

Trévou-Tréguignec

The sandiest beach on this stretch of coast is the perfect crescent of Plage de Trestel, with great views of the Sept Iles. There's good swimming, and lots of space for kite-flying or windsurfing here, but if you want something a bit quieter, albeit more pebbly, walk round to the west to the Plage aux Choux (named Cabbage Beach for its sea kale).

Tregastel beach.

Action stations

Canoeing
Centre Nautique et d'Animation de Glomel
base de Creharer, 22110 Glomel, T02 96 29 65 01, animation-glomel.com.
Learn to canoe on the Nantes-Brest Canal, including all the excitement of navigating the locks.

Horse riding
Club Hippique Trégastel
13 route du Calvaire, 22730 Trégastel, T02 96 23 86 14, equitation-tregastel.com.
This great riding club operates coastal treks near Trégastel. From age four.

Ecurie du Gallais
Rue du Bois-es-Lucas, 22380 St-Cast-le-Guido, T02 96 41 04 90, ecurie-du-gallais.com.
See Sleeping, page 94.

Kitesurfing
Sylphe
6 rue de Kerpeux, 22190 Plérin, T06 62 41 73 03, kitesurf22.com.
Based in the Sylphe club in St-Brieuc Bay, Tadeg Normand provides two-hour taster classes for groups of three. Note: you need to weigh at least 50 kg and be willing to stick at it – so this is one for teenagers, mums and dads.

Mountain biking
Station VTT Arguenon-Hunaudaye
1 place du Martray, Maison des Associations, 22270 Jugon Les Lacs, T02 96 31 70 75, jugon-les-lacs.com. Bike hire half-day €11 adult, €7 child, half-day supervised ride with bike hire €15.
One of the leading mountain bike centres in France, it offers beginners classes for kids and adults.

Multi-activities
Base Sports Nature de Pont Querra
Le Pont Querra, 22210 Plémet, T02 96 25 97 22, sportsnature.cideral.com.
This base is located in the centre of Brittany, near Loudéac, with its national forest. Hiking is the main event and can be enjoyed independently or with a guide, but there are many other activities on offer, including mountain biking (from age 8) and kayaking. If your children can swim, paddle as a family on two-seater kayaks (€7.50 adult, €5 child).

Sailing, windsurfing & kayaking
There are around 30 sailing centres across Côtes d'Armor. Here are some great ones for families:

Binic Loisirs Nautique
Quai de Pordic, 22520 Binic, T02 96 73 38 45, binicvoile.com.
During the school holidays, Nicolas Le Dantec and his instructors offer daily training aboard Optimists and catamarans, as well as windsurfing in St-Brieuc Bay. (Activities also available on Wed, Sat and Sun during the rest of the year.) In summer, children can join a trip aboard a caravel – a relaxed and safe sailing experience for those over five. Sea kayaking is also available.

Centre Nautique d'Erquy
Maison de la Mer, Le Port, 22430 Erquy, T02 96 72 32 62, everquy.org.
Sailing, sand-yachting, sea-kayaking and paddleboarding

Binic sailing school.

in the St-Brieuc Bay. The cadets club takes kids over five years old. Special trips, equipment hire and private lessons are also available.

Centre Nautique Paimpol Loguivy De La Mer

En Mairie, 22500 Paimpol, T02 96 20 94 58, pole-nautique-paimpol.com.
Sailing and kayaking school offering equipment hire, private lessons and activities throughout the year.

Ecole de Voile de Fréhel

Plage des Fêtes, Sables-d'Or-Les-Pins, 22240 Fréhel, T02 96 41 55 47, ecolevoilefrehel.free.fr.
This small, family-friendly sailing school offers classes in windsurfing and catamaran and dingy sailing. You can also take part in excursions aboard a caravel, or hire your own boat if you want independence.

Ecole de Voile de Louannec

Plan d'Eau du Len, 22700 Louannec, T02 96 23 20 63, louannec.com.
Close to Perros-Guirec there is a salt-water lake. In July and August the Louannec Sailing School organizes Optimist and catamaran sailing courses for children from six to 14 years of age, enabling them to take their first steps in sailing on safe and sheltered waters. Adults can try their hand at windsurfing.

Point Passion Plage de Perros-Guirec

Plage de Trestraou, 22700 Perros-Guirec, T02 96 23 37 17, pointplage.fr.
The Perros-Guirec 'Point Passion' Beach Centre offers a raft of great activities, including windsurfing and catamaran and dinghy lessons. You can also climb aboard the *Ar Jentilez* for a gastronomic feast as you sail towards les Sept Iles.

Surfing
Ecole de Surf de Bretagne de Perros-Guirec

2 rue Maréchal Joffre, 22700 Perros-Guirec, T02 96 23 18 38, ecole-surf-bretagne.fr. 'Moby Kid' taster course for age 5-8 Mon-Fri 1½ hrs/day €110, 5-day course from age 8 Mon-Fri 2 hrs/day €120.
Three-day, weekend or week-long courses for children and adults on Trestraou beach in Perros-Guirec. There are paddle-boarding adventures along the coast and occasional free days for beginners in summer.

Seven Island Surf Club

102 bd de la Corniche, 22700 Perros-Guirec, T02 96 91 46 20, 7islandsurfclub.com.
Located on Trestraou Beach, looking out on the Sept Iles, the Seven Islands Surf Club can satisfy your requirements whatever your level. Surfing workshops take place every Wednesday for youngsters (aged 5-12) and on Saturday for adults.

Woodland adventure
Indian Forest Bretagne

Les Tronchées, 22400 Morieux, T02 96 32 80 80, aventure-nature.com/48//Parcours_Acrobatiques.html. €7 adult, €16 child (12-15), €14 (9-11), €10.50 (5-8), €7 (3-4).
Zip wires and fun in the trees for all ages.

Vivons Perchés

Sarl Vivons Perchés, Crec'h Ar Beg, 22560 Pleumeur-Bodou, T06 22 53 46 45, vivons-perches.com. Family of 4: €20 mini forest (minimum age 2), €40 small forest (minimum age 6), €56 middle forest, and €70 high forest.
More than 100 challenges over eight courses of increasing difficulty, with zip lines, Tarzan vines and monkey bridges. There's a mini forest for those as young as two. With younger children, it's a more enjoyable experience if there are two adults. Book a day or two in advance, as it is very popular. For something more quirky, adults can try a spot of sumo wrestling – laughter guaranteed.

Big days out

Aquarium Marin de Trégastel

Bd du Coz-Pors, 22730 Trégastel, T02 96 23 48 58, aquarium-tregastel.com. Apr-Jun and Sep Tue-Fri 1000-1800, Sat-Mon 1400-1800, Jul and Aug daily 1000-1900, Oct and Mar Tue-Sun 1400-1700. €7.50 adult, €5 child (4-16), €20 family.

Brittany is full of aquariums, but this one within the pink granite caves of the area is one of the best. There are three zones to explore, each describing a different habitat of the English Channel. Close by is Trégastel Forum (forumdetregastel.com), a seawater leisure centre with an indoor pool, a hammam, jacuzzi and work-out room.

La Vapeur du Trieux

La Gare, av du Général de Gaulle, 22500 Paimpol, T08 92 39 14 27, vapeurdutrieux.com. Early May-mid Sep. Return fares with stop: €22 adult, €11 child, under 4s free when sitting on parent's knee, €60 family. Advance booking recommended.

This steam train ride from Paimpol to Pontrieux runs along the Trieux Valley. There's a stop at La Maison de l'Estuaire de Traou-Nez, where you can taste local specialities served by costumed waitresses, and listen to Breton musicians. Every Saturday from early July to mid-August, the magician Tino Oudin amazes children with his magic tricks on the platforms at Paimpol and Pontrieux. Sights along the route include the 15th-century Château de la Roche-Jagu and the Leff-Pontrieux viaduct.

Le Village Gaulois

Cosmopolis, 22560 Pleumeur-Bodou, T02 96 91 83 95, levillagegaulois.free.fr. Apr-Jun and Sep Fri 1400-1800, Jul and Aug daily 1030-1900. €4.50 adult, €3.50 child.

Asterix fans may not find the Gallic hero running around here, but they will find an authentic reconstruction of life in a Gallic village. Managed by the MEEM association (Mondes d'Enfants pour les Enfants du Monde), it allocates 60% of its profits to schools in Togo, West Africa, and is run partly by volunteers, who live in the village under canvas and cook on wood-fired hearths.

Visitors can take part in Celtic-themed games such as a giant puzzle, wooden swing boats, a cairn maze and fishing with wooden fish. Kids can even mill grain to make flour for their own galettes. Le Village Gaulois is on the same site as the Cité des Télécoms (see page 80) and Planétarium de Bretagne (see page 83).

Zooparc de Trégomeur

Le Moulin Richard, 22590 Trégomeur, T02 96 79 01 07, zoo-tregomeur.com. Apr-Sep daily 1000-1900, Oct-Mar Wed, Sat and Sun 1330-1730. €13.50 adult, €9.50 child (Apr-Oct), €12 adult, €8 child (Nov-Mar).

This fabulous zoo in Trégomeur, just inland from Binic, is one of the newest attractions in Brittany. The majority of animals and plants are from Asia and Madagascar, including miniature pandas from China. There are four to six daily shows, an afternoon feeding time, and a petting area. There's a bouncy castle for little kids, as well as a great shop full of recycled games and toys.

❢ Reduced rates at the following attractions are available upon presentation of a receipt from the Trieux steam train: Planétarium de Bretagne, Cité des Télécoms, Office de Tourisme de Lannion, Zooparc de Trégomeur, Village Gaulois, Parcours Aventure Vivons Perchés, and Cap Plongée.

Aquarium Marin de Trégastel.

The big three forts

Château de la Hunaudaye
Le Chêne au Loup, 22270 Plédéliac, T02 96 34 82 10, chateau-hunaudaye.perso.neuf.fr. Apr to mid-Jun and mid-Sep to early Nov Wed, Sun, public holidays 1430-1800, mid-Jun to Sep daily 1030-1830, closed Nov-Easter. €5 adult, €3.50 child, under 6s free.
The original 13th-century castle was rebuilt in the 15th century and has plenty to interest and entertain kids. There's a French-language guide called *Y a pas d'âge pour le Moyen Age* (You're never too young for the Middle-Ages) for seven to 12-year-olds, suggesting two trails to follow. In summer, there are children's workshops on themes such as archaeology and weaving, and in September a Children's Day features workshops on chainmail, stained glass and paper-making. Take the path around the outside for good views of the towers. Right by the castle is a lake with picnic tables and a crêperie, open for drinks and ice creams in summer. Look out for events at the castle in summer.

Château de Tonquédec
22140 Tonquédec, T02 96 54 60 70, chateau-tonquedec.com. Apr-late Jun and late Sep daily 1400-1800, late Jun-late Sep daily 1000-1900, Oct Sat and Sun 1400-1730. €5 adult, €2.50 under 12s.
Situated on a spur overlooking the Léguer River, this fascinating castle, has drawbridges, turret stairs and dank cellars. It was essentially a fortress rather than a home, but domestic details remain in the tracery of chapel windows, fireplaces in former tower rooms and some fine latrines! See who can spot the most masons' marks on the stonework. From the castle, you can take a well-signed 10-km walking circuit of Tonquédec, past the Châteaude de Kergrist, chapels and fountains as well as a beautiful river valley.

Fort La Latte.

Fort La Latte
Cap Fréhel, T02 99 41 57 11, 22240 Plévenon, castlelalatte.com. Apr-Sep 1030-1830, early Jul-late Aug until 1900, Oct-Mar Sat, Sun and school holidays 1330-1730. €5 adult, €3 child (6-12), under 5s free.
This pink sandstone ship, as it is known due to the way it hugs the sea cliffs, has a spectacular setting. There's a sense of excitement in crossing the first drawbridge, used as a film set for *The Vikings* (1958) with Kirk Douglas and Tony Curtis. A second majestic entrance with portcullis leads into the inner courtyard. There are plenty of classic castle features to stir young imaginations. Look down into the alarming *oubliette* (dungeon) near the gatehouse, and imagine the reality of being imprisoned in such a space. The tower gives panoramic views, but if you want to test your nerve continue up into the look-out point by the flag-pole, but do cling onto the rope provided, especially in high wind! Look for the 'cannonball oven', one of those ideas that sound good but are hopelessly impractical – it took two hours to make the missiles red hot, by which time enemy ships would have moved on. Look out for entertainment and shows in the summer months.

Don't miss Ile de Bréhat & Les Sept Iles

Set off for the Sept Iles (Seven Islands) archipelago and discover 40 ha of wild Brittany, the undisputed realm of sea birds, including puffins. If you plump for an excursion to the Ile de Bréhat, keep an eye on the coastline to spot the Sillon de Talbert (Talbert Causeway), The Trieux estuary and the fishing village of Loguivy-de-la-Mer.

Ile de Bréhat

Off the coast of Paimpol is Ile de Bréhat, one of Brittany's loveliest islands. In fact, Bréhat consists of several islets centred on two small islands (car-free) that are joined by a bridge at low tide. It is easily accessible by a regular 10-minute boat journey from Pointe de l'Arcouest. Ferries arrive at **Port-Clos** on the south island, where you can hire bikes and then pedal the short distance to the island's main village, Le Bourg. The hub of activity is the main square, which is thronged with hotels, restaurants and cafés and hosts a regular market. There's plenty to do on Bréhat. As well as cycling or ambling around the lanes and paths, the old fort, next to the island's only campsite, is home to the **Verreries de Bréhat**, where you can marvel at glassblowers at work and maybe have a go yourself. Alternatively, visit the **Birlot tidal mill**. Built in the 17th century, it was restored in the 1990s, thanks to a group of locals, and visitors can watch buckwheat being ground when the tide goes out (twice a day); the miller opens the sluice gate and water from the lagoon turns the wheel. If you're just looking to relax and catch some rays while the kids play, the best beach is **Grève du Guerzido**, opposite the mainland.

Essential information

Vedettes de Perros-Guirec, Gare Maritime, Plage de Trestraou, 22700 Perros-Guirec, T02 96 91 10 00, vedettes-perros-guirec.com. Various options are available: a two-hour trip (including the islands and Pink Granite Coast) €16 adult, €10 child.

Les Sept Iles

One Breton writer beautifully described these round-backed islands as so many whales lurking out to sea. The seven islands lie about as many kilometres north of the popular Rose Granite Coast, but few humans have set foot on them. Monks tried to establish a base here but gave up. The main occupants are the seabirds that nest in vast numbers. Imagine thousands of gannets, razorbills, guillemots, fulmars, shags, great black-backed gulls, lesser black-backed gulls, and herring gulls all nesting in crannies in the rocks! It was the hunting to near-extinction of puffins on Les Sept Iles that brought the Ligue pour la Protection des Oiseaux, the French society for the protection of birds, into existence in the early 20th century.

Ile de Bréhat.

Gannet colony, Ile Rouzic.

These delightful birds with their big bright beaks became the emblem of the association. These days puffins can be seen on the islands from spring to July. The archipelago attracts a phenomenal number of birds that otherwise rarely nest in France. From spring through to September, for example, one side of the **Ile Rouzic** turns white as snow with the density of gannets that gather to reproduce here, the only place in France where these splendid marine birds nest. Guillemots, fulmars, kittiwakes and many shearwaters are among the many other species that thrive here. There's also a small colony of grey seals.

Visitors can find out lots more at the Station LPO de l'Ile Grande, La Réserve Naturelle des Sept Iles, 22560 Pleumeur-Bodou, T02 96 91 91 40, bretagne.lpo.fr/dept/22. June and September daily 1400-1800, July and August daily 1000-1300, 1430-1900 (closed Sat and Sun mornings).€2.50 adult, €1.50 child, €6.50 family.

Pink Granite Coast from the air

From Lannion, you can take a flight over the Pink Granite Coast (see page 70) lasting 15 minutes (€65 for 2 people), or go further afield to the Côtes des Ajoncs or above the Manoirs of the Léguer valley (€105/30 mins). Contact Aéro-Club de la Côte de Granite, T02 96 48 47 42, accg.asso.fr.

More family favourites

Abbaye de Beauport

Kérity, 22500 Paimpol, T02 96 55 18 58, abbaye-beauport.com, mid-Jun to mid-Sep 1000-1900, Oct-May 1000-1200, 1400-1700. €6 adult, €3.50 child (11-18), €2.50 (5-10), €13 family.

Hugging the shore just south of Paimpol, this abbey is well geared to families. Kids can go in search of wild flowers with which to create a box of scents in a two-hour workshop, or learn about strange sea creatures and make their own sea monster out of clay. Older children might like the summer night walks when dreamlike projected images of talking apples and a library illuminated by fireflies reveal details of the monks' daily life. But just exploring the ancient abbey's nooks and crannies is fun. Built in a position to profit from natural resources, trade and pilgrimage, it has a beautiful location, and sudden glimpses of the bay and islands appear through stone arches as you wander around the remains.

Centre de Découverte du Son

Kérouspic, 22140 Cavan, T02 96 54 61 99, decouvertesonore.info/centre. Daily in school holidays and Sun in low season 1300-1800. €6.50 adult, €4.50 child (3-14).

This sound park is a magical way to spend a morning or an afternoon. Take a gentle stroll through a forested area, sharing in your children's delight as they discover things to blow into and bang together, from huge xylophones to musical pulleys. There are intriguing sounds along the way, from waterfalls to fairy music, plus a small shop with books on how to make your own sound instruments. A modest attraction that hits all the right notes.

Haras National de Lamballe

Place du Champ de Foire, 22405 Lamballe, T02 96 50 06 98, haraspatrimoine.com. Tue-Sun, guided visit at 1500. €5.50 adult, €3 child (6-12).

This makes a great family outing, and is heaven for horsey kids. The stud is housed in a former château, so the horses live in fine

Visit Cité des Télécoms

Why? This extensive attraction devoted to how telecommunications have developed over the decades has loads of hands-on and interactive exhibits, and is a great place for tech-heads from five years of age and up. It looks back – the founding fathers Morse and Marconi have their place here – but also forwards to speculate about the future: for example, will cars drive themselves in 20 years' time? Inside the adjoining Radome is the antenna, built in 1961-1962 to receive the first live television pictures from America via Telstar, and information on everything from the first undersea cables to the internet. You can even snowboard against a projected background and try to spot the places you've visited on a satellite image taken of Brittany from space.

Where? Cosmopolis, 22560 Pleumeur-Bodou, T02 96 46 63 80, cite-telecoms.com.

How? Apr-Sep and school holidays Mon-Fri 1000-1800, Sat and Sun 1400-1800. €7 adult or child, €19.60 family. Joint tickets to the Planétarium de Bretagne (see page 83) available.

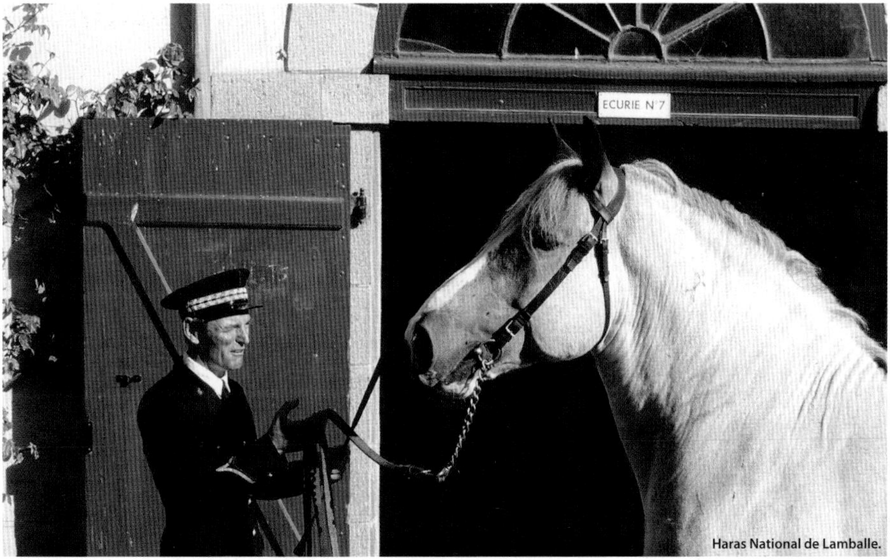

Haras National de Lamballe.

style. Guided tours (in English in summer months) reveal how the horses are raised. An impressive display is put on every Thursday at 1730 in July and August. As well as admiring the horses, you can see demonstrations by saddlers, blacksmiths, displays of riding and driving and an array of carriages.

Labyrinthe Végétal Paimpol
Chemin de Goasmeur, Plounez, Paimpol, T02 96 20 44 06. Jul and Aug daily 1330-2000 (last admission 1830). €6 adult, €4.50 child (4-12).
Lose yourselves in this massive summer corn maze. With more than 8 km of paths, there's treasure to be found, and often a theme, such as the korrigans (Breton fairies), all helped along by clues, riddles and costumed actors. It's so big, there's even a play area within the maze. Good family fun.

Les Forges des Salles
22570 Perret, T02 96 24 90 12, lesforgesdessalles.info. Easter-Oct weekends 1400-1830, Jul and Aug daily 1400-1830. €5 adult.
A very interesting social history is enshrined in this former forge-workers' village from the 18th and 19th centuries. You can inspect the schoolroom, accounts office and workers' cottages, where period objects including beds and washing utensils bring to life the daily routines of the villagers. As well as the remains of working areas, where iron was smelted and shaped, you can also see the chapel (unusually a Protestant one, following the faith of the noble Rohan family who started the enterprise). The grand house, with its terraced gardens, belonged to the master of the forge. A little stream running through the site is the boundary between Morbihan and Côtes d'Armor, so you will be in two departments on your visit.

Maison de la Baie
Site de l'Etoile, 22120 Hillion, T02 96 32 27 98, saintbrieuc-agglo.fr. Mon-Fri 1030-1830, Sat and Sun 1330-1830. In low season call for opening hours. €3 adult, €2 child (6-12).
This excellent local environment museum, set high on a bluff

overlooking Baie de St-Brieuc, centres on a Galerie des Oiseaux that encourages even the youngest of kids to consider the 50,000 birds that winter in this enormous bay. A recreated stretch of seashore with life-sized models of birds and real fish is at the heart of the display. There are interactive displays and, best of all, a wall of illuminated boxes that get you to guess which animal might have inspired a certain tool – crabs and pincers, long-billed birds and tweezers. Outside there's a kids' play area and 'interpretation path'.

Model boats

Perros-Guirec marina on the east side of town has a fun miniature port (Bassin du Linkin, T02 96 91 06 11) where anyone over three years of age can sail model ferries and other boats. Open July and August.

Musée de l'Electricité

56480 St-Aignan, T02 97 27 51 39. Mid-Jun to mid-Sep 0930-1230, 1430-1830, closed Sun morning. €3.50 adult, €1.80 child (under 18).

Not far from the barrage (technically just in Morbihan), this unusual and very enjoyable little museum explores electricity and all its uses and applications. Barn-like buildings (complete with nesting swifts) house old railway signalling devices and early hydroelectric machinery. Ask for a demonstration! Upstairs is a room with interactive models showing

Musée de l'Electricité.

Hit or miss?

Armoripark

22140 Bégard, T02 96 45 36 36, armoripark.com. Jul and Aug daily 1100-1900, Apr-Jun and Sep certain days only (check before you go) 1100-1800. €11 (Jul and Aug), €8 (at other times) adult €10 (Jul and Aug) €7 (at other times) child (4-12), under 4s free.

For those times when only an adventure park will do, Armoripark fits the bill, though there's no particular wow factor and some attractions look in need of a refurb – not that kids will notice when they're tearing around having fun. Highlights include a waterpark with slides, trampolines, pedal karts, human table football, a luge track, bouncy castles, mini-golf, bowling and, best of all, a mini farm where children can meet Lulu the grey donkey, Nigelle the cow and Leon the old goat among others. You can check out old farm machines beside the stone dovecote, and picnic nearby, or head to the snack bar, which has outside seating. There are good playgrounds, especially the one for toddlers. Low-tech fun guaranteed.

how electricity works and a fascinating collection of utensils and domestic items – a washing machine and toaster from 1935, for example. One room is devoted to the building of the Barrage de Guerlédan. This is a good place for older children and adults.

Planétarium de Bretagne

22560 Pleumeur Boudou, T02 96 15 80 30, planetarium-bretagne.fr. Feb-Apr, Jul-Dec daily, May-Jun Sun-Fri. €7.20 adult, €5.80 child (5-17), joint tickets to the Cité des Télécoms available.

Combined with the Cité des Télécoms (see page 80), on the same site, Brittany Planetarium makes a great day out for kids with a scientific bent. It helps if they speak French, as the best shows are in French only. However, its hemispheric projection room, where you can see images of the heavens in 3D, hosts shows in English.

Terrarium de Kerdanet

Kerdanet, 22170 Plouaget, T02 96 32 64 49, terrariumdekerdanet.over-blog.com. Call for opening times. €5.50 adult, €4.50 child (under 12).

Kids obsessed with all things reptilian will love this jungle-like reptile and amphibian discovery centre, home to plodding tortoises and some of the world's deadliest snakes. You are obliged to join a guided tour in French, but there's a hands-on session at the end where you can touch pythons, boa constrictors and adders.

Rain check

Bowling

• **Bowling Le Bélem**, 8 rue Tramontane, 22100 Taden, T02 96 85 13 08.
• **Bowling Le Cyclope**, 14 rue Paris, 22000 Saint-Brieuc, T02 96 61 30 01.
• **Bowling l'Eclipse**, ZC Le Lion de Saint Marc, 22300 Lannion, T02 96 14 14 74.
• **Bowling Le Strike**, 3 rue Louis Malle, 22950 Trégueux, T02 96 94 04 89.
• **Bowling Les Haubans**, rue de Pleumeur, 22700 Perros-Guirec, T02 96 49 08 24.

Cinemas

• **Cinéland**, 1 rue Jacques Tati, 22950 Trégueux, T02 96 01 55 44.
• **Club 6**, 40 bd Clemenceau, 22000 Saint-Brieuc T08 92 68 01 22.
• **L'Eden**, rue Vallée Besnault, 22380 Saint-Cast-le-Guildo, T02 96 41 95 94.
• **Le Douron**, place de Launceston, 22310 Plestin-les-Grèves, T02 96 35 61 41.
• **Les Baladins**, 6 rue Saint-Nicolas, 22200 Guingamp T02 96 43 73 07.
• **Les Baladins**, 34 av Du General-de-Gaulle, Lannion T02 96 37 26 10.
• **Les Baladins**, rue Rohellou, 22700 Perros-Guirec T02 96 91 05 29.
• **Ves le Large**, 4 route Dinard, 22100 Dinan T02 96 39 13 83.

Indoor play

• **Woupi**, 1 rue Louis Malle, 22950 Trégueux. T02 96 94 10 20.

Indoor swimming pools

• **Aquabaie**, rue Pierre de Coubertin, 22000 Saint-Brieuc, T02 96 75 67 56.
• **Espace Aqualudique Goëlys**, Rue Pierre de Coubertin, 22520 Binic, T02 96 69 20 10.
• **Espace Aqualudique Ti Dour**, 49 av de Park Nevez, 22300 Lannion, T02 96 05 09 00.
• **Forum de Trégastel**, plage du Coz-Pors, 22730 Trégastel, T02 96 15 30 44.
• **Piscine Ar Poull Neuial**, Guingamp, T02 96 13 50 00.
• **Piscine Caneton**, rue du champ Garel, 22100 Dinan, T02 96 39 56 13.
• **Piscine Communautaire Jugon**, Jugon-les-Lacs, T02 96 31 30 16.
• **Piscine de La Planchette**, rue Plumaugat, 22250 Broons, T02 96 84 60 30.
• **Piscine de Plein-air de St-Nicolas-du-Pélem**. T02 96 29 52 51, 02 96 29 51 27.
• **Piscine Islandia**, rue Gardenn Toul Ar Verzhid, 22500 Paimpol, T02 96 20 54 57.
• **Piscine La Chèze**, rue Vincent Ferrier, 22210 La Cheze, T02 96 26 65 31.
• **Piscine La Tourelle**, Le Pont des Vallées, 22510 Plemy-Moncontour, T02 96 73 56 27.
• **Piscine Lamballe Communauté Lamballe**, rue des Olympiades, 22400 Lamballe, T02 96 50 13 80.
• **Piscine Les Aquatides Loudéac**, Les Livaudières, 22600 Loudéac, T02 96 66 14 40.
• **Piscine Les Pommiers Léhon**, Bourg de Léhon, 22100 Léhon, T02 96 39 21 00.
• **Piscine Municipale Lanrelas**, Lanrelas, T02 96 86 50 47.
• **Piscine Municipale Pléneuf**, route Plumaugat, 22250 Lanrelas T02 96 86 50 47.
• **Piscine Ophéa**, Quintin, T02 96 58 19 40.

Dinan

This higgledy-piggledy medieval town is a history lesson come to life. To kids, it may seem a bit fusty at first, but with the help of parents they can dig a little deeper to discover a fascinating world of castles, battles, knights and dark dungeons.

This bijou town has an ancient centre and a modern buzz; it's somewhere to get your head swivelling from side to side as one architectural gem follows another, from the impressive ramparts to handsome medieval buildings. It is one of those places that are enhanced by people filling the streets, creating a gregarious ambience.

William the Conqueror, before his invasion of England, drove Conan, Duke of Brittany, out of Dinan castle. The event is recorded in the Bayeux Tapestry, which shows Conan sliding down an escape rope from a wooden tower.

Two hundred years later, in the 13th century, the town became part of ducal possessions in Brittany, and stout ramparts were constructed. During the Wars of Succession, Dinan was unsuccessfully besieged by the English supporters of Jean de Montfort. The most famous soldier of the age, Bertrand du Guesclin, was involved in this conflict, and it is the best-known incident in Dinan's history.

Allow a full day for visiting the town. Parking outside the ramparts is best, as then everything is accessible on foot. You can drive down to the port to avoid a steep hill.

Get your bearings

It is easy for families to lose themselves in the mass of narrow streets, but the **clock tower** in the rue d'Horloge is a good point for orientation. It is actually an ancient bell tower, and was given its finest bell by Anne de Bretagne in 1507. For a small fee you can climb to the top (Apr-May 1400-1800, Jun-Sep 1000-1830) to look down on thronging crowds and enjoy the best views of the town. Superb half-timbered houses can be found in the street below: No 6, Hôtel Kératry (1559), now containing a **Celtic Harp Centre** (T02 96 87 36 69, harpe-celtique.com) and offering workshops for six- to 12-year-olds during the summer months, No 13 with its stone effigy outside, and No 33, in a rather more faded state. In the nearby place des Merciers and rue de la Mitterie (or mint, where coins were once produced) are many other fine examples.

Don't miss

Château-Musée de Dinan

T02 96 39 45 20, dinan.net/chateau-dinan.htm. Jun-Sep 1000-1830, Oct-May 1330-1730, closed Jan. €4.25 adult, €1.75 teenager, under 12s free.

Prepare to be spooked in the town's atmospheric castle. Entry is through the chapel, where the duke had his own little private niche with a fireplace. On the way down to the gloomy kitchen there are examples of Roman remains from the area, including a second-century plaque. Upper rooms with huge fireplaces house temporary exhibitions, and there is access to the walkway at the top for

Essential information

Tourist office, 9 rue du Château, T02 96 87 69 76, dinan-tourisme.com.

fine views over the town. In the tower of Coëtquen the highlight is the Salle des Gisants, a murky deep basement where the uneven floor formed from the very rock is often partly under water, and greening effigies of medieval knights lie heedless of their eerie resting place under a finely vaulted ceiling.

Le Petit Train de Dinan

T02 99 88 47 07, ttdf.com. Departs rue de l'Horloge (Théâtre des Jacobins), place Duclos (Hôtel du Ville), Port de Dinan (Face à la Capitainerie), Jun, Sep-Oct 1100-1700, Jul and Aug 1000-1800 daily except Sun morning. €5 adult, €4 child.

Orientate yourselves on this charming little train ride, with commentary in French and English. It is the most pleasant way to explore the town, as Dinan is hilly and difficult to pace with youngsters in tow. You'll discover the old town with its wooden houses, the St-Sauveur Basilique, the resting place of Bertrand du Guesclin, the clock tower, the Duclos square and the town hall, the ramparts, the impressive viaduct (250 m long and 40 m high) and the English garden.

Musée du Rail

Gare du Dinan (Dinan train station), T02 96 39 53 48, museedurail-dinan.com. Jun-Aug 1400-1800. €4 adult, €3.25 child.

For Thomas the Tank Engine and Chuggington aficionados, this rail museum is a must. Set in the eastern wing of Dinan's railway station, it has full-scale models and a vast track on which you can watch the trains chug around. Models of local buildings help set the scene, and there is plenty of station memorabilia to transport kids back to a bygone age, such as old station clocks, signs, platform lanterns and scales. The beautiful old French railway posters show landmarks of the region such as Carnac and Mont St-Michel.

Port of Dinan

Below the viaduct, the port of Dinan clusters around an attractive old stone bridge over the river. Cafés and restaurants line the waterside, ideal for people- and boat-watching. You can hire a boat, a canoe or a kayak here, or take an organized cruise down to Léhon. On the opposite bank, the Maison de la Rance (quai Talard, Port de Dinan, 22100 Lanvallay, T02 96 87 00 40, codi.fr/la-maison-de-la-rance-p117.php, Apr-Nov Tue-Sun 1400-1800, Jul and Aug 1000-1900) has an exhibition presenting many aspects of river life. There are displays and interactive puzzles for all the senses, including smell! A neat feature explains how tides are governed by the phases of the moon.

Rampart walk

After the Wars of Religion, during which Dinan was a Catholic stronghold, the need for town defences was over and the ramparts fell into disuse. They were later threatened by redevelopment, but when the Gate of Brest was destroyed in 1881 a public outcry led to their classification as a historic monument. Now there is a fine walk (just under 3 km) around the ramparts, in places on their summit, in others at their foot. Look for the arrow slits converted for the use of cannons in the Tour Penthièvre, and admire the view over the port from the Tour Ste-Catherine. A leaflet from the tourist office outlines this path.

La Fête des Remparts de Dinan

T02 96 87 94 94, fete-remparts-dinan.com.
In July Dinan hosts one of the largest medieval festivals in Europe. It's especially exciting for children, who can enter a world populated by ancient beasts, wolves, knights, highwaymen and bears and find their way through enchanted forests. There are historical re-enactments and jousting, and in the centre of town there's a medieval market with food and handicrafts of yore. You can follow one of six tours that take place around the castle.

Thursday is market day in place du Guesclin; you can stock up on picnic and self-catering goodies.

Around Dinan

Léhon

A couple of kilometres upriver from Dinan lies one of Brittany's least-known 'little towns of character'. Its beautiful stone houses decorated with bright flowers cluster around the abbey beside the River Rance, where you can take a riverboat or enjoy a spot of fishing. There's a basic but fun municipal swimming pool if you fancy a dip. There's plenty of history here too. The spectacular Abbaye de Léhon is the resting place of 13th-century knights, and there is free access to the remains of the château, which lays claim to being the oldest hilltop fortress in Brittany. It was besieged by Henry II in 1168 and destroyed and then rebuilt. From the squat towers, the flag flying from the chatêau at Dinan is clearly visible.

Megaliths

Two Neolithic sites very near Dinan are well worth a visit. Asterix fans can have fun taking photos of each other with a menhir on the back, Obelix-style, at the leaning **Menhir of St Samson**. The engravings have weathered badly, so try to go on a bright day when sunlight brings out traces of its patterns. Park on the main road (D57) by the blue heritage site sign.

The so-called **Druids Cemetery** at Preslin-Trigavou, set in a grove of young oak, is an alignment of 65 quartz stones in rough lines. The Druid allusion is not founded on any evidence: the site is late Neolithic (c2000 BC). One legend says that it came into being after weary fairies dropped the stones they were carrying to build Mont St-Michel. The live music Festival of the Megaliths, held in July, was inaugurated in 2009.

Grab a bite

Auberge des Terres Neuvas

25 rue du Quai, T02 96 39 86 45. Closed Sun and Wed eve except Jul and Aug, lunch only Oct-Mar.

Great for a treat on a day out in Dinan and good for older children. Cécile and Grégory Correaux keep a very stylish dining room and outdoor terrace down at the port. A few meaty options, but fish is *the* dish here: from whelks to oysters and prawns to salmon, or try one of the various casseroles (*en cocotte*). The two-course lunch menu is excellent value at €12.

La Cale de Mordreuc

22690 Pleudihen-sur-Rance, T02 96 83 20 43, lacaledemordreuc.com. Closed Mon eve, Tue.

Take a 10-minute drive out of Dinan on a pleasant evening to eat outside with lovely views over the Rance estuary. If the tide is up you may see a regular visiting seal in the water or taking a turn up the jetty. The restaurant has even adopted her as their logo. Reliably good meat and fish dishes here, and for dessert there might be delicious peach soup.

La Petite Cantine – Crêperie Grill

17 rue de l'Apport, T02 96 87 56 75. 1200-1400, 1900-2200, closed Mon eve out of season.

Handy cheap and cheerful little place right in the old centre with surprisingly imaginative specials. Good crêpes, but also grills, omelettes and home-made burgers, so something for all the family. The *tarte tatin*, made in-house, is delicious.

Explore the craft shops

Chic shops and craft studios are everywhere. A leaflet, available from the tourist office (see page 85), plots the craft studios on a plan of the town. Many are in **rue Jerzual** and **rue des Petits Fossés**, the most attractive of all Dinan's old streets, leading down to the port.

Off the beaten track

Lac de Guerlédan

Otherwise known as the Lake District of Brittany, this is Brittany's largest lake. Set on the southern boundary of Côtes d'Armor, just west of Mûr-de-Bretagne, it's a wonderfully remote place to spend a few days with the family. It is the perfect place for messing about on the water, and it also offers extensive trails for walking and cycling. The Quénécan Forest and Abbaye de Bon Repos are not to be missed.

Joining the Nantes–Brest canal at its western and eastern ends, the 12-km-long lake was created in the 1920s with the building of the dam, which provides hydroelectricity for the region; visit the **Musée de l'Electricité** at St-Aignan (see page 82) to find out about its history. A good time to visit Guerlédan is in mid-August when the Fête du Lac takes place – a day-long festival featuring markets, classic cars, water-based activities, fireworks and traditional Fest-Noz (Night Festival) with Breton music and dancing, kids games and great food.

Get your bearings

The lake's main village is Beau Rivage on the north bank. With its choice of accommodation, restaurants, beaches and moorings, this is a good springboard for exploring the surrounding area. From here you can tour the banks of the lake on horseback, on foot or by bike. In Beau Rivage you'll also be able to hire kayaks, pedalos or try your hand at waterskiing (from age 10 if a confident swimmer), or simply take a leisurely boat trip.

South of the lake is the **forest of Quénécan**, an area known as 'Swiss Brittany', which covers about 28 sq km. The area is accessible to walkers from March to October via the GR37 and GR 341 footpaths; twitchers will be interested to learn that more than 70 species of birds winter here.

In the heart of the forest are **Les Forges des Salles** (see page 81), an important site for iron

Mûr-de-Bretagne

This small town a few kilometres east of Lac de Guerlédan is a good base for enjoying active holidays on and around the lake. The tourist office (T02 96 28 51 41, guerledan.fr) by the church is the main source of information on the lake and its activities. In summer the town has a market every Friday evening (1800-2030), with musical entertainment. In July and August the Cap Armor initiative, which encourages participation in sporting and cultural activities, opens an office in the centre of town, where you can sign up for organized events such as Breton games, horse riding or waterskiing. It is also worth a look at the **Chapelle Ste-Suzanne** at the top of the town (Jul and Aug 1000-1200,1500-1800) to see the fine 18th-century painted ceiling and unusual double-arched entrance below an elegant tower. In September, a well-attended Foire Biologique (Organic Fair) is also held in the town.

Top fact

The Barrage de Guerlédan took seven years to build and is 45 m high by 206 m long.

and steel-making in the 18th and 19th centuries. The self-contained forge-workers' village once had 150 inhabitants, and visitors can see the workers' cottages, the manager's house and the forges.

At the western end of the lake are the attractive remains of the 12th-century Cistercian **Abbaye de Bon Repos** ('good rest'). There are daily guided tours in English in July and August, a popular farmers' market on Sunday mornings and regular exhibitions by contemporary artists. If you're here in August, the evening son et lumière shows at the abbey are spectacular (pays-conomor.com). Excerpts from Breton history are energetically performed against the façade of the ruined abbey, cleverly lit to create a changing backdrop. An Iron Age village, galloping horses and packs of hounds add to the drama. Good fun for all ages.

Grab a bite
Café de l'Abbaye

Bon Repos, 22570 St-Gelven, Lac de Guerlédan, T02 96 24 91 06. Apr-Nov 0830-2130, Nov-Apr 1000-2000.

Highly popular, this very busy café/brasserie has a basic menu of sandwiches, omelettes and quiches: the daily specials like *moules frites* are recommended by locals. Or you could just have an ice cream, sitting on the terrace across the water from the abbey and watching the world go by.

Lake Cruise
Les Vedettes de Guerlédan

Beau Rivage, Caurel, T02 96 28 52 64, guerledan.com. Apr-Oct.

Take a 1½-hr cruise on the lake (Jul and Aug daily 1500, €7.50 adult, €4.50 child). Or make more of the occasion with a dining cruise: prices from €37 to €59 depending on the chosen menu (check the website for details).

Pitch for the night
Camping Nautic International

See page 90.

Pick of the pitches

Bellevue

Route de la Libération, 22430 Erquy, T02 96 72 33 04, campingbellevue.fr. Early Apr-late Sep. €16-21.50 pitch for tent or caravan with 2 people, €4-5.20 adult, €3.50-4.50 child (7-12), free-€3.20 child (2-6); mobile home sleeps 4 €310-630/week.

Well situated in the resort of Erquy about 2 km from the cliffs of Cap Fréhel and the long beach of Les-Sables-d'Or, this pretty site with many shrubs and flowers has a good family atmosphere and all the amenities you would expect in a four-star site, including a heated pool, toddler paddling pool, playgrounds, crazy golf, volleyball and table tennis, plus a games room. Next to the campsite are tracks for riding bikes or horses. As well as pitches and mobile homes, furnished tents are available.

Camping Claire Fontaine

26 rue de Toul Al Lann, 22700 Perros-Guirec, T02 96 23 03 55, bm-webdesign.com/camping-perros. Apr-Sep. €15.50-19.50 pitch for 2 people and car, €6-8 extra person over 7, €3-4 child (under 7); B&B €39/night, €350-480/week.

Located near beautiful Trestraou beach and the centre of Perros-Guirec, this lovely campsite benefits from all the advantages of a lively resort – festivals, bars, restaurants, nightlife – without being so close as to be subjected to the drawbacks. The campsite nestles discreetly within 3 ha of grounds scattered with large trees and flowerbeds. Besides its empty pitches for tents and caravans, there are some typically Breton gîtes, B&B rooms with access to a kitchen, and bungalows scattered around the property.

Camping de Traou-Mélédern

22260 Pontrieux, T02 96 95 69 27, campingpontrieux.free.fr. Year round. €4 Pitch, €3.50 adult, €2 child; mobile home for up to 4 €260-360/week; gîtes for up to 5 €300-380/week.

An excellent position for this quiet site by the Trieux River, near characterful Pontrieux. Has spacious pitches for tents and caravans and accommodation to rent. Regulars of many nationalities appreciate the helpful owners and very clean facilities, including a small kids' playground. There are also a couple of gîtes to rent, each sleeping up to five.

Camping Nautic International

Route de Beau Rivage, 22530 Caurel, T02 96 28 57 94, campingnautic.fr. Mid-May to late Sep. €5.80-9 pitch, €1.80 car, €3.80-6 adult, €1.90-3.30 child (under 7).

For stunning lakeside camping beside Lac de Guerlédan (see page 88), you won't find much better in Brittany. Situated at Beau Rivage, this campsite is spacious and nicely landscaped. Facilities include a large swimming pool and tennis and badminton courts. There are lots of games suitable for children up to 14, a TV room and projection room. Handy for all sporting options on the lake, it's also close to restaurants and places of interest. Mûr-de-Bretagne, less than 6 km away, has climbing, sailing lessons and an outdoor centre.

Le Château de Galinée

Rue de Galinée, 22380 St-Cast-le-Guildo, T02 96 41 10 56, chateaudegalinee.com. Early Apr-early Sep. €32-49.60 pitch for 1 person, extra adult €4-6.80, €2.50-4.80 child (7 and over); mobile home for up to 4 €37-74/night.

This family holiday park with 273 pitches and two- or three-bedroom mobile homes, 'cottages' (upmarket mobiles) and tented bungalows is just 3 km from the sea and 5 km from the seaside resort of St-Cast-le-Guildo (St-Cast for short). It's a great base to explore the Emerald Coast towns of St-Malo, Dinard and Dinan. It's family-run and quieter than other holiday parks, with a relaxed feel, grassy open spaces in which to kick a football, plus everything from a mini farm to a mini zip line. The **Galinée Mini Club** is open to kids aged five to 10 and offers painting, drawing, plasticine workshops and treasure hunts. There's a modern outdoor pool complex with good water slides, plus a newish indoor pool and nice playgrounds. Sports include badminton, basketball, crazy golf, football, fishing, mini golf, table tennis and volleyball. There is entertainment during July and August, including a family disco, plus a restaurant and takeaway in a thoroughly modern setting.

Le Ranolien

Rue Squewel, 22700 Perros-Guirec, T02 96 91 43 58, leranolien.fr. Early Apr to early Sep. €17-41 pitch with 2 people, free-€5 child (3-7); *roulottes* (gypsy caravans) for 4 €39-€124 child.

Le Ranolien, a member of the Yelloh! Village chain, is one of Côtes d'Armor's more impressive holiday parks. Situated on the Pink Granite Coast in Perros-Guirec, just 1 km from the beach, it offers secluded pitches, *roulottes* (gypsy caravans) and cottages for up to six people. Mums and dads will appreciate the beauty and wellness spa offering massage and beauty treatments. Other amenities include a mini cinema, a vast outdoor pool complex with water slides, including a four-lane slide, and a covered, heated pool for cool or rainy days. The mellow stone Breton farm buildings have been converted to house a pizzeria and crêperie. There are fabulous play areas and a mini club for four- to 12-year-olds, with art workshops, sports, tournaments, treasure hunts, cabaret rehearsals and performances. Great for fans of *The X-Factor*.

Les Capucines

Voie Romaine, 22300 Trédrez Locquémeau, T02 96 35 72 28, lescapucines.fr. Late Mar-early Oct. €14.40-20.30 pitch for 2 people and a car, €4-5.50 extra person over 7, €2.90-3.60 child (under 7); mobile home for 4 €280-590/week.

Les Capucines is a quiet, friendly, family camping site just 1 km from the beach. Set in a well-kept landscaped park of 4 ha, each of the 100 pitches is enclosed by hedges. There's a small heated pool, a paddling pool for toddlers, a playground, crazy golf, tennis court, games room and a library. If you don't want to bring your tent or caravan, hire a two-bedroom mobile home.

Yurts

Augès François

8 Impasse Poul-Bissy, 22220 Plouguiel, T02 96 92 32 38, yourte.biz. €55 per couple with breakfast, €5 child (under 16).

These super-deluxe yurts near Tréguier, west of Paimpol, are equipped with flatscreen televisions, large comfy sofas, fully-fitted kitchens and regal-style beds. They even have windows. There's a separate bathroom and toilet yurt.

Farm favourites

Ferme de Malido

22400 St-Alban, T02 96 32 94 74, malido.fr. Family rooms €66.

This working farm offers six homely B&B rooms just 4 km from the sea. It has its own mystery maze with two playful artworks, two themed mini mazes and an area with wooden balancing and skill games that offer the chance to win a basket of farm produce. There are night tours of the maze, spit roast pig evenings, Celtic nights and visiting circus acts. The rooms include two triples and two two-roomed family units. There's a shared kitchen and cosy breakfast salon for limited self-catering. For self-catering proper there are two five-bedroom gîtes but you may need to come with friends and extended family to fill these.

Randoyourtes

Eric Charroy, 22570 Plélauff, T02 96 24 90 15, randoyourte.com. May-Sep. €25/person.

These three Mongolian yurts are set in the countryside near Carhaix-Plouguer and the pretty village of Plélauff by the Nantes–Brest canal. With pretty wooden doors, brightly painted furniture and wall hangings, they sleep a family of four comfortably. Bikes and pull-alongs are available to hire with the yurt. Horse riding and canoeing are available nearby too.

Youth hostels

Youth hostels (*auberges de jeunesse*) are generally a good

bet for cheap accommodation (see aubergesdejeunesse.com) and open to people of all ages. The Pass Bretagne offers a sixth night free after getting five stamps from different establishments belonging to the scheme (details on breizh-trotters.com).

Auberge de Jeunesse Les Korrigans

Rive Gauche, 6 rue du 73ème territorial, 22300 Lannion, T02 96 37 91 28, fuaj.org/Lannion-Les-Korrigans. Year round. €10.50/person.

A great find in the centre of Lannion, named after the mischievous fairies said to populate the area. Its 12 rooms, each with two brightly painted bunk beds, a table and chairs, have enchanting names such as Mare aux Fées (Fairies' Pond) and Vent des Songes (Wind of Dreams). Linen and continental breakfast are included in the rates, and low-priced meals and picnics are available; there is also a shared kitchen for self-catering. Other amenities include a tavern with internet access and a pool table. Guests can hire mountain bikes, and coastal hiking packages are available.

Best of the rest

Emerald Coast Gîtes

La Touche, 22400 Hénansal, T+44(0)845 489 0140, babyfriendlyboltholes.co.uk/similar-baby-friendly-holiday-properties-14709.htm. Gîtes for 2-8 plus cots €300-1500/week.

This fabulous collection of seven one- to four-bedroom gîtes is perfect for families. Inclusion on the Baby Friendly Boltholes website guarantees upmarket and stylish child-friendly amenities, from toys to heated toddler pool (in addition to a large heated pool for adults). For older kids there's a multi-activity play centre with swings, slides and a climbing wall, a mini football pitch, basketball hoop and trampoline. For parents, there's a well-stocked bar that overlooks the play area, a great place to mingle with other families.

Emerald Coast gîtes.

Gîtes-en-Tregor

Route de Kerfons, 22300 Ploubezre, T02 96 47 17 86, gites-en-tregor.com. Ker Louarn €250-475/week, Ker Toud €325-525/week, La Grange €500-850/week.

Run by Clara and Martin Cronin (see page 71), a British couple who moved to Brittany with their two children specifically to run gîtes for families, these three beautiful holiday cottages near the market town of Lannion, a 15-minute drive from the north coast beaches, are a real find. Ker Louarn (The Fox House) and Ker Toud (The Owl House) both sleep up to four, whilst La Grange (The Barn) is perfect for a large family or two families. It's also fully accessible for disabled guests. Ker Toud and La Grange can be rented as one large interconnecting property. There's everything you need from English channels on the TV to firewood for the open fire, bikes to borrow, high chairs, baby cots and baths. There's a real farmhouse feel, with cider apple trees and a field with donkeys, a pony and a horse.

Gîtes La Julerie

22130 Corseul, T02 96 27 24 23, lajulerie-gite.com. Gîtes sleep between 4-8, €435-1290/week.
Just 10 km from the historic town of Dinan and 20 km from the beach, these four beautiful Breton-style gîtes with all mod cons are tucked away in a rural setting where you'll hear owls at night. There's a fabulous indoor heated pool, a large games room with ping-pong and a nice playground with a sandpit in the garden. You can dine outside on patio tables and chairs and there's barbecue equipment. Linen and towels are included.

Hôtel des Agapanthes

1 rue Adrien Rebours, 22620 Ploubazlanec, T02 96 55 89 06, hotel-les-agapanthes.com. €43-63 doubles; room in the garden (sleeps 4) €82.
Well situated near the coast between Paimpol and the ferry to Bréhat, this smart, comfortable hotel has nice rooms (some small) in two buildings, some with sea views and a little terrace or balcony. There's a good family room in the garden sleeping up to four. Everything here – reception, bedrooms, even the lavish breakfast buffet – is well presented with lots of attention to detail.

Le Manoir des Portes

La Poterie, 22400 Lamballe, T02 96 31 13 62, manoirdesportes.com. €55-113 double, extra bed €15.
Just outside the town, this stylishly decorated hotel has an international clientele. Hervé Jamin and his team have created an atmosphere of calm competence and assured comfort. Bright, tastefully furnished bedrooms, an excellent restaurant with menus created daily and pleasant grounds add up to the ideal treat for families with older kids.

Les Terrasses de Trestel

Plage de Trestel 22660, Trévou-Tréguignec, T02 96 15 10 10, location-bord-de-mer-appartement-vacances-piscine-tourisme.terrasses-trestel.fr.
Situated between Tréguier and Perros-Guirec, next to a lovely arc of beach, this two-star holiday village has cute little houses and apartments that sleep two to seven people. The decor is simple but adequate, and most properties have sea views. There's a small pool and crazy golf in the garden, but the beach is the main source of entertainment.

Manoir de la Pichardais

22130 Créhen, T02 96 41 09 96, manoirdelapichardais.com. Double €67 plus €16-24 per child.
In a quiet location, this delightful manor house has been in the de Courville family since the 17th century. There are two large period bedrooms, one in Renaissance style, the other in an airy mix of blues, with an adjacent room suitable for children. All rooms are beautifully proportioned, with some exquisite monumental fireplaces.

Petites Maisons dans la Prairie

Petites Maisons dans la Prairie

Le Mourvet Noir, 22170 Plélo, T02 96 79 52 39. Gîtes from €400-775/week.
These ultra-romantic yet family friendly gîtes are like something out of *Elle Decoration*. Created by the Lamour family of the famed Au Char à Bancs (see page 21), this is a chip off the old block, with style oozing out of every throw and rocking chair. Book a self-catering gîte (Rose, Louise, Marie, Joséphine, Jeanne, Anne or Florence), each of which sleep between two and six guests. There's a small playground with a wooden castle and a slide,

and there is lots of room to run around or play football. Each cottage has also its own private garden in which kids can play in view of their parents. In summer, the Lamours provide children with free tickets to go to Char à Bancs (3 km away), where there are pedal boats and pony rides. There's also plenty to see and do in the area, including beaches, castles, forests, walking and cycling.

Val Rive

1 quai du Val de Rance, 22100 Léhon, T+44(0)1438-312366, French-lettings.co.uk. €275-525/week.

This impressive group of five apartments and two historic cottages near the little town of Léhon (see page 87) are perfect for families with kids past the toddler stage and for groups of families and friends who want to holiday together but be independent. Situated beside the River Rance, it is a picturesque spot, just a kilometre down the road from the port of Dinan, with its lively restaurants and bars. Bring your bikes for riverside cycle rides. There's a great patisserie, Le Fournil de L'Abbaye, just around the corner, for fresh croissants (from 0715). A public pool, Les Pommiers (T02 96 39 21 00), is five minutes' walk away in Léhon, and there are tennis courts (T02 96 39 95 31) nearby too.

Villa Cyrnos

10 rue du Sergent l'Héveder, 22700 Perros-Guirec, T02 96 91 13 36, villacyrnos22.monsite-orange.fr. €70-80 double.

On the way down to the port, this large house in well-kept gardens has five bedrooms, including two adjoining rooms suitable for families. Old family photos create a homely feel, and Roger Guyon is an obliging host. Ask for a room with a sea view; at the very least you can enjoy a panoramic perspective from the breakfast room.

Cool & quirky

Château du Val

Notre Dame du Guildo, 22380 St-Cast-le-Guildo, T02 96 41 07 03, chateauduval.com. Treehouse €115.

Stay in a treehouse in the grounds of an 18th-century granite château near the coast at St-Cast-le-Guildo. This place has a great family atmosphere with plenty of parkland to run around in and the beach nearby. If you tire of the treehouse option, there are rooms in the château or cottages in the grounds.

Ecurie du Gallais

Le Logis du Gallais, rue du Bois-es-Lucas, 22380 St-Cast-le-Guildo, T02 96 41 04 90, ecurie-du-gallais.com. Family room €74 with breakfast. Horse riding €20/1 hr-€160/10 hrs.

Calling all horse riding fans, Ecurie du Gallais is a beautiful stable with farm accommodation for a riding-based holiday. Rides take in Cap Fréhel and Fort la Latte and you can even reach Ile de Ebihens at low tide across the sands. Even very small children can enjoy rides around the farm. Bedrooms are comfortable and bright, with the occasional horsey touch and a few teddy bears dotted around the place. There's a family room for four as well as a garden to play in.

Les Ecuries de Kerbalan

Kerbalan, 22200 Gommenec'h, T02 96 52 32 11, lesecuriesdekerbalan.com. €650/week.

Really pretty cabins in the trees and smart gypsy caravans inland from St-Quay-Portrieux. This place really stands out from the rest. A good place to discover your inner hobbit!

Métairie de St-Valay

St-Valay, 22100 Taden, T06 79 39 14 18, roulottes-de-bretagne.com. €395-420/week.

Pretty gypsy caravans just outside Dinan, surrounded by orchards. Each caravan has its own terraces with table and chairs.

Splashing out

Hôtel Aigues Marine

5 rue Marcellin Berthelot, Port de Plaisance, 22220 Tréguier, T02 96 92 97 00, aiguemarine-hotel.com. €85-126 family room.

Situated on the waterfront, with a short uphill walk to the town centre, this bright, comfortable hotel has large well-equipped rooms with balconies overlooking the river, and offers excellent service. In the restaurant, chef Yoann Peron's fish dishes are particularly good, and the breakfast buffet is a treat in itself. There is an outdoor pool, plus a gym and a sauna.

Hôtel Le d'Avaugour

1 place du Champ, 22100 Dinan, T02 96 39 07 49, avaugourhotel.com. €87-290.

Overlooking the busy place du Champ, this is a comfortable and well-furnished hotel. Bedrooms are double-glazed, but you may want to ask for a room at the back to overlook the lovely garden. This is surprisingly large and has the bonus of a rampart terrace with a view of the château. The hotel has a lift, a bar and a charming breakfast room. Staff give visitors a very warm welcome, including children.

Hôtel-Restaurant de l'Abbaye

12 rue Marie Paule Salonne, 22130 Plancoet, T02 96 84 05 01, abbaye-hotel.com. Double from €83, apartment from €123.

This old convent is a great family hotel for discovering the Emerald Coast. Located in the lovely town of Plancoet, it combines sophistication with a relaxed family feel. There's a lovely swimming pool, sauna, tennis courts and ping-pong, or children can play in the extensive gardens where there are swings beneath the trees. There's a pretty restaurant with a good kids' menu at around €14 for a three-course meal. Families can book an apartment with interconnecting rooms.

La Demeure

5 rue du Général de Gaulle, 22200 Guingamp, T02 96 44 28 53, demeure-vb.com. €85-145.

Proprietor Carinne Solo's passion is decor, and each room, whether in the new wing or the original building, has a different style and feel. You can even buy items of decoration that take your fancy! The overall tone is smart and chic. One suite has a corner kitchen and roof-top terrace for sipping your evening drinks. The breakfast-room overlooks a pretty walled garden. More suited to older children.

La Maison du Phare

93 rue de la Tour, 22190 Plérin-sur-Mer, St-Brieuc, T02 96 33 34 65, maisonphare.com. €80-110 double.

A stylish green-shuttered B&B in a former merchant's house just past the port. Excellent designer-styled rooms, some with balcony or terrace, and one on the ground floor. Fine sea views and well placed for St-Brieuc centre or the coastal resorts, with easy parking and a bus route passing the door. A good choice for families with older kids.

Eating Côtes d'Armor

Quick & simple

Auberge du Guerlédan

35 rue Roc'Hell, 22530 Caurel, T02 96 26 35 16. Daily mid-Jul to Aug, rest of year closed Tue and Wed.

This charming and popular auberge has good-value three-course menus. Traditional dishes include the very Breton grilled *andouillette* (tripe sausage) or a meltingly tender pork fillet with mushrooms. There are also snails on offer, uncommon in Brittany restaurants, and the usual galettes and ham and frites for kids.

Auberge du Tregor

3 rue St Yves, 22220 Tréguier, T02 96 92 32 34, aubergedutregor.com. Tue-Sat 1200-1400, 1900-2100, Sun 1200-1330.

Near the cathedral, this beautiful old stone house has a pretty dining room. Christian Turpault works wonders in the kitchen, while his wife welcomes diners with good-value set menus and a tempting carte. Goat's cheese with bacon and apples, followed by scallops and prawn with artichokes in a vanilla sauce might leave room for an apricot version of Breton far (a custardy pudding with Armagnac). Families are well taken care of.

Chez Camille et Margaux

44 rue Charles Carte, 22400 Lamballe, T02 96 31 05 35. Mon-Sat lunch, Thu-Sat dinner.

A very individual little restaurant with an imaginative menu (try the salmon crumble of spiced bread with pine nuts), and specializing in savoury tarts using locally sourced ingredients. Welcoming and friendly service. Also serves speciality teas.

Crêperie de Bon Repos

Bon Repos, 22570 St-Gelven, T02 96 24 86 56. Year round, closed Mon except holidays.

This no-frills crêperie gets very busy, especially with locals, and as everything is freshly and carefully cooked be prepared to wait. The *blé noir* (buckwheat) crêpes are excellent, with an unusual light and delicately crisp texture. The fillings are generous.

Crêperie Chez Marie

9 rue Mer, 22380 St-Cast-le-Guildo, T02 96 41 98 66. Daily in school holidays 1100-2130.

Kids will love this intriguing seaside crêperie with outsized flower frescoes on the walls and the odd goblin or witch inside. As well as tasty galettes and crêpes, you'll find steak and chips, fish dishes and omelettes and salads.

Crêperie des Grèves

23 rue des Grèves, 22360 Langueux, T02 96 72 56 96, lacreperiedesgreves.fr.

The dining room here is a riot of nautical themes, with sails, nets, old photos and lighthouse paintings. There are books on the hearth that kids can look through and a play area by the sea that is visible from the dining room. A good-value traditional menu, with galettes, crêpes and cider. Children's main, dessert and juice from €9.50.

Digor Kalon

89 rue Maréchal Joffre, 22700 Perros-Guirec, T02 96 49 03 63, digor-kalon.com. Daily 1830-late.

Kids will love the crazy eclectic decor at this quirky tapas-cum-French restaurant and bar. It's a lively venue for offbeat music and very welcoming to families out for the evening. There's a kids' menu with ham and chips and *moules frites*, and delicious desserts. There is also a nice little courtyard out back if the weather is fine.

Fleur de Blé Noir Crêperie

9 rue du Commandant Malbert, 22410 St-Quay-Portrieux, T02 96 70 31 55. Thu-Tue 1200-1400, 1900-2200, closed Thu lunch and Sun dinner out of season, also Nov-Dec.

Opposite the casino and beach, this little crêperie has two *salles*, the upper with good sea views, and an outdoor terrace. Very tasty open-textured savoury and thick sweet crêpes made with quality ingredients. Try La Bisquine if you like caramel sauce and ice-cream. Friendly service, nice atmosphere.

La Bretannière

Place du Martray, 22270 Jugon-les-Lacs, T02 96 31 63 32. Apr-Jun Wed-Sat lunch and dinner, Jul and Aug daily 1200-2130, closed Sep-Mar.

This standard-looking crêperie/pizzeria, with a small dining room and large outdoor terrace, serves very tasty dark galettes with generous fillings such as scallops and creamed leeks, as well as omelettes and pizzas. An excellent budget choice.

La Fauconnière

Cap Fréhel, 22240 Plevenon, T02 96 41 54 20. Easter to mid-Jun Thu-Tue 1215-1430, mid-Jun to Nov daily.

This restaurant (and *salon du thé* until 1800) on the cliff-top, with panoramic ocean views, can only be reached on foot. It isn't cheap, but fish dishes are reliably excellent, and the chef presents dishes with panache. It attracts families in summer, especially for the bargain *menu du jour* on weekdays. Watch the changing hues of sea and sky from every table.

La Ferme de Kerroc'h

Route de Bréhat, 22620 Ploubazlanec, T02 96 55 81 75. Apr-Oct Wed-Sun 1200-1400, 1900-2130, Jul and Aug daily.

On the main road to the Bréhat ferry, this grill/crêperie offers a high standard of country cooking in an attractive old house with fine stone doorways. Simple dishes, such as chicken in white wine sauce with rice, are full of flavour and attractively presented. Recommended.

La Kabane

By Fort La Latte parking. Apr-Sep.

By the car park for Fort La Latte, this charming little cabin bar with deckchairs and garden tables is a good stop for hot and cold drinks, such as the Breton beer Coreff and apple juice for the kids. Cool music plays in the background and service is super-friendly.

La Moana

32 rue Maréchal Joffre, 22520 Binic, T02 96 73 65 89.

One street back from Binic's marina, this cosy restaurant serves genuine Italian cuisine with home-made pasta and pizza plus a good choice of seafood dishes.

La Stalla

48 rue du Port, 22430 Erquy, T02 96 72 01 03.

For pizza and pasta, you can't go wrong with this seafront Italian restaurant. The 'menu bambino' for under 12s features all the old favourites from margarita pizza to spag bol.

Le Crapaud Rouge

28 Plage de Port Goret, 22410 Tréveneuc, T02 96 70 36 21, lecrapaudrouge.com.

This lovely seaside restaurant serves all the Breton staples including *moules frites* and galettes in the perfect setting.

Le Crêperie du Roy

4 rue aux Blés, 22200 Guingamp, T02 96 43 75 36. Closed Tue eve, Sun.

Delicious galettes of all sorts here: try the ham, cheese and onion-stuffed 'Guingampaise' with a potato on top. There are also hot salads and a cheap daily dish such as *blanquette de veau* (veal in a white sauce). Popular with local workers.

Le Ker Bleu

Plage Trestraou, 17 bd Joseph Le Bihan, 22700 Perros Guirec, T02 96 91 14 69. Apr-Sep daily 1200-2300, check for times in low season.

This great seaside restaurant serves galettes, crêpes, pizza, pasta, seafood and drinks all day in summer. Sit on the decked terrace for views of the Sept Iles Bird Reserve.

Le Manoir Elfique (Manoir de Kerloas)

Allée Kerloas Bras, 22300 Ploulec'h, T02 96 46 36 64. Mon, Wed-Fri 1700-0100, Sat and Sun 1200-1500, 1800-0100.

A new cultural venture in a 15th-century château, with a café-bar offering food ranging from tapas to boeuf bourguignon. Events include exhibitions, concerts and story-tellers.

Le Moulin Vert

15 rue Duguesclin, 22300 Lannion, T02 96 37 91 20. Daily 1200-1400 and from 1830.

You can't miss the green windmill signs outside this

attractively decorated corner restaurant. Menus decorated with local scenes, bright tablecloths and plants all contribute to a pleasant atmosphere. The simple food is excellent, focusing on salads, galettes or pasta dishes: try a warm salad with Breton sausage. Very popular with locals and tourists alike.

Le Palus/Restaurant La Homardine

Palus Plage, 22580 Plouha, T02 96 70 38 26, lepalus.com. Apr-Oct daily, closed Tue in winter.

A varied choice is available in this large establishment comprising a brasserie/crêperie and restaurant. Upper and lower dining rooms overlook the beach and sea. Seafood – mussels in cream, oysters, langoustines – is the speciality, but there are steaks and crêpes too. Set menus from €20-30.

Thématique

Place de l'Eglise, 22530 Mûr-de-Bretagne, T02 96 26 01 35. Tue-Sat 0900-1800, Sun 1100-1400, closed Wed.

Very pleasant English-owned café/*salon du thé*, with a bookshop and internet access. Have drinks and sandwiches or salads inside or on the terrace overlooking the little market square.

Ty Coz

35 place Champ de Foire, 22400 Lamballe, T02 96 31 03 58. Daily 1200-1400, 1900-2100, closed Wed, Sun lunch out of season, Tue eve in winter.

Near the Haras, this highly recommended crêperie is very popular with locals. Ty Coz means 'old house' in Breton, and the atmospheric dining room has exposed beams and fireplace. It holds a Crêperie Gourmande label, which means you can be sure of locally sourced ingredients in your pancakes. The house cider is excellent.

Via Costa

Plage du Moulin, 22680 Etables-sur-Mer, T02 96 70 79 57, viacosta.fr.

You'll find a rare burst of fashionable beach chic at this Brazilian-themed restaurant

lounge. And yes, it still manages to be family-friendly: there's a children's menu and delicious pizzas. Alternatively, get a babysitter and come back in the evening for cocktails.

Posh nosh

A l'Air du temps

4 rue du Gouët, 22000 St-Brieuc, T02 96 68 58 40, airdutemps.fr. Tue-Sat 1200-1400, 1900-2130.

Funky-chic-trad decor in an old house with huge fireplace and beams. Specialities are fish and meat dishes *en cocotte* (casserole), with imaginative starters such as goat's cheese and Serrano ham with rhubarb compote. Vegetarian dishes if required. There's a three-course dinner with limited choice for under €20, and there are tasty options for kids as well.

Au Biniou

121 rue Clémenceau, 22370 Pléneuf Val-Andre, T02 96 72 24 35. Year round.

Near the beach of Le Val-André, this stylish fish restaurant is surprisingly child-friendly. An under-10s menu at €12 features roast chicken and tagliatelle. Book ahead.

Aux Pesked

59 rue du Légué, 22000 St-Brieuc, T02 96 33 34 65, auxpesked.com. Tue-Fri 1200-1400, 1900-2300, Sat 1900-2300, Sun 1200-1400.

On the way to the Port de Légué, with a large fish sculpture outside, this is a gastronomic delight for fish-fanciers. The *menu du pêcheur* features the catch of the day, and there is a superb chef's *menu de dégustation* at €85. It's best to bring children at lunchtime (midday Tue-Fri only), when two or three courses for around €25 make a good-value treat.

La Boissière

90 rue de l'Yser, 22200 Guingamp, T02 96 21 06 35, restaurant-la-boissiere.com. Tue-Fri 1200-1330, 1915-2100, Sat 1915-2100, Sun 1200-1330.

Excellent service and superb food in a dining room that manages to feel both elegant and cosy. Chef Thomas Montfort changes the menu regularly, offering a very reasonable no-choice three-course lunch on weekdays (maybe mussels, salmon with black olive sauce and finishing with Breton far) and à la carte in the evening. Attention to detail is evident at every turn, from the 1950s-style washroom to the blissful plate of home-made sweets served with coffee. Good children's menu from €12.

La Cuisine du Marché

4/6 rue des Frères Merlin, 22000 St-Brieuc, T02 96 61 70 94, lacuisinedumarche.net. Tue-Sun 1200-1400, 1900-2200, closed Sun eve, Mon.

A bright and busy restaurant that is equally popular with locals and visitors. There's lots of choice on the menu, including good-value set menus, with daily blackboard specials.

Local goodies

Au Fournil Gourmand

16 place du Général Leclerc, 22300 Lannion, T02 96 37 60 65. Tue-Sat 0730-1930, Sun 0730-1300.

Despite changing from its famous wood-fired oven to gas for baking, the quality here is still excellent. The pizzas and fruit-tarts are delicious, or try their Flûte Gana speciality bread.

Barnabé

Corner of rue du Port and rue du Petit Fort, 22100 Dinan, T02 96 85 03 12. Daily 0800-2000.

This baker's shop at the bottom of rue du Petit Fort has delicious cakes made to traditional Breton recipes, as well as salted caramels and excellent cider to take home.

Dinan market

If you are in Dinan on Thursday morning for the market, make a bee-line for the stall of Erika Hicks, a local cheese-maker who produces superb organic Cheddar (yes, in France!) and also the French cheese tomme.

Glacerie Morice

Quai de Courcy, 22520 Binic, T02 96 73 79 27. Daily in high season and weekends in low season.

Famous ice cream parlour in Binic with more than 70 speciality and traditional flavours.

Pâtisserie du Théâtre

3 rue Michelet, 22000 St-Brieuc, T02 96 33 41 68. Tue-Sat 0845-1915, Sun morning only.

Tiny shop with delicious cakes and coffee. Also sells chocolate and sweets, attractively gift-wrapped if required.

Terre de Terroirs

5 rue St-Gilles, 22000 St-Brieuc, T02 96 33 02 01. Tue-Fri 0900-1300, 1530-1900, Sat 0800-1300, 1500-1900, Sun 1000-1200.

Delicatessen with minimalist decor, selling superb regional produce for a superior picnic, including cheeses, cold meat, foie gras and smoked salmon.

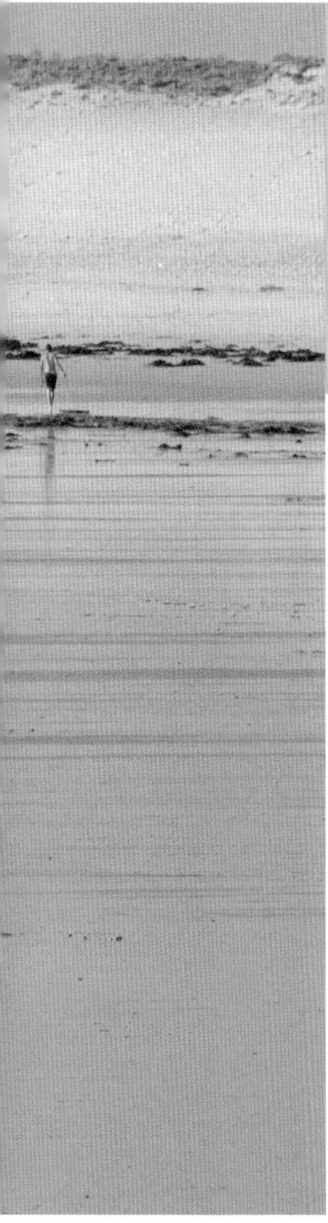

Finistère

Contents

Horse ride on Pointe de la Torche.

You must

❶ Ride in the shark lift at Océanopolis, Brest.

❷ Hold a snail at L'Escargot du Pays de Cornouaille.

❸ See the glowing minerals at the Musée des Minéraux.

❹ Have a go at sand-yachting on Trez Bellec.

❺ Go on a singalong storytelling walk in the Parc Armorique.

❻ See the wolves at Domaine de Menez Meur.

❼ Feel like you're at the end of the world at Pointe du Raz.

'The end of the earth', as Finistère literally translates, is a magical place for families. Here nature is writ large, from crashing Atlantic breakers on its westerly surf beaches to the Parc Naturel Régional d'Armorique in the east, where there are wolf museums and storytelling in the woods.

It is often considered to be the real Brittany, and there is a fierce pride in Breizh roots. Combining incredible land and seascapes, this place has a magical, otherworldly feel where adventure and exploration are around every corner. Who knows what you might find? Glowing minerals, an aquarium with a shark lift, treetop circuits, labyrinths, theme parks, landscapes that inspired Gauguin, castaway islands with black dwarf sheep, towering lighthouses, and several cracking castles.

Finistère excels when it comes to messing about on the water. There are facilities galore for sailing, kayaking, surfing and windsurfing, as well as sand-yachting and kitesurfing.

If you sail direct to Finistère, chances are your ferry will dock in **Roscoff**, home to the Onion Johnnies and many childhood delights, including little train rides and seaweed tours. The first large town you come to is **Brest**, heavily bombed in the Second World War and now a modern university city, but with plenty to engage kids, including Océanopolis on the outskirts of town.

Northwest of Brest is the westernmost point of France at **Pointe de Corsen**, and also the tallest standing menhir in France near **St-Renan**. Lovely salty seaside towns like **Le Conquet** are perfect bases for family holidays. Further south is the **Crozon Peninsula** with its fabulous beaches and the beginnings of the **Parc Naturel Régional d'Armorique**, with one-off attractions for families.

Part of Finistère's appeal is its links with the past. Visit little towns of character like **Locronan** and you could be stepping back into the 19th century. **Dourarnenez** is a delightful town for exploring maritime history. Head out west again and you'll come to the natural vantage point of **Pointe du Raz** where you can see the **Ile de Sein**. The **Bay of Audierne** is a paradise for water sports, and **Pointe de la Torche** one of the world's top surf spots.

The south coast of Brittany provides gentler bays and beaches where buckets and spades reign supreme. Places like **Lesconil**, **Benodet** and **Port Manec'h** all come out tops for young sailors. Don't miss out on the wonderful old town of **Pont-l'Abbé** and **Concarneau** or the arty streets of **Pont Aven** where Gauguin once painted. Then there's the departmental capital of **Quimper** with its beautiful medieval centre and surprisingly modern shops and restaurants.

Finally, make sure you pick up a Cultural Passport to Finistère. It offers reductions at 20 attractions (passeport.culturel.cg29.fr).

Woodland treasures found in Domaine de Menez Meur.

Out & about Finistère

Fun & free

Get to the point

Pointe du Raz, the most spectacular point on the Finistère coast, feels like the end of the earth. In fact, this is not quite the most westerly point of France, but the rocky heights are impressive. The visitor centre (required parking €5) is set 500 m back from the point to preserve its natural splendour. Offshore, the almost flat Ile de Sein is usually visible. Don't miss the nearby Baie des Trépassés (Bay of the Dead) for surfing and sunbathing (see page 106). Pointe du Van, opposite Pointe du Raz, is less busy than Raz and just as beautiful, with wonderful views, marked walkways through the heather and butterflies to spot. There's a cute little visitor centre and a tiny café with crêpes and ice cream. Parents need to be mindful of kids on these cliff walks, but stick to the path and you can't go wrong.

Pointe du Raz lighthouse.

Beautiful botanics

The National Botanical Conservatory in Brest is a Noah's Ark for plants. Its gargantuan glasshouses enclose four exotic environments with endangered and ornamental species from around the world. There's a superb 48-ha park where kids can let off some steam, as well as a playground, a crêperie (open every day), sport trails and paths. Make the most of this free experience by catching an exhibition at the information pavilion. Eden Project meets Kew Gardens, Breton-style.

Conservatoire Botanique National de Brest (**National Botanical Conservatory**), 52 allée du Bot, 29200 Brest, T02 98 41 88 95, cbnbrest.fr. Garden 0900-1800, until 1900 in spring and 2000 in summer; information pavilion April-October Wednesday and Sunday from midday; glasshouses July-September Sunday-Thursday 1400-1730.

That takes the biscuit

Brittany is renowned for its butter biscuits and several retail outlets offer free tours of their kitchens. The Willy Wonkers of Brittany, some even allow kids to try out their baking skills. Though the tours are free, you'll probably end up spending a small fortune in the attached shops, as you won't be able to resist the biscuits in traditional tins, Kouign Amann (buttery cake), ciders, pâtés and so on. Here are some of the best:

Atelier de la Galette Biscuiterie de Pont-Aven
8 rue du Général de Gaulle, 29930 Pont-Aven, T02 98 09 14 20, biscuiteriedepontaven.com. Apr-Sep daily 0900-1200, 1400-1700 (1800 summer), Oct-Mar Mon-Fri.

Biscuitier de Douarnenez
93 av de la Gare, 29100 Douarnenez, T02 98 74 39 44, biscuterie-douarnenez.com. Tours Jul and Aug Wed and Thu 1700.

Biscuiterie de la Pointe du Raz
Route de la Pointe du Raz, 29770 Plogoff, T02 98 53 10 13, biscuiteriedelapointeduraz.com. Tours daily Apr-Sep, Oct-Mar Mon and Fri, 1000, 1100, 1400 and 1500.

Biscuiterie François Garrec
Route de Fouessant, RD44, 29950 Bénodet, T02 98 57 17 17, garrec.com. Tours Mon and Sat 0900-1830.

Biscuiterie Jos Péron
Jos Péron, route de Quimper, BP7, 29370 Coray, T02 98 59 36 35. Tours mid-Apr to Jun 1400 and 1530, Jul and Aug 1400, 1500 and 1600, Sep 1400 and 1530.

Find buried treasure

The Menhir de Kerloas near Plouarzel is the tallest upright standing stone in France, at almost 11 m. Legend has it that hidden treasure beneath the menhir was revealed when the stone went off to drink from the ocean on the first stroke of midnight on Christmas Eve. As it returned on the second stroke, no one had time to steal it.

Be enchanted

The enchanting Fôret de Huelgoat surrounds the famous 'Chaos', a jumble of vast granite boulders, many bigger than houses, tumbled into incredible shapes. The rocks hold a fascination for all ages, and kids love to try out the 100-tonne Trembling Rock. There are loads of good stories connected to the site: that it is the work of giants, or the petrified remains of discarded lovers thrown into the chasm of the Gouffre. You can also follow a little canal through the woods to the remains of one of the oldest lead/silver mines in France.

Visit a snail farm

Come face to face with half a million snails at L'Escargot du Pays de Cornouaille – one of only 10 snail farms in France. Located on the D765 between the towns of Bannalec and Rosporden, in the hamlet at the crossroads of La Croix Lanveur, it is a boon for minibeast lovers of all ages. You get to hold lots of snails, including the Petit Gris variety, indigenous to Brittany. There are loads of fascinating snail facts to hear – when snails are born, for example, their birth weight increases 500 times in five months (in human terms, a baby would weigh 1.5 tonnes at that age). Not only is the whole place free, but there's the chance to taste the snails afterwards – if your kids dare.

L'Escargot du Pays de Cornouaille, La Croix Lanveur, 29140 Kernevel, T06 72 20 27 21, organic-snail.com; complimentary guided tours in English every Wednesday and Friday from mid-June to mid-September 1000-1900.

That's (free) entertainment

Free shows and concerts are held at Brest port every Thursday in July and August (Les Jeudis du Port) and the waterfront is lively with bars and restaurants.

The Festival of Cornouaille (festival-cornouaille.com) in July (programme and tickets from March) fills the centre of Quimper with music, song and dance. Many events are free with the chance to learn Breton dancing and listen to traditional instruments and watch children parade in colourful costumes.

Visit **Ville Close** in Concarneau for free shows all summer long at the Carré des Larrons, a little open-air amphitheatre (see page 125).

Parc Naturel Régional d'Armorique

See page 128.

Fôret de Huelgoat.

Best beaches

Baie des Trépassés.

Baie des Trépassés

This breathtaking beach between two craggy headlands with caves under the cliffs is a good place for beachcombing. It is a great surf beach and there's a lifeguard in summer, but beware the strong currents. A hotel/restaurant is right on the beach, and the Pointe du Raz (see page 104), the second most westerly point in France, is a short drive away, or a 45-minute walk along the coastal path (not suitable for very young children).

Beg Meil

The Plage des Dunes is a long strand of thick white powdery sand and rocks near the semaphore station on the point along this gentle southern coastline. There's a raised pool at one end (parents to be vigilant), a Second World War bunker to clamber on, and cormorants preening on the rocks. The beach of Cap Coz to the north is much longer and more sheltered. The deep Baie de la Forêt looks across to Concarneau (see page 124).

Benodet

A traditional hot-spot for the yachting fraternity, Benodet has four beaches, the best being Plage du Trez, a long stretch of sand at the mouth of the Odet estuary with safe, calm waters and backed by concrete beach huts. It's perfect for lazing on, but it has plenty of activities too, including swimming lessons at the Mickey Club, pedaloes and sea canoes. Kids love the gigantic bouncy giraffes. There are good shops, a strollers' promenade shaded by pines, and lots of choice for eating out. You can also catch a ferry to the Iles Glenan, a 45-minute trip away. The little **Plage St-Gilles** is popular with kids for its rock pools. Picnics are not permitted.

Brignogan-Plages

This small resort gets crowded in summer. The sheltered Plage des Crapauds is best for families, with organized events for kids and sports equipment for hire. There are plenty of rock pools for a bit of *pêche-à-pied*, and the quirky rock formations visible at low tide set an adventurous scene for all kinds of games. Just to the northwest, the Plage des Chardons Bleus is a long stretch of fine sand.

Camaret and around

There is a delightful town beach here, in a very pretty setting with easy access to all facilities. It's a good place for paddling, and a coastal path wends its way up onto the cliff tops. Round the headland of the Pointe de Toulinguet is the wilder surfers' Plage de Pen Hat, where strong currents make swimming unsafe. The Peninsula Le Labyrinthe wooden maze, fun for kids, is not far away.

The vast expanse of sand at Kerloc'h (on the D8 just outside the town) has exceptional views across to the Château de Dinan rock formation, said to be the home of mischievous *korrigans* (fairies). Facilities are limited to a beach bar, but there are plenty of rock pools and caves.

Carantec

There are six beaches on the Carantec Peninsula on Finistère's rocky northern edge but Kélenn is the most entertaining for families. It has a sailing centre, play area, volleyball pitch, picnic site and café terraces. You can even rent a cute blue-and-white or red-and-white striped bathing hut in summer. At low tide you can walk out to the fine sand beaches and protected creeks of Ile Callot (pay careful attention to the tide times posted there before crossing) where children from six years and up can take drawing and painting lessons in summer. Information from the Carantec tourist office (T02 98 67 00 43, carantec-tourisme.com).

Keremma

For something completely unspoilt – conservation has kept the buildings at bay – enjoy this impressive 5 km of clean sand backed by grassy dunes. It's the perfect place for hoisting

Hit or miss?

Centre de Découverte des Algues (Seaweed Discovery Centre)
5 rue Victor Hugo, 29680 Roscoff, T02 98 69 77 05, algopole.fr. Free.
Charge for talks and events from around €5 adult, €3.50 child.

This is a great place to find out more about the wonders of algae, the first plants to appear on our planet. However the centre itself isn't of much interest to kids unless you've come for a scheduled event. Most talks, films and events are in French but can be captioned on request in English. This place really comes into its own when you take a trip along the shore at low tide with a scientist guide to look at the rich diversity of plants and animal species. Such oddities as sea lettuce and all the old and new uses for seaweed are talked about. A 75-minute guided tour taking you behind the scenes at Roscoff's fish auctions includes a children's quiz, a children's corner with activities and a video that takes you on board a fishing boat heading to the high seas. If you're just popping into the centre, one of the best parts, especially for mums, is the shop, full of beauty products made from algae and its derivatives. There are wonderful seaweed soaps and scrubs, Thalado face creams and masks and interesting seaweed pot pouris to smell. There's even a Briezh tea made of seaweed. Cup of seaweed cha, mum?

kites and playing beach games, and a popular spot with horse riders too. The nearby Maison des Dunes (400 m) has nature exhibitions and events in summer, and a short walking circuit with explanatory panels. The Bay of Goulven is a prime birdwatching area.

L'Aber

There are no facilities here except a refreshment van in summer, but there's a fabulous pebble and sand beach, with the clear waters of the Bay of Douarnenez to enjoy. At low tide you can explore a semi-island with an old fort and lots of nooks and crannies. Take care not to get cut off. The estuary behind is teeming with bird-life and has an old lime kiln.

Lac du Drennec

If you are looking for a relaxing day inland with small children, what could be better than this lake in a beautiful hilly setting? There are two swimming beaches, one by the café/crêperie and sailing centre, but you can swim anywhere around the shore along the 7-km walking circuit. There are also children's playgrounds, tennis and table tennis, or you could get out on the calm water in a kayak.

Le Conquet

Les Sables Blancs just north of the town is a favourite spot for surfing, kite-flying and sun-bathing on a 2.5-km stretch of glorious white sands, but stock up on provisions in the town first. Explore the adjoining Kermorvan Peninsula on foot and watch the ferries plying their way to the islands of Molène and Ouessant out in the Atlantic Ocean. Or how about a bit of dolphin spotting?

Le Pouldu: Les Grands Sables

Set in a gentle coastline of bays and low cliffs that once attracted artists like Gauguin, Le Pouldu has several beaches. The most central is Les Grands Sables, reached by steep steps or a sloping road from the parking above. The Ti Soaz beach club offers games and trampolining for kids (3-10) in summer.

Le Pouldu: Plage de Bellangenet

Just to the west of Les Grands Sables, Blue Flag Plage de Bellangenet has level access from the parking area, with a café, speciality ice cream and mini-golf nearby. It also has open showers.

Le Pouldu: Plage de Kérou

This is the site of the local surf school and popular with the young set. Try the new craze of Stand-up Paddle.

Locquirec: Plage du Port

You'll be spoilt for choice with nine sandy beaches around the promontory of this very family-friendly little town. The Plage du Port by the harbour has a beach club for kids.

Locquirec: Plage Les Sables Blancs

If you fancy a more open beach than Plage du Port, try Les Sables Blancs west of the centre.

Meneham

This is an idyllic curve of sand, with boats bobbing on the tide and seaweed drying in stacks on the dunes. Just behind the beach (150 m) is the restored fishing village of Meneham, a protected site with an ancient bread-oven, an *auberge* for food and ice cream, and the chance to see artisans at work. Kids love the custom officers' lookout, wedged between enormous boulders that provide opportunities for energetic scrambling.

Morgat

The Blue Flag beach is right at the heart of this very attractive resort, with shops, cafés and restaurants all around. Brightly coloured houses and flapping sails contribute to the holiday atmosphere. There are lots of sporting facilities for all the family on hand, and a beach club for younger kids.

Pointe de la Torche

This surfing and sand-sports mecca has a real buzz in high season, and has a good vibe for teens. Miles of sand backed by dunes provide plenty of quiet spots when the beach nearest the parking is crowded. Stroll out to the point for stunning views, and the chance to clamber over a Second World War bunker or admire a large Neolithic dolmen.

Porz Carn

This sandy crescent is great for building sandcastles and swimming, and more sheltered than the 32 km of sand running north along the Baie d'Audierne. The little café shack does a roaring trade in summer. It's also a popular place with kite-flyers, as the Atlantic breezes kick in nicely along this shore. For more action, it's an easy stroll to the Pointe de la Torche (see above).

Port Manec'h

Set at the mouth of the Aven Estuary with a magnificent private château behind, this was one of the great holiday centres of the belle epoque and it still shows. There's handy road parking behind original white beach huts and a great sailing and kayaking school (Cardinal Sud: Club Nautique de Port Manec'h de Kersidan). The bay is perfect for swimming or messing about in a boat, and has a pontoon a little way out to sea. There's a pretty café, La Châtaigneraie, a grassy slope for sand-free picnics, and a kiosk for ice cream. While away a few hours with a fishing net in the rock pools, or when the crowds descend, stroll through the pine trees along the Sentier André Jolly to the little port area.

Raguènes (Névez)

The Ile Raguènes, with its two lonely houses, is accessible from a rocky strand at low tide. It's a great place for seeking out crabs and mussels in the rock pools. Just to the east is a long sandy beach known locally as **Plage Tahiti** for its balmy atmosphere and perfect for a simple day of doing nothing. (You can get drinks and ice creams in summer, but it's best to take a picnic.) Nearby (2.5 km) is **Kerascoët**, Brittany's most picturesque thatched village with a welcoming café.

St-Nic – Plage de Pen Trez

This long and popular stretch of golden sand backed by pebbles has safe swimming and easy parking above the beach. Parts of the beach are used by high-speed sand-yachters and there is a kitesurfing zone. There are lots of campsites nearby for budget beach holidays.

Trez Bellec

This magnificent stretch of surf beach near Telgruc-sur-Mer is made for family fun. When the tide goes out there's a huge area for sand-yachting, kite-flying and simply running wild, all flanked by magnificent cliffs. The busy sailing school, Centre Nautique de Telgruc-sur-Mer isn't flash, but it does the job well. Behind is a gentle valley with a basic campsite, Camping Pen Bellec.

Le Pouldu.

Action stations

Boat trips

Locamarine

Port de Plaisance, 29750 Loctudy, T02 98 87 95 95, locamarine-loctudy.fr. Call for rates.

Locamarine provides yacht or motor boat hire, with or without a skipper, to explore the coast of southern Finistère, the Glénan islands or for a fishing trip. It also offers jet-skis and trips on giant inflatables, including a motorboat-drawn banana.

Vedettes Rosmeur

29160 Crozon-Morgat, T06 85 95 55 49, grottes-morgat.com. €11 adult, €8 child (4-12), €3 under 4s.

Take a cruise into the grottos of Morgat, with commentary in English, to see the amazing colours of the 80-m-long Cave of the Altar, the Cave of Ste-Marie, the Devil's Chimney and the Devil's Bedroom.

Canyoning

Face Ouest

1 route de Keruguen, 29570 Roscanvel, T02 98 27 44 76, faceouest.fr. Courses for adults and children (over 12).

Get with the in-crowd and try out Aquacord. A combination of climbing and canyoning, it takes place at Pen Hir Point on the Crozon Peninsula. Before setting out on your first adventure, you will be kitted out in a wetsuit, helmet and harness. One for adrenalin-junkie teenagers.

Diving

Presqu'ilemersion

1 bd de la France Libre, 29160 Crozon, T06 18 05 91 76, presquilemersion.com. Initiation session from €42.

This diving school, based in Crozon, is open year round for novices and experienced divers. Equipment can be hired and diving instructors accompany all dives. Courses for children (from age 6) are available.

Horse riding

Centre Equestre de l'Arrée

Garzuhel, 29190 Brasparts, T02 98 81 47 34, centre-equestre-arree.fr. Year round. From €10/30 mins.

Riding for adults and children (from age 5), from short pony rides and lessons to all-day treks.

Ferme Equestre de Neiscaouen

Neiscaouen, 29560 Landévennec, T02 98 27 37 11.

At the land end of the peninsula, this centre offers short rides along the estuary and riding holidays. Phone in advance.

Les Petites Ecuries

Rue de Kéréon, Crozon, T06 62 87 13 09, les-petites-ecuries.chez-alice.fr. Year round.

One- or two-hour excursions for novice or experienced riders.

Haras de la Mer Blanche

Chemin de St-Sébastien, 29170 Fouesnant, T02 98 56 51 37, harasmerblanche.com.

In Fouesnant, near Benodet, the Mer Blanche Stud Farm welcomes beginners and experienced riders. Offers pony rides and rides along the beach for adults and children (over 6). Also raises foals.

Sailing, windsurfing & kayaking

Carantec Nautisme

Plage du Kelenn, BP17, 29660 Carantec, T02 98 67 01 12, carantec-nautisme.com. Mar-Jun and Sep to mid-Nov Mon-Sat, Jul and Aug daily. Catamaran hire €36/hr, double kayak hire €16-22/hr; courses available.

In the heart of Morlaix Bay, Carnantec water sports centre takes full advantage of this amazing stretch of water. Sea kayaks, racing catamarans and schooners are available, with sailing for all ages. You may also get to see the birdlife, grey seals and whales in the area.

Centre Nautique Crozon-Morgat

Port de Plaisance, 29160 Morgat, T02 98 16 00 00, cncm.fr. Year round.

For a whole variety of water sports, equipment hire and tuition, the Centre Nautique de Crozon-Morgat has bases on the beach and at the port in Morgat. You can enjoy the safe waters of the Bay of Morgat or Bay of Douarnenez for sailing (including motor and catamaran), surfing and windsurfing, or why not learn to kitesurf? Sea-kayaking (single or double seat) can be arranged at any time of year. From age four.

Club Léo Lagrange

2 rue du Stade, BP13, 29570 Camaret-sur-Mer, T02 98 27 90 49, club-leo-camaret.net.

On the Crozon Peninsula, this club offers sailing (from age 5), surfing, windsurfing and also diving (from age 8). A seaside summer camp allows kids aged 13-16 to learn water sports whilst taking French classes.

Visit Locronan

Why? This pretty granite village dates back to the 10th century and is a must if your family likes the experience of stepping back in time. It was used during the filming of Roman Polanski's *Tess*.

Kids will be magnetically drawn, not to the magnificent 15h-century church (though this is well worth a look), but to G Larnicol Biscuiterie Chocolaterie (place de l'Eglise) to sample the incredible cakes, biscuits and chocolates. This is a great place to pick up a Kouign Amann – a traditional buttery cake (see page 145).

There are other lovely little shops that kids will enjoy rummaging through. La Tribu de Lulu sells toys, hairclips, stickers, fun wellie boots and clothes. Next door is Savonnerie de Bretagne for all your soaps and bubble baths.

There's a tiny little museum adjoining the tourist board (1000-1200 and 1400-1700, €2 adult, children free) that traces the history of the town's sailcloth industry, at its peak in the 16th century.

Where? Just off the D7 east of Douarnenez.

How? There are no cars allowed in the village. Park just outside, €3. locronon.org.

Club Nautique Plouguerneau

Port du Koréjou, Maison de la Mer, 29880 Plouguerneau, T02 98 04 50 46, cn-plouguerneau.com.

Just a paddle from Europe's tallest lighthouse built at sea, Plouguerneau water sports centre's kindergarten welcomes children from four to seven and the kids' club from six to eight. Provides sailing and windsurfing lessons, or you can simply hire the equipment and go.

Ucpa Benodet

Le Letty, 29950 Bénodet, T02 98 57 03 26, benodet.ucpa.com.

The magnificent lagoon setting, looking out to the Glénan Islands, is the perfect place to learn the art of sailing catamarans and dinghies, windsurfing and kitesurfing. There are two-, three- or four-day packages as well as week-long courses, including all meals and accommodation. There are also lessons for families not staying at the centre.

USAM Voile

Maison du Nautisme, CN Moulin Blanc, 29200 Brest, T02 98 02 36 73, usam-voile.fr. Minimum age 5. 5-day courses from €153 for ages 5-7.

For over 30 years, the USAM has been giving beginners' classes and advanced lessons to young and old in catamaran and dinghy sailing and windsurfing. Based near Océanopolis, this club stands out with its wide range of activities and options.

Surfing

The strong tides make for great surfing. For more information see surfingbretagne.com.

Ecole de Surf de Bretagne La Torche

Pointe de la Torche, 29120 Plomeur, T02 98 58 53 80, ecole-surf-bretagne.fr. 1½-hr course for over 8s from €29.

La Torche is the place in Brittany to go surfing. This surf school offers various classes, with or

Learning to surf, Baie des Trépassés.

without accommodation. If you are not sure whether you have what it takes, try the Discovery Package comprising one to three sessions. The school also organizes a lot of special events: competitions, open days and tests. There's kitesurfing and sand-yachting classes too.

Ecole de Surf Bretagne Audierne

Pointe du Raz, Quai Anatole France, 29770 Audierne, T02 98 70 07 98, ecole-surf-bretagne.fr. 1½-hr course for over 8s from €29.

With Pointe du Raz on one side and Pointe du Van on the other, this school is an ideal place to learn how to surf.

Via ferrata Bertheaume Iroise Aventure

Fort de Bertheaume, 29217 Plougonvelin, T02 98 48 26 41. Weekends, public hols and school hols, Apr-Jun and Sep 1400-1800, Jul and Aug 1100-1900, €15/person.

Have fun on two giant rope slides above the sea, 200 m long and 38 m high. From nine years.

Woodland adventures Arbreizh Adventure

Bois de Keroual, 29820 Guilers, T06 64 24 06 41, arbreizh.com. Weekends, public hols and school hols 1000-1800. €15 adult, €10 child, €7 from 5 years.

This treetop adventure circuit just to the west of Brest will keep families happy for hours. From five years.

Toulinguet headland, Crozon.

Parcours d'aventure Karaez Adrénaline

Vallée de l'hyères, Kerniguez BP60125, 29833 Carhaix-Plougher, T06 50 19 15 98, karaezadrenaline.com. €18 adult, €14 child (11-16), €10 (7-10), €6 (5-6).

In Carhaix between the Montagnes Noires (Black Mountains) and the Monts d'Arrée, the Karaez Adrénaline Adventure Trail is a treetop assault course involving balancing skills and games. Seven circuits of increasing difficulty enable everyone from the age of five to 90 to take part. There is also a maze.

Walking

The coastal path (GR34 – red and white waymarks) gives access to the most spectacular walking in Brittany. If you can manage the logistics of linear walking, this is more satisfying than circuits through the not particularly attractive interior. An exception to this is at Landevennec, where the forest provides some lovely paths. The best walking is from Camaret to Morgat, a distance of about 40 km, making a fantastic two-day hike, but if you have less time or younger kids, the short walk (6 km) from Camaret to the Pointe de Pen Hir has unbeatable sea views. Continuing to the wonderful sands of Kerloc'h doubles the distance, but you can return along quiet roads directly to Camaret. Obviously you can shorten the walk to suit your child. The wildest walking is the 10 km from the Pointe de Dinan through Lostmarc'h to the Cap de la Chèvre.

Big days out

Aquashow

Rue du Goyen, 29770 Audierne, T02 98 70 03 03, aquarium.fr. Apr-Sep daily 1030-1830, Oct daily 1400-1800, Nov-Mar open during school hols 1400-1800; birdshow at 1600. €13.80 adult and child over 11, €10.80 child (4-11), €2 (2-3), €50 family.

Not far from the Pointe du Raz, this small and friendly aquarium is a real find. It features conger eels, lobsters, rays, sharks, seahorses, cuttlefish, octopus and more, and has a touch pool and 3D cinema. Despite its name, it also features birds. In a magnificent show, birds of prey and owls fly literally a few centimetres above your head. After your visit have a drink and a snack on the terrace overlooking Audierne's port.

Breizh Park

Route de Dinan, 29160 Crozon, T02 98 27 28 99, breizhpark.com. Year round with reservations, summer 1400-1900. Treetop adventure €12 adult, €10 under 12s; paintball (over 12 only) €15; mini-golf €3.50; horse and carriage ride €35 for 5 people.

Active families will love Breizh Park with its treetop climbing, paintballing, mini-golf and horse and carriage rides.

La Récré des 3 Curés

Parc de Loisirs, 29290 Milizac, T02 98 07 95 59, larecredes3cures.fr. Low season Wed, Sat and Sun 1400-1800, May-Sep Wed, Sat and Sun 1100-1830, Jun-Aug daily 1000-1900. €14 adult, €12 child (under 12), free for kids under 1 m. Karting €10 for 8 mins.

In Milizac, near Brest, La Récré des 3 Curés guarantees a great family day out. There are slides, giant trampolines, a 1900s merry-go-round, Niagara ride, boat rides, mini farm, pirate ship and teacups. The 25-m-high Big Wheel provides a great view over the entire park. You'll find many picnic areas as well as wooded areas offering a stroll in the shade if you want to get away from the frenzy.

Le Port-Musée Douarnenez

Place de l'Enfer, 29100 Douarnenez, T02 98 92 65 20, port-musee.org. Apr-Jun, Sep-Nov Tue-Sun 1000-1230, 1400-1800, Jul and Aug daily 1000-1900, €7.50 (€5.50 low season) adult, €4.50 (€3.50 low season) child (6-16), under 6s free, €20 (€15 low season) family.

This modern museum on the quayside features a fascinating collection of boats and boating paraphernalia from Europe, Asia, Africa and Oceania. Outside, on the water, are four boats to explore. The area around the museum has some great shops like **Bacyrouge et Tricouvert** (36 rue de Port Rhu, 29100 Douarnenez, T02 98 92 42 80) selling model boats, wooden seagulls, nautical cushions, Breton stripey tops and woollen fishermen's jumpers, old ropes and diver's helmets.

Parc d'Attractions Odet Loisirs

Kerrun Moustoir, route de Quimper-Coray-St-Brieuc, 29370 Elliant, T02 98 59 18 25, odet-loisirs.fr. Apr-early Nov Wed, Sat and Sun, school hols 1400-1900, Jul and Aug daily 1100-1900. €7.50 over 3 years.

This may not be the most technically advanced theme park in the world, but kids are sure to have a ball here. Just outside Quimper in a hilly, landscaped setting with lakes, it has over 50 activities for all ages. Trampolines, climbing frames, bouncy castles, a Tyrolean rope slide stretching 175 m over water, a natural labyrinth, waterslides, plus a covered play area, adventure trail and picnic area make it a satisfying day out for a reasonable entrance fee.

Océanopolis

See page 116.

Parc de Loisirs Bel Air

Domaine de Bel Air, Keridreuff, 29710 Landudec, T02 98 91 50 27, parc-loisirs-belair.com. Apr-Jun and Sep Wed, Sat and Sun 1100-1900, Jul and Aug daily 1100-1900. €7/person, free for kids under 1 m.

Another of Brittany's traditional theme parks that relies on old-fashioned fun. There's an aquatic complex, waterslides, pedal boats, fishing, bouncy castles, swings, slides, trampolines, pedal cars, giant chess, a little train, hammocks and more. If you like the park, you can camp next door at Domaine de Bel Air (belaircamping.com).

Parc Naturel Régional d'Armorique

See page 128.

Phares de Penmarc'h

St-Pierre, 29760 Penmarc'h, T02 98 58 72 87, penmarch.fr. Apr-early Nov daily 1030-1900. Vieux Phare (Old Lighthouse) €3.50 adult, €2 child (7-16), under 7s free; Eckmuhl Lighthouse €2 adult, €1 under 16s.
Everyone loves a lighthouse, and there are three of them at Penmarc'h, including the Eckmühl Lighthouse and the Old Lighthouse. Enjoy panoramic views from the 60-m-high Eckmühl Lighthouse, 307 steps up. Its walls are made entirely of local Kersanton granite and the internal staircase is lined with opaline glass tiles. Don't miss the 15th-century chapel at the foot of the lighthouse, or the exhibition on the ground floor of the Old Lighthouse that tells the story of lighthouses in Finistère and Penmarc'h, with historic documents and audiovisual displays. If you have time, have a look at the *Papa Poydenot*, the last lifeboat with oars.

Mini ravers

Les Vieilles Charrues, T02 98 99 25 45, vieillescharrues.asso.fr. Mid-Jul. Prices were yet to be confirmed for 2011 at time of going to press but a 3-day pass will be in the region of €75, including access to the campsite and a day ticket €32 (half price for children aged 9-14 and free for under 9s).
France's answer to Glastonbury, Les Vieilles Charrues, held on the outskirts of Carhaix-Plouguer in Finistère, is one of France's largest and most eclectic music festivals with over 80 acts and 215,000 spectators. It has stayed true to its principles as a non-profit making community project with over 5000 volunteers giving their time and energy. It began in 1992 as a modest village fete for students celebrating their graduation. Recent acts have included The Killers, Bruce Springsteen, Lenny Kravitz, The Ting Tings and Moby up front plus a mix of uber-cool, up-and-coming French bands like Naïve New Beaters. Check out this year's line up on the website and rest assured you'll discover new artists to keep your iPod cred high. Despite its size, it retains a village fete spirit with free milk ('a glass of white') served by local farmers to festival-goers camping on the 12-ha site, and a fancy dress theme, which kids love, such as aliens or the Wild West – an in joke as it's held in the far west of France. Ticket prices are reasonable. When Springsteen was touring the world, Vieilles Charrues charged the lowest price to see him.

Don't miss Océanopolis

You'll notice the striking poster for Océanopolis throughout Brittany – the little girl's head full of coral reefs, sharks and turtles. It's one of the region's best-loved attractions and on a scale you'd be more likely to find in Florida than in rural France. But being Brittany, the emphasis is on education as much as spectacle.

The attraction is divided into four pavilions: Temperate, Polar, Tropical and Biodiversity. Families journey through each of these very different ocean worlds. The Tropical pavilion begins with windows into a huge tank housing a warm water reef, the archetypal undersea world of the Caribbean or Indian Ocean. Huge swordfish, clownfish, reef sharks and more glide by. It's as close to scuba-diving as you can get without taking the plunge. The highlight of this pavilion is the shark lift – a short journey down through the shark tank in a glass-sided elevator. At the bottom you step out into a rainforest where tanks reveal the life of the Amazon.

The Polar pavilion is dominated by the penguins and artic seals, which swim swiftly through vast tanks. It's mesmerizing watching the difference between their movements above and below

Essential information

Port de Plaisance, Moulin Blanc, 29210 Brest (3 km east of Brest), T02 98 34 40 40, oceanopolis.com. May to mid-Sep daily 0900-1800 (1900 Jul and Aug), mid-Sep to Apr 1000-1700, closed Mon except school hols. €16.50 adult, €11 child (3-17), under 3s free, pushchair park €2, English audioguide €2. Buy your tickets in advance (online is easy and the tickets are undated, which gives flexibility) and get in without queuing.

water. Don't miss the multiscreen film *Antarctica*, which takes viewers on a helicopter flight over the icy continent. The Temperate pavilion explores Brittany's underwater environment, including its sharks and seals. There's an oceanography exhibit, a jellyfish aquarium and a fabulous touchpool. Kids can learn about tides, currents and so on. The Biodiversity pavilion looks into the all-important ways we can protect our oceans.

Temporary exhibitions on themes such as mermaids or sea monsters cater well to young visitors, and are thought provoking. There are two daily seal feedings (1000 and 1500) and penguin feedings (1030 and 1530). In the Tropical pavilion you can watch a scuba-diver feeding the reef fish (1130 high season and 1500 off season).

The design of Océanopolis allows you to dip in and out of pavilions, so it doesn't get too overwhelming despite there being so much to see. Outside there are plenty of picnic areas and a great nautically themed playground where kids can let off steam before going back inside. There are three restaurants to choose from: a brasserie, self-service and takeaway. Kids will want to investigate the two shops for ocean-inspired games, toys and books. Enter at your wallet's peril.

Across the road from Océanopolis are some great nautical shops: **Swell Addiction**, **Bekayak**, **Bleu Evasion** and **Uship** sell everything from state-of-the-art kayaks to fishing tackle.

More family favourites

Parc botanique de Cornouaille & Musée des Minéraux

29120 Combrit-Pont-L'Abbé, T02 98 56 44 93, parcbotanique.com. Mar to mid-Nov daily 1000-1200, 1400-1900, Jul and Aug 1000-1900. Closed mid-Sep to mid-Oct. €6.50 adult, €3.50 child.

If you like gorgeous gardens, this is for you. There's a lovely English garden and an enchanting water garden. A particularly stunning time to visit is in the spring when the camellias, magnolias, cherry trees and the rhododendrons are in full bloom. Kids might like the little mineral museum attached.

Les Jardins de Rospico

Kerangall, 29920 Névez, T02 98 06 71 29, jardins-rospico.com. Last week of Mar to mid-Jun and 2nd week Sep to mid-Nov 1400-1800, mid-Jun to early Sep 1100-1900, daily except Sat throughout. €6.50 adult, €2.50 child (6-16), under 6s free.

This is a tranquil place to come after the beach. Themed gardens include Mediterranean, water, Japanese and English. Kids will like the open spaces, the brightly coloured mobiles, the dragon sculpture and the giant bulrushes that you can walk right through.

Maison des Jeux Bretons (House of Breton Games)

Place de la Mairie, 29120 St-Jean-Trolimon, T02 98 82 13 45, saintjeantrolimon.fr. Mon-Fri 0830-1200, 1400-1730, closed Thu and Sat morning. Voluntary payment.

Try your hand at a traditional Breton game. There's around a dozen to choose from.

Maison-Musée du Pouldu

10 rue des Grand Sables, Le Pouldu, 29360 Clohars-Carnoet, T02 98 39 98 51, museedupouldu.clohars-carnoet.fr. Call or see website for opening hours. €4 adult, €2 child (12-16), under 12s free.

If your kids have any interest in art, this is a great voyage of discovery about the painters who left Paris in the late 19th-century for Brittany, including Paul Gauguin. This house is a glimpse into that period. You can also follow the town's *chemin des peintres*; its 11 landmarks conjure up the stunning landscapes that inspired the artists. Choose the long route at 5 km, or the short one at 2 km. Details from the museum.

The shop and café at Les Jardins de Rospico.

Théâtre guignol

The French equivalent of Punch and Judy dates back 200 years. You can catch shows at seaside towns across Brittany during the summer, with tickets around €6. There are always goodies and baddies and a smattering of political satire, all in French of course, but kids get the gist and love the stripey-circus-tent atmosphere, the popcorn and the brutal humour.

Musée Bigouden

Château des Barons du Pont, Pays Bigouden, T02 98 66 09 03, museebigouden.fr. Apr-May Tue-Sun 1400-1800, Jun-Sep daily 1000-1230, 1400-1830. €3.50 adult, €2.50 (12-26), under 12s free.

The tall lace *coiffe* is synonymous with Brittany, and its vital story, linked to Breton identity, is told here. Visiting this museum of social history also allows you to see the keep of the former château, though it's odd to be looking at a 1960s Formica kitchen one minute and climbing a medieval stone staircase the next. Exhibits look at the changing role of Breton women and the wearing of the famous headdress, at work and play, and even while watching football.

Musée du bord de mer

29 av de la Mer, 29950 Bénodet, T02 98 57 00 14. Mid-Jun to mid-Sep 1000-1300, 1400-1830 (Sun closes 1800). €4 adult, €2 child (5-12), under 5s free.

Cute maritime museum, exploring sailing in Bénodet and La Belle Plaisance. Lots of old-fashioned games for children.

Le Labyrinthe de Pont-Aven et sa Mini Ferme

Kergo, 29930 Pont-Aven, T06 78 18 35 98, labypontaven.canalblog.com. Early Jul and Aug 1000-2000, 1-21 Sep 1000-1800; €6 adult, €4.50 child (3-12), under 3s free (also free for the third child before 1200). Night time Jul and Aug Wed and Sat 2130-0100; €9.90 adult, €7.90 child (under 16).

This incredible maze is a great one for kids who like a challenge. To find the exit, you must solve the riddles given by Kergloz, the evil magician. There are lots of twists and surprises along the way. If you have teenage kids, you might like to try the evening experience with the added excitement of using torches. For little ones, there's also a great Breton mini farm with local breeds such as Ouessant sheep and black pigs.

Musée de la Fraise

12 rue Louis Nicolle, 29470 Plougastel-Daoulas, T02 98 40 21 18, musee-fraise.net. Jun-Sep Tue-Fri 1000-1230, 1400-1800, Sat and Sun 1400-1800, school holidays until 1730, Oct-May Wed-Fri and Sun 1400-1730, closed Jan. €4 adult, €2 child (12-18), under 12s free.

How much fun does a strawberry museum sound! This is one of those little attractions that Brittany does so well. There are exhibits on traditional Breton houses, maritime heritage, Breton costumes and the local apple tree ceremony. In summer there are strawberry tastings.

Musée de l'Amiral

Penhors-Plage, 29710 Pouldreuzic, T02 98 51 52 52, museedelamiral.com. Feb-Jun, Sep-Dec Tue-Fri 1000-2000, Sat and Sun 1400-1800, Jun-Sep open until 1900, Jul and Aug daily 1000-2000. €5.50 adult, €2.90 child (5-14), under 5s free.

This cheerful, nautical museum has over 10,000 shells from all over the world, from giant clams to intricate microscopic shells found in the sand. There are also hundreds of birds to learn about, along with fossils, coral, minerals and sharks. Hunt out souvenirs and keepsakes in the shop, and then head to the outside play area, which has many nautical curiosities scattered around and views of Pointe du Raz.

Roscoff

Roscoff has lots of great attractions for kids. There's the cute merry-go-round by the port where you can ride Asterix or a Disney character for €2 (the chance for a free ride if you pull the bobbly ball off its hook during a ride adds greatly to the fun). There's a little train that takes you for a tour around the town and plenty of interesting shops to explore full of pirate-themed treasure.

Maison des Johnnies et de L'Oignon Rosé

48 rue Brizieux, 29680 Roscoff, T02 98 61 25 48. Call for opening times and talks. €4 adult, €2.50 child (10-18), under 10s free.

In a former traditional Breton farm, the Maison des Johnnies explains the history of the Roscoff onion. And just who are/were the Johnnies? It is the name given to the onion sellers who, from the middle of the 19th century, used to set off from Roscoff in the summer to sell their onions door-to-door in Great Britain, first on foot, and later, on bikes. In 1929, there were some 1500 on the road. Today, there are about 20. It's an often forgotten story that is told here with photographs and films. The museum also shows off the Roscoff onion – its health benefits (vitamin C) and AOC (Appelation d'Origine Contrôlée) label, granted in 2009. There are tastings of onion-based products, and a discovery trail in a little train, including a visit to an onion grower. If you're in Roscoff around 20 August, watch out for the Onion Festival (roscoff.tourisme.com).

Musée de Pont-Aven

Place de l'Hôtel de Ville, 29930 Pont-Aven, T02 98 06 14 43, museepontaven.fr. Open daily Feb, Mar, Nov, Dec 1000-1230, 1400-1800, Apr-Jun, Sep, Oct 1000-1230, 1400-1830, Jul and Aug 1000-1900. €4.50 adult, under 18s free.

The Pont-Aven School brought more than 20 artists together in Brittany between 1886 and 1896, including Gauguin. They were looking for new forms of artistic impression or 'the right to go where no-one has gone before'. This is the fruit of their labours. A great exhibition for anyone studying art.

Musée des Beaux Arts

40 place St-Corentin, 29000 Quimper, T02 98 95 45 20, musee-beauxarts.quimper.fr. Open 1000-1200, 1400-1800, closed Tue except July and Aug (closed Sun morning Nov-Mar). €4.50 adult, €2.50 young person (12-26), under 12s free.

Here you'll find a wealth of Breton domestic and outdoor scenes like the *Pardon of Kergoat* by Jules

Castles of Finistère

Château de Kergroadez

29810 Brélès, T02 98 32 43 93, kergroadez.fr. Guided tours inside the castle: Jul and Aug 1100-1800 (closed Sun morning), Jun and Sep Thu 1430, Sun 1500, Oct-May by appointment. €4 adult, €2.50 child over 6, under 6s free. Gardens: mid-Apr to Oct, €1.50 adult, €1 over 6, under 6s free.

This granite Renaissance castle close to Brest offers lots of family activities and events in summer, candlelit night-time tours, storytelling evenings, donkey trails, concerts, festivals and a sound and light show, usually in the last week of July.

Château de Kerjean

29440 St-Vougay, T02 98 69 93 69, cdp29.fr. €5 adult, €1 child (7-17), under 7s free.

This castle and fortress is a symbol of the Renaissance in Brittany and is a lovely place for kids to explore, with plenty of parkland where they can run wild and have a picnic. Guided tours and special exhibitions.

Château du Taureau

Baie de Morlaix, T02 98 62 29 73, chateaudutaureau.com. €13 adult, €6 child (under 12), under 4s free.

Set in one of the most beautiful bays in Brittany, the offshore Château du Taureau is visited by boat, starting from Carantec, Plougasnou or Roscoff. Choose one of the guided tours, with storytelling, theatre and songs thrown in.

Le Domaine de Trévarez

29520 Sant-Goazec, T02 98 26 82 79, cdp29.fr, call for opening times. €5 adult, €1 child (7-17), under 6s free.

This turreted belle-epoque castle has wonderful gardens to explore. In 2011 (Jun-Oct) look out for the amazing natural sculptures by Patrick Dougherty in the grounds. Kids will love them.

Pont-Aven

Pont-Aven developed into an artists' colony in the 19th century, attracting first Americans, then a group that included Gauguin, Emile Bernard, Maurice Denis and Paul Sérusier in the 1880s. They developed a new style – sometimes called Synthetism – in rather flat, boldly blocked and coloured renderings of local landscape and life.

Pont-Aven.

Breton. Another room illustrates Breton legends: *Les Lavandières de la Nuit* (1861) by Yan Dargent shows an unfortunate traveller ensnared by a herd of flying sheets! The most famous tale is St-Guenolé persuading King Gradlon to throw his daughter Dahut into the waves. Set your kids the task of finding Gauguin's goose.

Parc Animalier du Quinquis

29360 Clohars-Carnoet, T02 98 39 94 13, parcanimalierduquinquis.com. Apr daily 1400-1900, Jun to mid-Sep daily 1030-1900, Mar and Oct Wed and Sun and school holidays 1400-1900. €8 adult, €4 child (4-12), under 4s free.

If your kids like animals and lots of space in which to run around, this animal park will be a hit. Wander along ancient paths to see deer, ponies, donkeys, small monkeys, wallabies and many more on this 8-ha site. Kids can feed the animals by hand.

Peninsula Le Labyrinthe, Crozon

Menez-Kerbasguen, route de la pointe de Dinan, 29160 Crozon, T02 98 26 25 34, peninsulabyrinthe.com. Summer 1000-1900, Apr, May, Jun, Sep 1400-1800, afternoons only in school holidays. €7 adult, €6 child, under 5s free.

Humorous and well-planned entertainment designed for children, but fun for adults too: a huge maze made out of wooden panels with storyboard clues (English summaries). Exhibition about mazes and games for youngsters too.

Rain check

Bowling

- **Bowgali**, Persivien, 29270 Carhaix-Plouguer, T02 98 93 03 20.
- **Le Master**, 59 rue Prés Sadate, 29000 Quimper, T02 98 53 09 59, quimper.lemasterbowling.fr.

Cinemas

- **Cinéma Jeanne D'Arc**, rue Hugo Derville, 56110 Gourin, T02 97 23 50 42.
- **Cinéville Parc Lann**, rue Aristide Boucicaut, 56000 Vannes, T08 92 68 06 66.
- **Le Beaumanoir**, rue Douves du Noyer, 56120 Josselin, T02 97 22 22 93.
- **Le Bretagne**, quai Dupleix, 29000 Quimper, T02 98 53 23 11.
- **Le Ciné**, rue du Phare, 56170 Quiberon, T08 36 68 69 24.
- **Le Club**, 34 rue Berthelot, 29100 Douarnenez, T06 36 68 00 71.
- **Le Grand Bleu**, Kerampuil, 29270 Carhaix-Plouguer, T02 98 93 32 64.
- **Le Rex**, 21 av Miln, 56340 Carnac, T02 97 52 92 20.
- **Le Rialto**, rue de l'Hospice, 29600 Morlaix, T02 98 80 07 90.
- **Le Roha**, 5 rue de la Fontaine-Blanche, 29800 Landerneau, T02 98 21 33 11.
- **Les Arcades**, 38 Bd Dupleix, 29000 Quimper, T02 98 52 02 88.
- **Les Arcades**, 8 rue de Levenant, 56400 Auray, T02 97 24 06 52.
- **Les Studios**, 3 ave Foch, 29400 Landivisiau, T02 98 21 33 11.
- **L'Image**, 9 rue de Saltash, 29470 Plougastel-Daoulas, T02 98 40 30 79.
- **Multiplexe Liberté**, 10 av Georges Clémenceau, 29200 Brest, T02 29 61 13 13.

Ice skating

- **Patinoire Rinkla Stadium**, place Napoléon III, 29100 Brest, T02 98 03 01 30, rinkla-stadium.com.

Indoor play

- **Les Petits Monstres** (8 km east of Quimper), ZA Troyalac'h, 29170 St-Evarzec, T02 98 56 29 29.
- **Ty Marmouz** (3 km from the centre of Pont l'Abbé), ZA Ty Boutic, 29129 Plomeur, T02 98 87 30 19, tymarmouz.fr.

Indoor swimming and leisure centres

- **Aquacap**, route de la Pointe du Raz, 29770 Esquibien, T02 98 70 07 74, aquacap.fr.
- **Acquarive**, route de Kerogan, Creach Gwen, 29000 Quimper, T02 98 52 00 15.
- **L'Ile aux Mômes**, 15 rue Aimé Césaire, 29900 Concarneau, T02 98 97 10 28, lileauxmomes.fr.
- **Piljadour**, rue de la Piscine, 29270 Carhaix-Plouguer, T02 98 99 39 50, poher.com.
- **Piscine Spadiumparc**, bd Léopold Maissin, Le Moulin Blanc, 29480 Le Relecq-Kerhuon. T02 98 34 34 34, spadium.fr.
- **Zone de l'Hippo**, 5 rue du dr Piquenard, 29000 Quimper, T02 98 53 08 65.

Karting

- **BKI Brest Kart Indoor**, Golf de Brest Iroise, Parc Lann Rohou, 29800 St-Urbain, T02 98 41 82 42.
- **Kart West**, ZI de l'Hipppodrome, 29000 Quimper, T02 98 53 03 03, kart-west.fr.

Don't miss Sing-along forest walks with Addes

A gentle ramble through the canopied forest with nursery rhymes and local songs sung to a live guitar sounds a little odd, yet this is a truly magical experience for young kids and one not to be missed.

Addes is a group of young entrepreneurs who also happen to be passionate about the Monts d'Arrée region and its strong tradition of Breton storytelling and legends. In an area where you're hard pushed to find work, they started up their own company offering outings, rambles and walks themed around local legends, nature and kids. Ten years later, they now attract around 7000 visitors a year; half of those are children.

Their headquarters is a tiny village called Botmeur deep in the Parc Naturel Régional d'Armorique. Everyone assembles for the kids' walks at the school car park. Here, Katell, originally from Wales, welcomes participants and introduces Fred the guitarist, who looks straight out of troubadour central casting. Everyone is made to feel very welcome and then, while walking around the back of the school, Katell gets everyone to introduce themselves in song (not as intimidating as it sounds). The excited party continues onto pretty country lanes, which lead to song stops in forest glades and rocky clearings beside a stream.

Songs are sung in Breton, French, English and occasionally Welsh, but none of that seems to matter to the kids. They all join in whatever the language. A song like 'Five Little Ducks' (*Cinq Petits Canards*) is easily recognizable in French with the help of finger puppets. It's a great way of exposing your kids to other languages and encouraging them to have a go. When Katell sings a very cute French song about bears washing in the river, the meaning is loud and clear and everyone joins in with the chorus and actions.

There are plenty of things to spot along the way, like a woodpecker's hole in a tree, and Katell gives out little ladybird stickers to put on fingertips when the 'Coccinelle' song is sung. At the end, the kids get a little colouring booklet with all the songs inside. Everyone then heads back to the school hall for orange juice and butter biscuits and a cup of cider for the adults.

For older children, especially those who are learning French, there are nature and wildlife walks, including to the hidden beauties of the Yeun Elez, and an inspiring sunrise walk to blow the cobwebs away. A gold panning walk reveals the prospecting techniques and the alluvial minerals of Brittany. Moonlight walks are especially magical, with legends and stories about the little people, the Korrigans, who inhabit the area. You may even spot one!

Meet at **Botmeur School**, 29690 Botmeur, T02 98 99 66 58, arree-randos.com. Apr-Aug and Easter holidays. Children's walks €6/person, €5/person for a group of 4 or more; nature walk €6 adult, €4 child; sunrise walk €12 adult, €6 child; gold panning €13/person or €11 each for a group of 4 or more; moonlight walks €12 adult €8 child (7-14). Special wheelchairs for disabled. Must book in advance.

Let's go to...

Concarneau

Concarneau is the perfect family day out. Its stone-built Ville Close (walled town) is compact and walkable, with interesting shops and restaurants. But don't expect to be the only ones there. This place gets rammed with visitors, but you can escape to the new town or beach if it gets too much.

Kids will love the dramatic approach to Concarneau's Ville Close, over its ancient bridge. Unlike a castle, this is a working town where every timber-framed building is in use.

Get your bearings

Concarneau belongs to the national network of Villes et Pays d'art et d'histoire, and the Heritage Centre (02 98 50 39 17) offers tours of the town. For views over the area, climb up to the ramparts. Le Petit Train (T06 80 70 58 89, Apr-Sep) is a cute tourist train departing from opposite the entrance to Ville Close.

Don't miss

Musée de la Pêche (3 rue Vauban, Ville Close, T02 98 97 10 20, museedelapeche.com; daily Feb and Mar 1000-1200, 1400-1800, Apr-Jun, Sep and Oct 1000-1800, Jul and Aug 0930-2000, €6 adult, €4 child, €20 family and 3rd child free, under 5s free) is one of the first attractions you come to as you enter Ville Close. The museum celebrates all things fishy from a stuffed Coelacanthe, a prehistoric fish, to a magnificent sewing machine, used for making sails, that looks likes something you'd use to run up a pair of trousers for a giant. Don't miss the massive Japanese crab suspended high above your heads; it was caught in 1839 and measures more than the average height of a man.

The highlight of the museum is the chance to board a real fishing trawler, the 34-m *Hémérica*. Kids will love exploring the galley, the claustrophobic cabins and going up on the bridge.

Back inside the museum, there's a play area where kids can sit on old rope coils and barrels

and colour in a mermaid or octopus to put on the wall. There are also slapstick cut-outs of mermaids and deep-sea divers to put your head through.

Throughout July and August there are many special activities for children aged seven to 12, from treasure hunts to learning about sea legends.

Investigate the shops

Ville Close is full of interesting little shops and art galleries. They range from Breton tourist tat to upmarket artisan shops. Even touristy outlets like Triskell (8 rue Vauban, T02 98 97 03 26) will keep kids occupied, browsing the incredible Authurian-type swords, Breton flags and pirate gear.

Trésors des Mers (9 bis rue Vauban, T02 98 97 12 78) is a treasure trove of all things seasidey, from shells to driftwood sculptures.

Le Bois d'Angèle (5 rue St-Guénolé, T02 98 97 46 17) has beautiful wooden toys, including traditional jigsaws of the departments of France.

Go into any of the many gourmand shops including **Biscuiterie de Concarneau** (3 place St-Guénolé, T02 98 97 07 67) and you'll be offered Breton biscuits, cakes and sweets to sample.

And finally, there's the **Carré des Larrons**, a little open-air amphitheatre hosting free shows all summer, at the far end of Ville Close.

Let's go to... Concarneau

Essential information

Concarneau tourist office, Quai d'Aiguillon, BP529, T02 98 97 01 44, tourismeconcarneau.fr. Year round. By the port parking, close to the entrance to the Ville Close. There's a Lego play area and English-speaking staff.

Grab a bite

You can't go very far in Ville Close without stumbling upon a great little place to eat.

Crêperie Le Pennti (6 place St-Guénolé, T02 98 97 46 02) resembles a cottage from the outside, but is an Aladdin's cave within. Butter crêpes start at €2; ham, cheese and egg €5.70. It has a Le Routard recommendation, and there's fancier food if you want it.

Le Trimaran Restaurant (3 rue St-Guénolé, T02 98 60 52 90) is a lovely place to take the kids as it's decorated with fishing nets and buoys on the walls. There's *moules marinières* on the menu and a three-course lunch from €13.60.

For a beautiful view of Ville Close, head to **La Coquille Restaurant** (quai du Moros, T02 98 97 08 52, lacoquille-concarneau.com) in the fishing port. Reserve a table on the terrace and indulge in fresh seafood.

There are plenty of places to buy ice cream, but look out for the distinctive *glacé artisan*, huge swirling art forms of ice cream in fantastical flavours from Nutella to passion fruit. **Le Glacier de la Ville Close**, **Valérie Légnini** and **Auguste Glacier Fabricant** are very close to the entrance of the Musée de la Pêche. €2/scoop!

Something fishy

Concarneau is France's third most important fishing port, and more than 100,000 tonnes of tuna are caught each year by Concarneau-based boats. If you're all feeling adventurous you can join an organized trip on an old sardine boat to try your own hand at fishing.

Down by the breakwater, **Le Marinarium** (place de la Croix, T02 98 50 81 64, mnhn.fr, Apr-Jun and Sep 1000-1200, 1400-1800, Jul and Aug 1000-1900, Oct-Dec, Feb and Mar 1400-1800, €5 adults, €3 child (6-14) is one of the world's oldest marine biology centres. There's nothing flashy here, but plenty of hands-on exhibits, including a touch pool and the chance to look at plankton through a microscope, as well as gruesome exhibits from Victorian times, including a pickled dolphin.

Sailing

If you want to get on the water yourselves while in Concarneau:

Concarneau Voile (place de la Croix, 29900 Concarneau, T02 98 50 85 60, Mon-Fri 9000-1200 and 1400-1700, Sat 9000-1200) offers sailing from age four.

Ecole de Planche à Voile based on Plage des Sables Blancs (T02 98 50 85 60) offers sailing, kayaks and windsurfs. Catamarans from €35, kayaks from €6.

Beyond the centre

Take the Passage ferry from the Ville Close to the old fishing quarter on the left bank. Here, you can link up with the GR4 long-distance footpath to get views back over Concarneau and its bay. This is also the way to **Le Porzou** city sports complex (T02 98 50 14 50) with tennis courts, an indoor pool, children's play areas and picnic spots.

Several scenic walks start in Concarneau, such as the pushchair-friendly route through Kérandon wood, north of the centre, but the most pleasant is the coastal path from Quai de la Croix to the Plage des Sables Blancs, a sandy beach with a lifeguard daily in July and August and water sports. The **Glénans Sailing School** (T01 53 92 86 00, glenans.asso.fr) offers sailing, kayaking, rowing and diving.

On the outskirts of Concarneau is the **Château de Keriolet** (follow the signs to Castle Keriolet at the entrance of Concarneau, T02 98 97 36 50, chateaudekeriolet.com, Jun-Sep 1030-1300, 1400-1800 except Sat afternoon, €5 adult, €3 child, 7-15, €13 family), a fine example of 19th-century Gothic architecture. It is open for guided visits. The kitchens are a highlight for children, taking them back to a time when everything was done by hand – shock horror!

Take a trip to Iles Glénan

Take a day trip to these surprisingly tropical islands that lie 20 km from Concarneau.

Atlantique Voile Service (T06 82 17 09 92, atlantiquevoileservice.com).

Vedettes de l'Odet (T02 98 57 00 58, vedettes-odet.com) is a diverse company that offers scenic boat trips to the Glénan islands from Port de Plaisance (21 av du Docteur Nicolas, mid-Jul to Aug daily from 1100 and 1400, tours from €26 adult, €13 child, 4-12, €5 under 4s, €6 dog). It also offers kayaking tours, a submarine exploration tour or a trip up the River Odet.

Vedettes Glenn (T02 98 97 10 31, vedettes-glenn.fr, departs opposite tourist office, early Jul and Aug daily 1000 and 1415, €26 adults, €13 child, 4-12, €5 under 4s, €5 dog).

If you want to do a spot of fishing around these scenic isles, catch the *Santa-Maria* from the quay near the tourist office (T06 62 88 00 87, santamariapeche.com, Jul and Aug departs Concarneau Mon, Tue and Thu 0800-1200 and 1330-1730, Wed and Fri 0800-1230 and 1400-1830, €35 adult, €20 child, 4-12).

Concarneau is twinned with Penzance in Cornwall.

Special events

The popular and rather glamorous Transat AG2R La Mondiale transatlantic race begins in Concarneau in April and finishes on the *très chic* island of St Barts in the French Carribean, an island that has descendants of Bretons. Join in the buzz as you wave off the yachts. See transat.ag2rlamondiale.fr.

One of Brittany's most authentic festivals takes place in Concarneau in the last two weeks of August: Le Festival des Filets Bleus (Blue Fishing Nets), festivaldesfiletsbleus.com. It celebrates the fishing industry with traditional music and dancing, national dress, sea shanties and a smorgasbord of fishy food.

Parc Naturel Régional d'Armorique

Brittany's only Regional National Park, the Parc Naturel Régional d'Armorique runs across Finistère, taking in the islands of Ouessant and Molène, the Crozon Peninsula and Rade de Brest and the Monts d'Arrée. The further east you go the more remote it gets. It's a veritable playground for kids, with everything from storytelling walks in the woods to wild wolves and fluorescent rock museums.

Brittany excels itself when celebrating its natural beauty and concentrating on quirky, highly individual attractions that you won't find anywhere else in the world, all proving that you don't need flashy theme parks to keep children entertained. And, of course, parents love these places too, as they're highly educational and don't cost a fortune.

Park highlights

Singalong forest walks with Addes (see page 122).

Domaine de Menez Meur

29460 Hanvec, T02 98 68 81 71, pnr-armorique.fr. Mar and Apr, Oct and Nov 1300-1730 Wed and Sun (daily during school holidays), May, Jun, Sep daily 1200-1800, Jul and Aug 1000-1900. €3.50 adult, €2.20 child (4-12), under 4s free. Free talks and guides Jul and Aug.

This place has four marked routes to choose from but the 'Parcour animalier' or wildlife tour (3 km) is

entertaining and walkable even for little children. You'll discover wild flowers, towering pines, domestic animals and rare Breton breeds such as dwarf black sheep from Ile Ouessant, as well as wild boar, deer and wolves (in a large pen with their young). Feeding times for animals are posted at the entrance. Steep steps lead to lookout points where you can spot deer, and there are rocks and tree stumps to scramble on.

There's a spacious outdoor adventure playground next to parkland picnic tables. Nearby are domesticated birds, including peacocks, roosters and geese, plus huge white rabbits. It's a great idea to give your child a basket or bucket to collect things that have fallen on the ground, such as feathers, ferns and oak leaves to examine later. If you go in August, there are blackberries to pick.

Maison des Minéraux

Route du Cap de la Chèvre, St-Hernot, 29160 Crozon, T02 98 27 19 73, maison-des-mineraux.org. Jul and Aug daily 1000-1900, low season Mon-Fri 1000-1200 and 1400-1700, Sun 1400-1700. €4.80 adult, €3 child (8-18), under 8s free.

There's nothing particularly glittering about this museum on the geology of Brittany until you get to the fluorescent room, when it all becomes rather rock 'n' roll. When the lights are on, it's just a room with cases and walls covered in rocks, but when they click off it turns into a neon spectacle

Musée du Loup.

Domaine de Menez Muir.

worthy of any nightclub. You won't believe how the colours glow! During summer there are special activities for families on Thursdays, such as nature walks and science workshops.

As a wonderful added extra, don't miss the Metal Exhibition. Based on recycling, this is an interactive playground of reclaimed delights. Kids can bash oil drums, metal plates and pans, see sculptures made of forks and old bits of bike, and try and link up an electric circuit to power a fan. Electrifying!

Moulins de Kerouat

29450 Commana, T02 98 68 87 76. Jul and Aug daily 1100-1900, Jun Mon-Fri 1000-1800, Sat and Sun 1400-1800, mid-Mar to May, Sep and Oct Mon-Fri 1000-1800, Sun 1400-1800, closed Sat. €4.50 adult, €2.10 child (8-18). Many activites included in the price.

A living history lesson, Kerouat Mills takes kids back to the 17th century to discover the everyday life of the Fagot family. Kids can roll up their sleeves and take a shot at grinding wheat, baking bread, carrying timber with horses and a lot more. Follow the country lanes to discover a tannery and the replica of an old windmill.

Musée du Loup

1 rue du calvaire, 29410 Le Cloitre St-Thegonnec, T02 98 79 73 45, museeduloup.fr. Jul and Aug daily 1400-1800, Mar to mid-Nov Sun 1400-1800, €3.50 adults, €2.50 child (7-12), under 7s free.

Who's afraid of the big bad wolf? This museum plays into childhood myths about wolves, explores the wolf's biology, behaviour and history and honours the wolves that survived in the Monts d'Arrée until 1906. Some of the material is grisly, but there's lots of fun and humour in sound, pictures, cartoons and interactive stuff that kids will love.

Maison de la Réserve Naturelle et des Castors

Le Bourg, 29690 Brennilis, T02 98 79 71 98, bretagne-vivante.org. Mid-Jun to mid-Sep Tue-Sun 1400-1800.

The Venec peat bog has been a habitat for rare flora and fauna for 5000 years. Beavers were

Crozon Peninsula

Part of the Parc Naturel Régional d'Armorique, the Crozon Peninsula juts out into the sea south of Brest. It has charming villages, fortifications and scenic footpaths. Its southernmost tip culminates in Cap de la Chèvre, a windswept rocky outcrop.

Once a fishing port that brought in tuna and sardines, the main settlement is **Morgat**, now a pleasant summer resort boasting a long sandy beach with a kids' club in high season. It has the remains of an 18th-century gun battery and a 19th-century barracks. (The tourist office has designed a marked trail of the peninsula's 200 or so fortifications, which is headed by the impressive Vauban tower in Camaret-sur-Mer in the far west.)

Many people take a boat trip or hire a kayak to see the Cap, in particular the pretty cove of **Ile Vierge**, including the 8-m-long Altar Cave, with glimpses of seabirds and seals on the way.

On the west side of the cap is **La Palue** beach. Out of bounds to swimmers due to its strong currents, it is one of the best places in France for surfing. Many of the young surfers who gather here head over to Crozon during the first weekend of August when the Festival du Bout du Monde takes place – a world music festival that features many acts you'd see at Glastonbury or WOMAD.

introduced to the area relatively recently in 1968. The exhibition here has been designed as a general store, where kids can discover the wonderful world of beavers. Follow the beaver's footprints or explore the peat bog with a guide. Don't tread upon the *herbe d'oubli*, which could make you lose your memory!

Maison de la Rivière et du Lac

Moulin de Vergraon, 29450 Sizun, T02 98 68 86 33, maison-de-la-riviere.fr. Jul and Aug daily 1030-1830, rest of year Mon-Fri 1000-1200, 1400-1730.

Like Ratty in *Wind in the Willows*, you'll be in heaven here if you like messing about on the river. This fantastic river centre, in a former mill on the banks of the river Elorn, welcomes you to a watery world of discovery. Promoting environmental awareness, it teaches kids about fresh water environments and the importance of preserving them. They'll discover otter, salmon, rainbow trout and other riverine species, with activities such as fly-fishing and shore fishing. There are nature hikes, an interpretation path and guided tours.

Maison des Vieux Métiers Vivants

Ferme de Kerampran, 29560 Argol, T02 98 27 79 30, argol.fr. May, Jun and Sep Tue, Thu and Sun 1400-1730, Jul and Aug daily 1400-1800, €4 adult, €2 child (6-14).

A 'living museum' at its finest, here you'll find senior Bretons unravelling all the secrets of age-old crafts. Okay, it's in French, but there are hands-on demonstrations and plenty of audience participation, so it's easy to get the gist. Sheep shearing, butter-churning, making pancakes and baking bread the traditional way, horse-drawn cart rides, learning Breton dances and laundering linen at the local washing place will make kids either fall in love with the past or realize how easy everything is these days.

Musée de l'ancienne Abbaye de Landévennec

29560 Landévennec, T02 98 27 35 90, musee-abbaye-landevennec.fr. Apr-Jun Sun-Fri 1000-1800, Jul and Aug daily 1000-1900, Sep daily 1000-1800. €4 adult, €3 young person (8-26), €10.50 family.

This is not a boring old abbey ruin, but a vibrant alfresco setting for all manner of concerts and fairy tales told by strolling players. Sure there's a sixth-century abbey, where you can learn about cloisters, chapels and refectories, but there's also a flower garden based on the plants and herbs grown by the monks and loads of activities for youngsters, from writing with a quill pen to being an apprentice archaeologist.

View from Abbaye de Landévennec

Bird reserves

Keen birdwatchers may want to make a trip to the Réserve de Goulien on Cap Sizun and the reserves of the Sept Iles (see page 78), near Perros-Guirec. For further sites, consult:

bretagne-environment.org
bretagne.lpo.fr
bretagnevivante.asso.free.fr

Musée de l'Ecole Rurale

29560 Trégarvan, T02 98 26 04 72, musee-ecole.fr. Dec to mid-Feb Mon-Fri 1400-1700, Mid-Feb to Jun Sun–Fri 1400-1800, Jul and Aug daily 1030-1900, Sep 1400-1800, Oct and Nov Sun-Fri 1400-1700. €4 adults, €2.30 child, under 8s free.

The last thing your kids want to do on holiday is visit a school, but this one is worth it. In the small village of Trégarvan, right at the foot of the Ménez-Hom, the old school, built in 1907 and closed in the 1970s due to depopulation, has been turned into a museum. It brings alive what it must have been like at school over a century ago, or – as any six-year-old will tell you – in the olden days. There's an atmospheric classroom with long wooden desks, where visitors can sit and take dictation using quills and violet-coloured ink. Come in summer and you can take a gym lesson, play with toys such as marbles, skipping ropes and whirligigs, and join in traditional games such as hopscotch. You can even take part in science experiments. Best of all is the tiny shop where you can stock up on quills and ink, wooden multiplication tables and maps on little wooden slates.

Remember to ask for a summer events programme T02 98 81 90 08, contact@pnr-armorique.fr.

Ile Quessant

Remote and atmospheric Ouessant (T02 98 48 85 83, ot-ouessant.fr) is truly off the beaten track, lying way out in the Atlantic. You can reach the island by ferry, which leaves from Le Conquet, with Penn Ar Bed (T02 98 80 80 80, pennarbed.fr, €30.20 return) or by plane from Brest with Finistair (T03 2 98 84 64 87, finistair.com, €93 return).

Maisons du Niou
29242 Ouessant, T02 98 48 86 37. Jun daily 1400-1800, Jul and Aug daily 1100-1900, 1 to mid-Sep Sun-Fri 1400-1800.
Traditionally on Ile Ouessant women were in charge of the farm work and the survival of their families while their husbands sailed the world as merchant seamen. In this museum, comprising two houses, families can discover what everyday life was like on the island until the middle of the 20th century. The first is a traditional island home that is brightly painted inside and has haystacks outside, while the other displays traditional dress and explains the *proella*, a funeral rite, unique to the island, for those lost at sea and never found. There is an educational booklet for kids.

Musée des Phares et Balises
Phare du Créac'h, 29242 Ouessant, T02 98 48 80 70. Apr-Jun and Sep 1100-1700, Jul and Aug 1030-1800 (and 2100-2300 2 evenings/week), Nov-Mar 1330-1730, closed Mon, 1100-1700 school holidays.
If your kids have a thing about lighthouses, it's worth making the effort to get here. The museum is situated at the foot of the Créac'h lighthouse, which guides ships along one of the busiest maritime routes in the world. It displays the history of maritime beaconing, starting with the old machinery room where visitors get to ogle magnificent optical devices and a reconstructed lighthouse keeper's room. You can take a guide and discover more of the island's beacons from this starting point.

Inside the lighthouse on Virgo Island, Ile Quessant.

Pick of the pitches

Camping des Abers

51 Toull Treaz, 29870 Landéda, T02 98 04 93 35, camping-des-abers.com. May-Sep. €5.40/pitch, €3.15 adult, €1.80 child (under 7), €1.53 dog, €2.25 electricity; mobile home €270-570/week based on 5 sharing.

This campsite, one hour west of the ferry terminal at Roscoff, is set on the St-Marguerite Peninsula, alongside a lovely stretch of fine sand with little islands accessible at low tide. With 158 pitches and 22 mobile homes, it describes itself as *les pieds dans l'eau*, and the tent and caravan pitches really do slope down to the sea. The most luxurious of the caravans – sleeping up to six – are less than €300 for a week in June. Activities include pétanque, ping-pong, beach volleyball and an adventure playground. There are water sports in nearby L'Aber-Wrac'h and a riding centre close by. It also has a shop and a takeaway (Jul and Aug) and bikes for rent.

Camping-gîte de Loqueran

Bois de Loqueran, BP55, 29770 Audierne, T02 98 74 95 06, pointe.raz.free.fr. €3 pitch, €3 adult, €1.50 child (under 12), €1.50 car, family rooms from €52.

This communal gîte and campsite near Audierne is a find for those on a tight budget. The gîte, an attractive wooden chalet, runs like a youth hostel with shared kitchen and dining room, though family rooms have their own bathrooms. The campsite has 25 pitches with a toilet and shower block and shops close by. Kids will love the horses in the fields, the mountain bike and riding trails and the nearby beaches.

Camping Le Ty-Nadan

Route d'Arzano, 29310 Locunolé, T02 98 71 75 47, camping-ty-nadan.fr. €34-76.50/Castel Premium pitch for 2 people (includes electricity, waste water disposal, fridge, barbecue, garden furniture and 1-hr internet); €20-46 basic pitch for 2 with electricity; €47-119/mobile home for 4; 6-person wooden chalet €69-168.

If you're looking for an all-singing, all-dancing campsite, this is for you. This is a find for families with kids old enough to want plenty of activities, so long as you don't mind it being a 25-minute drive to the beach. Even teenagers addicted to their beds will be up early for the kayaking, paintball, quad biking, horse riding and much more. There's even an adventure park with treetop courses. Club Mousse (4-8 years) offers farm visits to Pont Scorff Zoo by minibus, painting, dressing up, insect hunting and puppet shows. Action Club (9-12 years) has its own wood houses in the forest, treasure hunts, mini discos, pancake competitions, sports games and films in English. There's a supermarket, bar, pizza restaurant/takeaway, and good nursery areas with baby baths. Babysitting is also available. If you want to splash out, book a six-person wooden chalet near the river.

Camping Les Hortensias

Kermen 29660 Carantec, T02 98 67 08 63, leshortensias.fr. €3 tent, €3.50 adult/child, €2.50 child under 7, €1.60 car, motor home €4.60.

This value-for-money, intimate campsite is part of an organic vegetable smallholding. There are none of the facilities of a big campsite, but that adds to the charm. There are showers though, and bouncy castles. It has amazing views over the sea and the beach is a 2.5-km walk via footpaths. There are also some beautiful gîtes and cottages on the site.

Camping Plage de Trez Rouge

Route de Camaret à Roscanvel, 29160 Crozon, T02 98 27 93 96, trezrouz.com. Mid-Mar to mid-Oct. €12.70-16.50 pitch and car, €4-5 adult, €2.50-3 child over 7, €1-1.50 from 2 years, mobile home for 4 €280-560.

Superb position by the 'Red Beach', so called for its striking cliffs. Good facilities and children's activities. Mobile homes have terraces with sea views and a rental of about €450 for four people in late June or early September. There's a bouncy castle for kids and it's just 50 m to the beach. Table tennis, a trampoline, playground and horse riding add to the fun.

Campsite Le Grand Large

Lambézen, 29570 Camaret-sur-Mer, T02 98 27 91 41, campinglegrandlarge.com. Apr-Sep. €6.60-13.60 pitch, €3.30-4.80 adult and child over 7, €1.70-3.30 child up to 7, mobile home €273-750/week.

This lovely campsite has amazing views over the port of Camaret, the bay and the straights of Brest, and is just 450 m from a sandy beach. There are 30 mobile homes and 100 pitches plus family facilities including an outdoor pool with a slide, a toddlers' pool, a play area, mini-golf, mini tennis court, table tennis, volleyball, boules, games room and a TV room. Diving, climbing and riding can be arranged. There's a little grocery shop, a snack bar selling takeaways and a bar overlooking the pool and sea. Concerts and discos in high season.

La Chaumière de Keraluic

Camping Keraluic, 29120 Plomeur, T02 98 82 10 22, keraluic.fr. Campsite May-Oct. €13.50-15.50 for 2 people and a car, €3.50-3/90 child over 8, €1.50-1.90 child under 8, gîte for 5 €495-795/week (€25 extra for high chair and baby bed), studios for 2 €195-435/week (€25 extra for high chair and baby bed).

Wonderfully placed in the southwest of Finistère, this campsite, family gîte and three studio apartments are surrounded by forest but only 6 km from the coast. There are just 25 large pitches, with a nice play area, table tennis and boules. There's a library plus a launderette and small shop selling freshly baked bread in summer. The pretty gîte sleeps up to five plus baby and the studio apartments are great for couples with a baby. There is Wi-Fi available throughout for a fee. Dogs aren't allowed during July and August.

La Ferme de Croas Men

Croas Men, 29610 Plouigneau, T02 98 79 11 50, ferme-de-croasmen.com. Camping Apr-Oct. €5 pitch for car and tent or caravan, €3.20 adult, €2.80 child (under 7), €2 child under 2; gypsy caravan or chalet (year round) €320-480/week, cabin €200-380/week, ridge tent €200-380/week.

If you like camping to be about getting back to nature, you'll love it here. The historic town of Morlaix and the sea are just 10 minutes away. Pitch your tent among fruit trees and lush vegetation providing privacy. There's a lovely recreation room with toys and board games, books, colouring sets and tourist info. If you don't want to stay under canvas there are gypsy caravans, chalets and dreamy little cabins with green shutters and wooden patios. Or you can go glamping in a new wood and canvas ridge tent. The amenity block has a mother and baby room, disabled access and laundry area. You can order farm produce, bread and croissants, and the farm is open every day to see the animals and have a tractor or donkey cart ride!

L'Orangerie de Lanniron

Château de Lanniron, allée de Lanniron, 29000 Quimper, T02 98 90 62 02, lanniron.com. Mid-May to Sep. €10.30-18.80 pitch with car, €4.30-7.50 adult, €2.80-4.80 child (2-9), under 2s free.

This must be one of the grandest settings for a campsite, in the grounds of a private château with 17th-century classical gardens, on the banks of the Odet. This is a one-stop shop for accommodation, with camping, gîtes, cottages, mobile homes and overnight hotel facilities. There is a new aquapark and bikes for hire and a nine-hole golf course and putting green to introduce kids to the sport. French lessons are available.

Farm favourites

Ferme Apicole de Térenez

Rosnoen, 29590 Le Faou, T02 98 81 06 90, ferme-apicole-de-terenez.com. Family room €50 with breakfast.

How cool is a stay on a bee farm? This one has its own free museum, children's playground, mountain bike hire and animals such as black Ouessant sheep. Lovely rocky beaches and the fossils of the Crozon Peninsula are just a 10-minute drive away. There are doubles or four-person rooms on a B&B basis. Kids will love the bunk beds, and cots and high chairs are available. A farm shop sells gingerbread, sweets, biscuits and royal jelly.

Ferme Insulaire de Quéménès

29259 Archipel de Molène, T06 63 02 15 08, iledequemenes.fr. Family rooms €519-595/2 nights.

This small island in the Mer d'Iroise is the subject of a durable development project. The sole inhabitants David and Soizic run a farm, and offer *chambres d'hôtes* with full board. There are only three rooms, with one bathroom between them. Visitors are collected by boat (weather permitting) from the island of Molène.

Best of the rest

Au Bon Accueil

Port Launay, 29150 Chateaulin, T02 98 86 15 77, bon-accueil.com. €62-82/night family rooms.

This friendly riverside hotel is on the threshold of the Monts d'Arrée in the Parc Naturel Régional d'Armorique and within a 20-minute drive of the beaches of the Baie de Douarnenez. There are 42 guest rooms, the best with views over the Brest-Nantes canal to the front. There are rooms for four or two interconnecting rooms. Alternatively there's a new residence, Au Fil de l'Eau with 12 apartments for two, three or four people. A value-for-money find, it also offers a heated pool, sauna, garden, mini-golf, table tennis and a fishing pontoon.

Auberge du Youdig

Kerveguenet, 29690 Brennilis, T02 98 99 62 36, youdig.fr. Doubles from €35, extra bed €15, gîte €220-570/week.

If you want a place to stay with oodles of character, this is it. Set in the heart of the Monts d'Arrée, not far from Huelgoat, it contains a scale model of the nearby 17th-century village of Brasparts created from old roof tiles. There's a B&B with three large rooms, and the inn serves hearty local food and hosts storytelling sessions. There are also five gîtes of varying sizes in renovated stone buildings, or the new *gîte d'étape* with three rooms sleeping up to 12.

Holiday house in Lesconil

5 rue des Sables Blancs, 29740 Lesconil, contact owner Pascale Bodere, T02 98 88 20 24. From €1350/fortnight.

This colourful, eclectic house is ideal for one or even two families if you like shabby chic. There are two big double bedrooms (one with an extra fold-down bed), one bedroom with twin beds and a baby cot, a huge kitchen/dining room and lounge. The garden is safe and enclosed, and there are lots of children's toys, beach equipment and two bicycles. It's just a minute from the beach, *boulangerie* and port.

Hôtel de la Baie des Tréspassés

29770 Plogoff, T02 98 70 61 34, hotelfinistere.com. €39-106 double.

It's all about the setting with this two-star hotel. If you want a surfing holiday or to discover the wonderful headlands of Pointe du Raz and du Van, this will do the job.

Hôtel de la Plage

42 bd de la Plage, 29160 Crozon-Morgat, T02 98 16 02 16, presquile-crozon.com/hotel-de-la-plage. €65-80 family room.

Good value at this friendly and newly refurbished hotel on the seafront. The first-floor restaurant has panoramic views, and a bar terrace across the road allows you to sip your drinks beachside. Book in advance to be sure of a bedroom with a sea view.

Colourful Morgat.

Hôtel Relais de la Pointe du Van

29770 Cléden, Cap Sizun, T02 98 70 62 79, hotelfinistere.com. €52-106 doubles.

Sister hotel to Hôtel de la Baie des Trépassés, this is all about location too. Sleep in a comfortable room facing the ocean, with the sound of waves breaking gently outside. It's ideal for walking the coastal path.

Hôtel Thalassa

Quai Styvel, 29570 Camaret-sur-Mer, T02 98 27 86 44, hotel-thalassa.com. Connecting rooms €100-130/night, apartments €410-980/week.

Close to the beach and the centre of town, this moderately priced hotel has 47 rooms, some of them interconnecting for families, plus 15 apartments. If you stay halfboard, children up to the age of three get free food and board (one child per room). Those aged 4-12 get 50% off at the sea-view restaurant. There's an outdoor heated seawater pool, sauna, solarium and gym, a garden and billiards room.

Kersimrah

Tres-Bellec, near Telgruc-sur-Mer. Just France, T+44(0)20 8780 4463, justfrance.co.uk (code FR2939.100.2). £499-1148/week. Sleeps 5. Price is inclusive of travel on P&O off-peak crossing for car and 5 passengers.

Cute and bijou three-bedroom barn conversion, with sweeping views down to the dramatic coastline and Crozon Peninsula. Recently renovated, it has stone walls and wooden ceilings. The little kitchen, dining and lounge area opens onto the front garden, which has a barbecue and table to catch the sunset over the bay. There is a single bedroom downstairs, shower (no bath), washer and dryer room. Upstairs, under the eaves, are a double room and a twin room. Great location for Trez Bellec beach.

Kervec Farmhouse
Lieudit Kervec, 29910 Tregunc, T+44(0)1425 650511, mybrittanyholidayhouse.com. Farmhouse £900-1000/week, Old Dairy £375-475/week, 15% discount if both places are booked together. Extra for bed linen, towels and cleaning.
This picture-perfect Breton farmhouse is down a leafy road, just north of Névez. Inside it needs a bit of updating but it definitely does the job, with a large lounge, rural kitchen with a vast stone fireplace, a great utility room, three decent-sized bedrooms and bathroom. The owner has young children, so you'll find kids' books, DVDs and toys lying around. There's an extensive garden and an outside dining area. If you want to bring along grandparents who like their privacy, the Old Dairy is next door. This one-bedroom barn conversion has ultra-modern interiors with double-height living space and a mezzanine bedroom. Just down the road is a bike hire place for cycling to Tahiti Plage or Port Manec'h Plage.

La Villeneuve Holiday Cottages
29340 Riec-sur-Bélon (5 km southeast of Pont-Aven), T02 98 06 99 38, brittany-gites-la-villeneuve-france.com. €400-1135/week 2-bedroom gîte.
This well-maintained collection of farmhouse, cottages and gîtes is a paradise for little children. Set in woods and grassland with large play areas it has a bouncy castle, badminton, table tennis, football, cricket, croquet and boules. The outdoor pool is heated from May to September. Bikes and helmets are available free, including a bike fitted with a child seat. There's a large

Playing shops at Kervec Farmhouse.

three-bedroom farmhouse, six two-bedroom cottages, two three-bedroom cottages and a detached three-bedroom chalet. The village of Riec-sur-Bélon is a 15-minute walk away, and you're within driving distance of some great family beaches like Port Manec'h. Best of all is 'chocolate hunt day'. Every Friday at 1800 children search the woods for hidden chocolates. The one who finds the most gets a prize and then all the booty is shared out – phew! There's a €3 charge per child but mums and dads get a glass of bubbly afterwards. It's a great way to start the weekend!

Le Keo

Bourg de Lampaul, 29242 Ouessant, T06 17 88 59 57, lekeo.com. €45 doubles, €85 family suite.

If you're heading over to the island of Ouessant then Le Keo is a traditional B&B close to the port. It doubles as a shop selling Breton crafts, puppets, old postcards and beer. There are three rooms, two of which interconnect to form a family suite with two beds. There's a nautical theme throughout and the owners will even take you on a tour of the island.

Le Nid d'Iroise

4 Hent Kergaradoc, 29840 Lanildut, T02 98 04 38 41, hebergement-nature-bretagne.com. Treehouses €110 for 2, extra bed €20, baby €10.

On the northwest reaches of Finistère, this lovely guesthouse in the quaint village of Lanildut has four bedrooms named the Boat, Cabin, Shellfish and Exotic. There are also wonderful self-catering wood cabins, covered with thatch and insulated with feathers, some in the trees. All have warm pine interiors and some have modern four-poster beds. The general feeling of well-being continues in the spa in the tropical gardens.

Camaret waterfront.

Le Ty Pouldohan

7 rue de Porz Breign, 29910 Tregunc, T+44(0)20 8780 4463, justfrance.co.uk (code FR2932.351.1). £1113-1350/week.

Le Ty Pouldohan is a charming house situated 3 km from the village of Tregunc and just 100 m from the sandy beaches of Pouldohan. The perfect location for a family holiday (the house sleeps 7), it is set in an enclosed garden with a barbecue and swimming pool.

Le Village Vacances de Beauséjour

Parc de Beauséjour, BP4, 29217 Le Conquet, T02 98 89 09 21, lesvillagesmer.com. Lodges for 5 €281-351/week.

These seaside villages in Le Conquet offer 40 wooden lodges for five or 10 guests. There are large play areas for children, plus more than 30 walking or cycling routes nearby, as well as dolphin-watching and boat trips. There are kids' clubs in summer. Great value for money.

Penty Kerveron

29160 Crozon, T02 98 27 20 41, locations-kerveron.com. €705-1450/week (sleeps 6) including bed linen, towels, logs for the fire and other bits and pieces.

The seascape views, sprawling garden and bracing Atlantic breezes make this 17th-century fisherman's cottage a Breton dream. It has four bedrooms and is furnished with antiques. The kitchen has a vast open fireplace complete with galette hotplate. Stroll the 300 m to the sandy beach or explore the old custom officers' coastal path, skirting the edge of the Crozon Peninsula.

'Stay and Sail', L'Ancrage

Kergalet, Lanvéoc, T02 98 17 01 31, brittanysail.co.uk. Apr-Sep. €425-575/week for 6.

Richard and Sue Curtis have two gîtes (sleeping 6 and 2/3) at their sailing school base near Crozon, and a family house (for 8) to let at Camaret. The gîtes are in outbuildings converted to a very high standard. Most of their 'Sail & Stay' bookings are for families. The total price for four is €2850 for a seven-day package, staying in a gîte and including five days cruising aboard the yacht *Cornish Legend*, with Richard as skipper. If any of the party would like to do a sailing course while onboard this can be included at no extra cost. Most children like to do the Competent Crew Course and learn about sailing, steering, knots and simple navigation.

Ty Keriquel

Keriquel I Vihan, Chemin de Park Vras, 29910 Tregunc, T+44(0)20 8780 4463, justfrance.co.uk (FR2932.260.1). £1190-1546/week.

Ty Keriquel is a lovely farmhouse situated in the hamlet of Keriquel and just 1.5 km from the beaches of Kersidan. The house sleeps up to seven and is set in a large garden and boasts an attractive terrace, private swimming pool and a barbecue and has plenty to keep the kids entertained including table tennis, badminton, a trampoline, slide and children's games and toys.

Splashing out

Grand Hôtel des Bains

15 rue de l'Eglise, 29241 Locquirec, T02 98 67 41 02, grand-hotel-des-bains.com. €157-318 double with breakfast, extra bed for child up to 12 with breakfast €68, cots free.

If you can afford it, this Relais & Châteaux beauty is a classic hotel that has kept pace with modern times. Set in the harbour town of Locquirec at the tip of a peninsula, it has a feel of New England about it, with tongue and groove wooden panels, eggshell-blue walls and painted wooden furniture. Most rooms have bay views, and family rooms for three are all on the bay side, with a double bed and a single and an extra bed or cot available. Alternatively families can book interconnecting rooms. Mums will probably want to spend some time in the spa, and there's a large indoor saltwater pool that children can use at certain times. There are also nine sandy beaches nearby as well as a good sailing and diving school.

Hôtel du Centre

Chez Janie, Le Port 29680 Roscoff, T02 98 61 24 25, chezjanie.com. Doubles €59-99, extra bed for child €30.

A rare boutique gem that's family-friendly and a good option for a day or two when you arrive off the ferry or before you depart. It has 16 rooms, four of which can interconnect to form 'family apartments' (though there are also some rooms with a double and a single and space to add a cot). Some rooms have views over the port. The decor is red and grey with soulful quotes by Breton poets on the wall over the beds. A former sardine bar has been transformed into a stylish basement bar with an outdoor terrace for casual meals of ham and chips, a milky pop and a Breizh Cola (menu Moussaillon €8). For mums and dads there are Caesar's salads at €11.50 or you can head upstairs to the posh bistro for a blowout.

Hôtel-Restaurant Le Goyen

Place Jean-Simon, 29770 Audierne, T02 98 70 08 88, le-goyen.com. €89-181 double.

This 26-room hotel at the northern end of the Baie d'Audierne has very pretty rooms, many with sea views and lovely French windows and balconies (though remember to request one, as most families are placed to the rear of the hotel overlooking a courtyard). There's a fabulous restaurant with a sophisticated kids' menu. Bike riding and boat trip packages are also available.

Le Manoir de Coat Amour

Route de Paris, 29600 Morlaix, T02 98 88 57 02, gites-morlaix.com. B&B family suites €155-170/night, gîte for 7 €700-1400/week, gîte for 3 €425-€765 week.

The name Coat Amour (Wood of Love) lends an appropriately romantic air to this hotel near the medieval coastal town of Morlaix. Offering B&B in palatial surroundings, this impressive *manoir* has the wow factor. It's a short walk to the restaurants in town, but an evening meal is available if booked in advance. There are family suites within the house, and two luxurious gîtes in the gardens. The units (one for 6/7, the other for 2 plus a child) have everything for a relaxing holiday. You can call on Bon Appetit (T02 98 78 00 81), a local catering company that will deliver meals to your gîte if you don't fancy cooking. Outdoor swimming pool in summer.

Cool & quirky

Les Roulottes des Korrigans

Coarem Edern, 29190 Brasparts, T06 84 57 96 24, roulottes-des-korrigans.com. Gypsy caravans for 4 from €69-99.

Deep in Les Montes d'Arrée, these gypsy caravans have cosy pine interiors. Kids will love beds tucked into cubbyholes. There's a lovely kids' playground and a sauna and jacuzzi for mums and dads, plus a crêperie, café, boutique and library. Fishing trips can also be arranged.

"Sur l'estacade"
C'est l'instant de perfection
le soleil descend sur la mer

Poetry on the walls at Hôtel du Centre, Roscoff.

Quick & simple

Amour de Pomme de Terre

23 rue des Halles St-Louis, 29200 Brest, T02 98 43 48 51. Daily 1200-1430, 1900-2200.

A good central place to eat, with huge platters of food featuring the eponymous potato in some form or another. The atmosphere is cheery, with an open kitchen, and chunky rustic tables packed into the small room. There's also a rather basic outdoor terrace opposite. Daily specials may be meat or fish, and the salads are also substantial. Try and find room for the banana *tarte tatin* if it's on the dessert board.

Auberge du Port

74 rue de la Marine, 29730 Le Guilvinec, T02 98 58 14 60. Mid-Mar to mid-Sep daily lunch and dinner.

This family-run restaurant has a slightly old-fashioned feel, with dark blue paint and tablecloths, but the food is excellent, particularly a huge plate of *fruits de mer* (shell-fish) fresh from the port. A simple meal of flavoursome fish soup, white fish fillet of the day in a tangy seaweed sauce, followed by home-made crème caramel costs just €16.

Bistrot à lire

18 rue Boucheries, 29000 Quimper, T09 63 00 19 53. Mon 1400-1900, Tue-Sat 0900-1900.

A bookshop with a café and outdoor terraces. Simple lunches and cakes available.

Café des Arts

4 rue Ste-Catherine, 29000 Quimper, T02 98 90 32 06. Mon-Fri 1100-0100, Sat and Sun 1500-0100.

On the quieter bank of the river, with a view of the cathedral from outdoor tables, this café/bar is popular with arty types and young people (good for teenagers). Linger over hot drinks, beer and cocktails, including non-alcoholic ones.

Café L'Ile Verte

34 Kérascoet, 29920 Névez, T02 98 06 80 66.

A great little café with a pretty garden in the heart of the incredible thatched village of Kérascoet. Leek tart is €3.80, apple tart €2.60, and crêpes from €1.90.

Chez Fanch

49 rue Anatole France, 29100 Douarnenez, T02 98 92 31 77, chez-fanch.com. Jul and Aug Fri–Wed 1200-1400, 1900-2200.

Breton flags, multilingual menus and whimsical drawings greet you on arrival at this restaurant just a few paces up from the port. It has a cosy interior, with a roaring fire in winter. The set menus from €11-41 are excellent value, with a good choice.

Crêperie Blé Noir

Vallon du Stang-Alar, 29200 Brest, T02 98 41 84 66. Daily from 1200.

The restaurant is near the parking area for the Stang Alar valley, with a lake and playground nearby. Crêpes, salads and a few gratin dishes, such as *scallops à la Bretonne* available. There's a choice of tasty pancakes, such as La Bretonne, with artichokes, ham and cheese. It's a very pleasant place in which to eat or have a drink outside, not far from Océanopolis.

Crêperie du Château d'Eau

Lieu Dit St-Roch, 29830 Ploudalmézeau, T02 98 48 15 88, creperie-du-chateau-deau.fr. Feb to mid-Nov daily 1200-2130. Rest of year Sat and Sun and school holidays.

Come to eat in this old 50-m-high water tower for 360° ocean and countryside views. It's open all day and there's a good choice of galettes, smoked sausages, and dessert crêpes. Try one of the crêpes named in honour of the keepers of the lighthouses, such as the Phare de l'Ile Vierge.

Crêperie du Sallé

16 rue du Sallé, 29000 Quimper, T02 98 95 95 80. Tue-Sat 1200-1400, 1900-2230.

In the heart of the old town, with tables on the street and a dining room with ancient beams and Breton-themed decorative

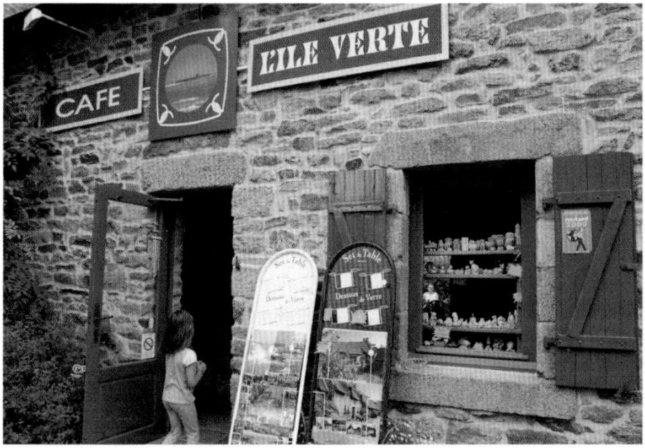

plates. The menu is fairly basic, but the crêpes are tasty with quality fillings. Particular recommendations include pear and hot chocolate, and apples with salted caramel. Queues form at lunch time during high season, so get there early, though service is pretty brisk.

Crêperie Hermine
35 rue Ange de Guernisac, 29600 Morlaix, T02 98 88 10 91, restaurantmorlaix.com. Mon-Sat 1200-1400, 1900-2130 (Fri and Sat 2200), Sun 1200-1330, 1900-2130.
This is perhaps the most popular crêperie in town, with a wide menu and efficient service in one of Morlaix's ancient houses. The seafood speciality fillings are fresh from Roscoff, and you can sample some of Brittany's 600 or more varieties of seaweed – something for kids to tell their friends back home!

Crêperie Les 4 Saisons
2 rue Burdeau, 29120 Pont l'Abbé, T02 98 87 06 05. May to mid-Sep daily 1130-1830, mid-Sep to April Mon-Sat.
An unpretentious place just off the main street serving memorable dishes, from the savoury *blé noir*, with goat's cheese, streaky bacon and a sort of creamy prune sauce, to the speciality dessert *crêpe au riz au lait*, a sweet rice pudding filling flavoured with caramel, chocolate or apple.

Goustadig
Rue de l'Abbaye, 29560 Landevennec, T06 15 71 10 20. Mid-Jun to mid-Sep, rest of year Sun and school holidays.
A cheap and cheerful *salon du thé* and crêperie by the old abbey, with rustic decor, simple well-cooked food and a nice atmosphere. You can devise your own filling for your crêpe from the lists of sweet and savoury ingredients, though there are some suggestions – goat's cheese with home-made green tomato chutney, and Roquefort with blackberry jam. Preserves are the house speciality.

Hôtel Brasserie Le Relais de la Pointe du Van
29770 Cléden-Cap-Sizun, T02 98 70 62 79, hotelfinistere.com. Daily 1215-1630.
Bag a table outside for the view over Baie des Trépassés or sit inside next to a large picture window. This spacious dining room has old school service (which can be a tad slow). However, the likes of fish soup (€8), *moules frites* (€13), pizza (€6), lasagne (€6) and banana splits (€8) should satisfy the whole family. And don't miss the chocolate *beignets*.

Krampouez Breizh Crêperie
21 place Aristide Briand, 29690 Huelgoat, T02 98 99 80 10, creperie-krampouez-breizh.com. Lunch and dinner, closed Wed (and Fri lunch Sep-Mar).
The best crêperie in town, according to numerous regulars. Combines an atmospheric setting in a beautiful old house with Gaelle's friendly service and delicious crêpes. The cheesy fillings such as Roquefort, Emmenthal and chèvre with walnuts are particularly good.

La Châtaigneraie

16 rue de la Plage, 29920 Port Manec'h, T02 98 06 64 15. Daily 1000-late.

Overlooking the beach, this is the perfect place to kick back with an early dinner with the kids after a day on the sands. Sit outside for fabulous views and cool breezes. Galettes are €3-7.50, *moules marinières* and chips or salad €9.70, *tartare de beouf* €14. The extensive wine list includes a chilled glass of Muscadet from just €2 (€14 for a bottle). There is a good ice cream kiosk in front of the restaurant during the day.

La Galère

41 bd Camille Réaud, 29100 Douarnenez, T02 98 92 17 95.

You can't miss this place, just across the road from Le Port-Musée (page 114). Outside stands a life-sized sculpture of a Breton lady with a skirt made of metal fish. This place is best on a sunny day when you can sit outside and watch the hustle and bustle. There's a kids' menu for €8.70, and mums and dads can dine on grilled sardines and Breton cider.

La Moussaillonne

38 rue Amiral Révèillere, 29680 Roscoff, T02 98 69 70 50, lamoussaillonne.com.

This cheery restaurant in the heart of Roscoff is perfect for families as it's stylish enough for parents and yet full of fun details for kids, such as funny clocks made out of knives and forks. It's bright and cheery with art on the walls and colouring pencils and paper for kids. An extensive menu includes sardines served imaginatively in the tin with yummy potatoes for €6.90, and there's a kids' menu, from €6.90 for a very generous pizza and a scoop of ice cream.

La Terrasse

31 place des Otages, 29600 Morlaix, T02 98 88 20 25. Mon-Sat 1200-1400, 1930-2130.

Popular with British visitors driving south from the ferry at Roscoff. Steak and chips is reliably good. It's worth seeing the belle epoque decor inside – wrought-iron staircase, huge mirrors and murals. People-watching from the terrace is fun.

L'Armen

9 rue Lieut Jourden, 29217 Le Conquet, T02 98 89 07 03. Jul and Aug daily 1200-1500, 1830-2200, rest of year closed Tue.

A pizzeria that also serves a selection of traditional dishes from set menus, such as fish terrine followed by turkey escalope in cream sauce. Friendly and good-humoured service creates a pleasant ambience here, as pizza deliveries stream in and out. Try a takeaway to eat by the estuary.

L'Autre Rive Café/Librairie

Restidiou Braz, 29690 Berrien, T02 98 99 72 58. Wed-Sun 1100-2100, school and public holidays daily.

A lovely café/bookshop with sofas and internet access, in idyllic forest setting just outside Huelgoat. Marc is a genial host and the whole atmosphere is

La Moussaillonne, Roscoff.

relaxed and civilized. A light menu of savoury cakes (using chestnut flour) and salad, soup and cheese/fish/meat plates is available at any time. Delicious ice cream too!

Les Boucaniers
3 rue Poncelin, 29217 Le Conquet, T02 98 89 06 25. Daily 1900-late.
This fine piratey establishment is an old-school tavern with guns on the wall, model galleons in glass cases, cannons on the floor and even a dusty old palm tree with a parrot. In other words it's a treasure trove of kitsch delights for kids, and the food's not bad either. A three-course meal costs €16 for a fish starter, *moules frites* and a *crêpe caramel au beurre salé*. Kids will enjoy ham and chips and ice cream for €7.50. It's a nice place to come after an afternoon at nearby Plage de Portez.

Les Boucaniers Restaurant sur la Plage
13 rue de la Mer, 29940 La Fôret Fouesnant, T02 98 56 81 71, lesboucaniers.eu. Jul and Aug daily until late, other times until 2200.
This laid-back but chi-chi restaurant is right on the beach with a choice of outdoor and indoor tables. The Pirate Menu for kids costs €9 including bream fillet or chicken wings with chips, or spaghetti bolognese, plus an ice lolly and a drink. Adults can have three courses for €14.50 at lunch time or go à la carte for more expensive dishes such as sea bass with red butter (€20).

Kouign Amann

The cake to try before all others is Kouign Amann, a round dense product made from repeatedly folded bread dough, sugar and salted butter, which is very rich and satisfying. The real thing needs no addition, but you do sometimes see apple versions.

Les Viviers de Térénez
Route de Térénez, Rosnoen 29590, T02 98 81 90 68, lesviviers.fr.
Fresh seafood, including sea trout and oysters from the hotel's own marine farm, is served on a sheltered terrace set in scenery reminiscent of the great Canadian lakes. It's a relaxing place to come with the kids for a lazy holiday lunch. Very close to the Pont de Térénez.

Tal an Iliz Crêperie
13 rue Amiral Réveillère, 29680 Roscoff, T02 98 61 22 06.
This has to be one of the prettiest crêperies in town with its blue paintwork, trad lace curtains and artfully rustic bike propped up outside. Crêpes are tasty and good value at €2 for a plain butter one, €6.10 for a more fancy Andouille oeuf fromage (with sausage and cheese). It's €9 for a main course, dessert and cider.

Tara Cantine de Mer
Le Port, quai Ouest, 29740 Lesconil, T02 98 82 27 43. Closed Thu lunch and Tue-Thu Oct-Jun.
This bright modern restaurant in a revamped boatyard is full of local art (Charlotte Coatalen Lambert's fish made out of bottletops) and funky map tablecloths. There's a private room at the back where kids can dine together, giving

mums and dads a chance to relax over their meal. A kids' menu is displayed on a cute blackboard in the shape of a girl and includes ham and chips or *moules frites* plus dessert for €6.

Posh nosh

Le Temps de Vivre

17 place Lacaze Duthiers, 29680 Roscoff, T02 98 61 27 28, tycoz.com/letempsdevivre. Jul and Aug daily, rest of year Tue evening-Sun lunchtime.

You can roll off the ferry in Roscoff and kick-start your holiday with a slap-up two-Michelin-starred meal here. Le Temps de Vivre ('take the time to live') says it all. This is for people who enjoy their food, so perhaps one for older children who can sit for a while. Dine overlooking l'Ile de Batz. Adults can enjoy a main course (such as fillet of duck with cider apple jus) and a dessert for €23. Children feast from €14.

L'Epée

14 rue du Parc, 29000 Quimper, T02 98 95 28 97, quimper-lepee.com. Daily 1030-2300 (food served 1200-1430, 1900-2200).

This suave brasserie by the river offers flavoursome food and cheerful service. The modern metallic decor and music set the scene for varied menus, with a three-course lunch at just over €20. A puff-pastry artichoke tart might be followed by crisp-skinned cod and imaginatively cooked vegetables. The chocolate panacotta is richly satisfying. Good ambience, and popular with all ages.

Ma Petite Folie

Port de Plaisance du Moulin Blanc, 29200 Brest, T02 98 42 44 42. Year round Mon-Sat 1200-1400, 1930-2200, closed Sun.

A fun place to eat, on board an old boat. The main dining room is on the lower deck, with ship's timbers and portholes. If you prefer the upper deck with views of the port, book in advance and specify where you want to sit. The menu is mainly fishy, with a daily special, but meat is available.

Restaurant Patrick Jeffroy

20 rue du Kelenn, 29660 Carantec, T02 98 67 00 47, hoteldecarantec.com. Mid-Jun to mid-Dec Wed, Fri and Sun 1200-1430, 1930-2200, Mon, Tue and Thu 1930-2200, rest of year Wed-Sun 1200-1430, 1930-2200.

It's a toss up whether the panoramic view of the Baie de Morlaix or the cuisine is best about this restaurant. Chef Jeffroy specializes in 'wicked marriages' such as Thai curry of hermit crab with warm artichoke, or a dessert of apple tart with lavender. There's a sophisticated kids' menu from €18 for youngsters willing to try avocado salad, pollack and strawberry sorbet.

Local goodies

Cheese & Co

13 place des Outages, 29600 Morlaix, T02 98 63 18 49. Tue-Sat 0930-1930, Sun 1000-1300 (Fri and Sat eve reservation only).

Just by the tourist office, this superb delicatessen specializing in cheese also offers a light but elegant menu, such as *tartan* or a plate of cold meat with cheese of choice. Jerome Grill is passionate about his products. A great place to buy the makings of a great picnic, and a nice stop for a coffee too!

Les Macaroons de Philomena

13 rue Hereon, 29000 Quimper, T02 98 95 21 40, macaron-quimper.com. Tue-Sat 0900-1900.

This shop is something of an institution and queues in the street are not unknown. Macaroons are taken to an art form, in every colour imaginable.

Les Saveurs de Guimiliau Boulangerie/Salon du Thé

41 rue du Calvaire, 29400 Guimiliau, T02 98 68 75 71. Daily 0630-1800, closed Mon mid-Sep to Easter.
Delicious bread and cakes. Also offers tea, coffee and hot chocolate at outside tables or in a pretty upstairs room. Excellent fare, served by very nice people.

Maison du Cidre de Bretagne

Ferme de Kermarzin, 29560 Argol, T02 98 17 21 67, maisonducidredebretagne.fr. Jul and Aug daily 1000-1300, 1400-1900, school holidays 1400-1900, low season 1400-1700 (closed Wed).
This is actually a cider museum (€5 adult, under 18s free). However, the shop is well worth a visit to stock up on locally made goodies such as biscuits, jams and honey.

Océane Alimentaire

Le Port, St-Guenolé, 29760 Penmarc'h, T02 98 58 43 04. Daily in summer, varied hours in winter.
Lots of fish products, such as rillettes of mackerel and tuna, seaweed items to eat and to beautify the body. Free exhibition too.

Penn Sardin

7 rue Le Breton, 29100 Douarnenez, T02 98 92 70 83, pennsardin.com. Daily 0930-1200, 1430-1900, closed Tue out of season.
The sardine shop is a truly Breton experience. Superb products and decorative tins.

Markets

Tourist offices will have maps or lists with details of the local markets. Some are morning-only, so get there early for your picnic ingredients. Cured meats, smoked fish and chevron cheese are good buys. The *traiteur* will have a range of prepared foods like quiches, salads and filled pastries. There is also a dedicated organic movement here, with quality goats' cheeses, vegetables and dense country bread available. Honey from native black bees is special, particularly in areas such as the Monts d'Arrée, where many types of heather flourish. Kids can learn about a whole new range of tastes.

Brest has a covered market, Halles St-Louis, with many food stalls open every day except Sunday afternoon.

Crozon, hub of the holiday area, has a market on Wednesday, and good food shops, including a fishmonger, in the pretty centre.

Douarnenez market is held on Monday, but fresh produce is available daily from Les Halles, the covered market.

Morlaix has a fabulous food market on Saturday mornings. Shoppers will also enjoy the cobbled streets of chic shops in half-timbered buildings.

Les Halles, rue St-François, Quimper, has all manner of good things – sushi, Moroccan specialities, local meats and cheeses, organic bread, fruit and vegetables plus many takeaway options for salads, sandwiches and savouries. Crêpes are freshly made in front of you, but go before or after the 1200 rush.

Le Faou's Marché des Saveurs in place aux Foires brings together fine regional produce from across the Parc Naturel Régional d'Armorique on Thursday afternoon (1600-1900) from early July to late August. You'll find wonderful bread, cheese, meat, honey, cider, dairy products, vegetables and, of course, crêpes.

Vannes et
sa femme

Morbihan

Vannes et sa femme.

Contents

You must

1. Take the helm at La Cité de la Voile.
2. Marvel at the Univers du Poète Ferrailleur.
3. Find the black widow spider that bit Spiderman at the Insectarium de Lizio.
4. Feed the animals at Brénature, St-Servant.
5. Puzzle over the standing stones of Carnac.
6. Live in the treetops at Parcabout on Ile de Groix.
7. Take a sailing lesson off Ile-aux-Moins in the Gulf of Morbihan.
8. Climb 213 granite steps in Le Grand Phare de Kervilahouen on Belle-Ile-en-Mer.

Morbihan is Brittany's less showy side. It's the kind of place that doesn't shout about its attributes but just gets on with the job of enchanting families. There's much to explore on its southerly coastline, but it would be a crime not to head inland to its castles, canals and crêperies.

It may not have the dramatic coastline of Finistère, but Morbihan ('little sea') packs a punch when it comes to family holidays. It has the world-famous standing stones at **Carnac** (a UNESCO World Heritage Site) and the beach-dotted **Quiberon Peninsula** to explore, not to mention Brittany's best new attraction, La Cité de la Voile (Eric Tabarly Sailing Museum) at **Lorient**, and the vast **Gulf du Morbihan**, a veritable *Swallows and Amazons* playground for any family that likes messing about in boats. **Vannes** is a town to put on any family itinerary with its attractive streets and little tourist train.

Offshore are the island gems of **Belle-Ile-en-Mer** and **Ile de Groix**, both boho-chic hangouts for in-the-know Parisian families and well worth the extra hop.

Venture inland and the little town of **Lizio** may seem like a sleepy old village, but there are quirky one-offs here that make Morbihan so special, such as the ingenious mechanical sculptures of the Univers du Poète Ferrailleur and the Insectarium where kids can force dad to eat a bug cake whilst coming face to face with Spiderman's creator.

Further north lie **Rochefort-en-Terre**, known as the prettiest village in Brittany, the medieval town of **Malestroit** and **Josselin** with its fairy-tale castle, half-timbered houses and doll museum. Or you could head out east to **La Gacilly**, home of eco beauty guru, Yves Rocher – certainly one for mums.

Les Buntings, near Serent.

Fun & free

Stand & stare

Morbihan's most famous attraction is its standing stones at Carnac. A history lesson, a fascinating puzzle and an awe-inspiring sight all rolled into one, it triggers many questions about the endeavours of man. This World Heritage Site is home to the most extensive Neolithic remains in Europe. The great thing is, it's free and you can stay as little or as long as you like depending on whether it fires up your child's imagination.

Thousands of standing stones range across the Breton countryside, interspersed by burial chambers and tumuli, a focal point for the ceremonies of early man. Some theories suggest the stones represent a lunar observatory that helped the ancients chart the movement of the stars, while some fringe theorists suggest they are the work of aliens.

Due to the intense interest in this area, most of the stones are fenced off and can only be accessed in part between November and March.

The Maison des Megaliths (May-Jun 0900-1900, Jul-Aug 0900-2000, Sep-Apr 1000-1700, free) at the Alignments du Ménec provides a little leaflet with diagrams of the whole complex, which ranges over several kilometres, as well as a model showing the inter-relationship of the alignments. There are three main groups, Alignments du Ménec, de Kermario and de Kerlescan, dating back to 4000 BC, pre-Stonehenge. A fourth, Le Petit-Ménec, may be an extension at a changed angle; don't miss this enchanting site a little off the beaten track.

Interspersed are numerous burial places and other enclosures or single menhirs, whose relationship to the main lines is uncertain. The Tumulus de Kercado and Tumulus de St-Michel contain burial chambers covered by mounds of earth, and in the area are hundreds of dolmen whose stone chambers are now exposed.

The sheer scale is what impresses at Carnac, and even if some of the site is inaccessible for reasons of conservation you can still get the sense of awe that such an elaborate construction must have inspired 6000 years ago. There's a viewing tower at Kermario for an aerial perception. Kids might enjoy the simple exercise of entering the Kerlescan alignments at the eastern end and walking up one of the rows, gradually going uphill and seeing the stones of the enclosure coming nearer.

It's worth taking a walk through the wood to the Géant de Manio menhir and nearby quadrilateral enclosure of Crucuno with its contrasting coloured stones. You can go inside the Tumulus de Kercado (c3800 BC), and see the carvings,

Standing stones at Carnac.

and there's a riot of decorative detail in the underground tomb of the group at Mané Kerioned to the north.

Strike a light

For a quirky free attraction that is pure gold, visit the Musée des Châteaux en Allumettes (Matchstick Castle Museum, 12 rue du Calvaire Bizole, 56250 Trefflean, T02 97 43 03 20, May-Oct Mon-Tue 1400-1900, Wed-Sun 0900-1200, 1400-1900). A collection of scale models of some of France's most famous castles and other monuments, all made from matchsticks, is the fruit of one man's obsession. They each take a year to build. Look out for Brittany's own Château de Josselin, which consists of 26,600 matches and Mont St-Michel, 50,000 matches.

Clown around

If you're in Carnac and have had enough of standing stones, head to the place aux Mômes near Carnac Plage, to catch free kids' shows, such as puppetry, story telling and clowns during the summer months.

Follow in the footsteps

Go to Les Aiguille de Port Coton, Belle-Ile-en-Mer to see the subject of Monet's famous painting *Les Aiguilles de Port Coton*, now in Musée d'Orsay in Paris (see page 175).

Touch & go

Capture mini-beasts with a triple-bug catcher bought from the Insectarium in Lizio (see page 159). Ladybirds, sandbugs and moths are easiest to find. Remember to release!

Step into the past

Wander around the amazing thatched cottages of Kerascoet à Névez. Don't miss the chapel with its Gothic bell tower.

I spy

Look out for the gnarled figures in the trees beside the D768 between Auray and Carnac.

Vannes vélos

Catch live music on the streets of Vannes during the summer months and enjoy a free 30-min cycle ride around the city of Vannes or along the Gulf du Morbihan on the orange and purple city bikes parked at the Gare Maritime. T+44 (0)845 226 57 51.

Keep track

Take part in a quest to track and record all the mammals living along the Nantes–Brest Canal, including bats, mice and otters. All you need is walking shoes and a picnic. The canal spans all four departments but Morbihan has one of the longest stretches of the canal. T02 96 61 06 64, gmb.asso.fr

Out & about Morbihan

Best beaches

The Quiberon Peninsula has a rocky west coast (with strong currents) and sandy beaches on the balmy eastern side. Stop at the pinch point of Fort du Penthièvre to see both sides of the picture!

If you are based inland, investigate the beaches of the inland lakes, Lac du Duc and Lac de Guerlédan (see page 88).

Arzon

The Plage de Fogéo-Kerjuanno is a gem – an unspoilt beach of fine sand backed by dunes, facing open sea on the southern arm of the Gulf of Morbihan. There's a picnic area with sea views, and a sailing school (see page 156). In summer the Mickey Club, 'Les Bélugas', will keep kids amused while you sneak off to the nearby thalassotherapy centre. The Petit Mont Neolithic monument is a short walk away.

Belle-Ile-en-Mer

See page 174.

Carnac Plage

Combine a wander among the standing stones (see page 152) with fun on Carnac Plage. Backed by the boulevard de la Plage, it has easy access to facilities. The nearby Lunapark has children's roundabouts, and you can hire sports equipment at the beach. Swimming zones are segregated for safety.

Erdeven

The Plage de Kerhillio is a large family beach. There's always something sporty going on, even out of season, when it's a popular surfing spot. There's good bathing, including a kids' pool, and you can hire kayaks from the beach club. A creek separates it from the naturist beach, Plage de Kerminihy.

Ile de Groix

For something different, take a boat from Lorient to the Ile de Groix and the Plage des Sables Blancs (see page 162), said to be the only convex beach in Europe. The water is lovely and clear, and perfect for snorkelling.

Quiberon: Grande Plage

In Quiberon itself, this is a popular choice for families, although it can be a scrum in high summer. There's a beach club for kids.

Quiberon: Les Sables Blancs

At the top of the Presqu'île, this long sandy beach has safe waters, with lifeguards in summer, and views across the Bay of Plouharnel. A good place for collecting shells.

St-Colomban, Bay de Quiberon

Not far from Carnac, this immense beach has no amusements or cafés. It's a lovely bay for swimming, and there's a water sports hut for the hire of windsurfing boards, paddleboards, kayaks and wetsuits, for adults and kids. A windbreak or beach umbrella is useful. When the tide is out, explore the rock pools or unfurl those kites. At high tide, most of the sand is covered.

Vannes

The Blue Flag Plage de Conleau, the nearest beach to Vannes, on its own 'almost island' in the estuary, is great for small children, with safe, sheltered bathing, a playground and carousels in summer. Surrounding woods provide shade and walks.

St-Colomban, near Carnac.

Action stations

Canal boating
Blavet Canal

This runs for 58 km between Pontivy and Hennebont, passing 28 locks. See canaux-bretons.net for information, and ninarion.fr for boat hire at Inzinzac-Lochrist, 20 km northeast of Lorient. Canoes and kayaks can be rented at the *base nautique* in Rohan (T02 97 51 50 33).

Nantes–Brest Canal

See page 156.

This is navigable from Redon in Ille-et-Vilaine to Pontivy in Morbihan, a distance of 184 km with 106 locks. Boats can be hired at Redon or La Gacilly in Morbihan (13 km from Redon).

Horse riding
Ecurie du Rohu

Chemin er Belanneguy, 56510 St-Pierre, Quiberon, T06 32 57 04 65, ecuriesdurohu.com. 5-hr course from €55.

Offers full-board riding holidays, lessons, hourly rides and excursions, whatever the weather. Young children (from age 3) can ride Shetland ponies (30 mins) led by an instructor.

Karting
Karting de Ploemel

Ploemel, T02 97 56 71 71, kart56.fr. From €13/10 mins.

Outdoor karting for everyone, seven years and up.

Grands Sables, Belle-Ile-en-Mer.

Sailing, windsurfing & kayaking
Centre Nautique de Kerguelen

Parc Océanique, Larmor-Plage, 3 km south of Lorient on D152, T02 97 33 77 78, sellor-nautisme.fr. Year round. Five 2½-hr sessions for 4- to 7-year-olds from €124.

Children over seven can sign up for the Moussaillons programme of sailing tuition, with up to six in a group. For older children there are canoeing trips on the Laita, Scorff and Blavet rivers or on the sea and sailing in the Rade de Lorient. Young children also catered for.

Club Nautique, Lac du Duc

T02 97 74 14 51, clubnautiquedupaysdeploermel.com.

The large Lac du Duc near Ploërmel has a good *centre*

Discover the Nantes–Brest canal

If your kids have a touch of the Ratties from *Wind in the Willows* and like nothing more than messing about on the river, water is never far away in Brittany, with many glorious rivers, and some large estuaries. In the west these are known as Abers, like the Aber Wrac'h and the Aber Ildut. In the ambitious 19th-century programme of canalization, large rivers such as the Oust, Blavet and Aulne were utilized, with artificial stretches constructed to connect the relevant valleys. The Nantes–Brest canal runs right across Brittany, with the Ille-et-Vilaine canal running north/south in the east and the Blavet linking Pontivy and the south coast in the centre.

Walking, cycling & boating

A monument of 19th-century economic and social history, the canal has reinvented itself for modern times as an exceptional leisure resource. The continuous towpath is perfect for walking, cycling or simply dawdling along looking at wildlife and nature. It provides an unproblematic, pretty much level route for strollers or a long-distance option for hardy walkers or cyclists ready to cover the 365-km length. A two-week holiday will nearly do it! Don't be deceived by the word canal – less than 20% is artificial, the rest is made up of wide-flowing rivers like the Blavet and Aulne, and the route passes through attractive towns and past chapels and châteaux. One of the most beautiful sections is north from the Barrage de la Potinais not far from Redon, following the Oust through sheer granite cliffs and past the serene Ile-aux-Pies.

Not all sections of the canal are navigable, and Lac de Guerlédan (see page 88) effectively divides the route into two. To the east you can hire a boat in Norte or Sucé-sur-Erdre (bretagne-fluviale.com) or Redon and sail as far as Pontivy. To the west, the whole 81-km stretch of Finistère is open, plus a short section in Côtes d'Armor. Boats can be hired at Châteauneuf-du-Faou (aulneloisirs.com).

If you are planning a trip on the canal, check for periods of *chômage*, when sections of the canal are drained for maintenance. September and October are commonly affected.

nautique providing sailing, kayaking and waterskiing.

Point Passion Plage du Crouesty

Parc du Fogéo, BP24, 56640 Arzon, T02 97 53 84 01, pointplage.fr. Sailing from €16/hr.

Hires catamarans, dinghies, windsurfing boards, kayaks and boats for making the most of the waters off Plage de Fogéo.

Pôle Nautique des Deux Mers

1 av de St-Malo, 56510 St-Pierre, Quiberon, T02 30 91 50 01, polenautique-quiberon.com.

Offers surfing, paddleboarding, windsurfing, sand-yachting, kayaking and also kiteflying, kite-landboarding and bike hire for children over eight.

Sand-yachting
Les Passagers du Vent

Av de l'Océan, BP21, 56340 Plouharmel, T02 97 52 40 60, aeroplage.com. Year round. €18/hr, €115/weekend course with 2 nights accommodation, breakfast and 4 hrs of lessons.

Based in Penthièvre, on a 6-km beach on the west coast of the Quiberon Peninsula. Beginners' sessions (1-2 hrs) are taught by qualified instructors.

Skydiving
Entre Ciel et Terre

27 rue de Ker Yol, 56270 Ploemeur, T06 16 39 24 23, entrecieletterre.com.

Parachute jumps from 15 years of age. €245/jump. €90/video.

Offers the ultimate thrill for older teenagers and adults.

Surfing
Ecole de Surf de Bretagne de Plouharnel
6 Av de l'Océan, 56340 Plouharnel, T02 97 52 41 18, board-kulture.com. 90-min introductory lesson from €29.
There are no currents here, making it ideal for beginners. Lessons are available over three days or a week, and a free open day is organized in summer. At surf camp everything is included: equipment hire, lessons and full board.

Quiberon Peninsula
The Spirit Surf Club (rue du Port de Pêche, 56179 Quiberon, T06 35 43 50 55, spirit-surf-club.com) runs courses for different ages with English-speaking instructors. The Surfing Paradise School (route de Port Blanc, ZA de Kergroix, BP23, 56510 St-Pierre, Quiberon, T02 97 50 39 67, quiberonsurfparadise.com) offers tuition in small groups for anyone over five providing they can swim 50 m (2 hrs, 30€).

West Surf Association
Centre Nautique, 56520 Guidel, T02 97 32 70 37, w.s.a.free.fr.
Lays on transport to the best surfing spots. Runs courses in the school holidays, and a summer surf camp for youngsters aged 12–17.

Woodland adventures
Camors Adventure Forest
Etang du petit-bois, 56330 Camors, T02 97 39 28 69, camors-adventure-forest.com. Daily in school holidays and Wed-Sun rest of the year. €20 adult, €15 junior, €10 child.
Treetop adventures – zip wires, aerial walks, rope ladders, Tarzan nets, even aerial skateboarding – for children and adults. There's also a toddler area (over 2s).

Forêt Adrénaline
Fontainebleau, Le Hahon, 56340 Carnac (on the N165), T02 90 84 00 20, foretadrenaline.com. €20 adult, €16 child (10-15), €10 (5-9), €5 (2-4). Family ticket offers 50% discount, cyclists get 20% off. See website for opening times.
Like its counterpart in Betton (see page 36), this is a treetop assault course where kids as young as two can enjoy ropes, swings and zip wires. There are 11 exciting trails for different ages (from age 2). The Spider Trail involves completing 25 challenges without a harness, above 1000 sq m of netting.

Parcours Aventure le Poisson Volant
Douar Gwen, 56270 Ploemeur, T06 80 24 05 06, poissonvolant.net. Summer daily, low season Wed, Sun, closed Jan to mid-Feb. €20 over 1.45 m, €15 (aged 6, under 1.45 m), €9 (3-6 years).
Offers three courses for different ages. At ground level, little acrobats as young as three can enjoy themselves in total safety.

Parc Aquanature de Stérou

Le Stérou, 56320 Priziac, T02 97 34 63 84, parc-aquanature.com, €9 adult, €5.50 child (both prices include Breton 4WD safari). Easter-early Nov daily 1100-1900, last 3 weeks Nov and Feb-Easter Sun and school holidays 1400-1800.
Kids relish the sense of freedom and adventure in this vast nature park. It spreads across six valleys, and has three waterfalls and 100 red and fallow deer. Activities include a nature school, with courses in school holidays for children aged six to 14, five walks (ranging from 1 km to 14 km), horse rides, pony and trap rides, and 4WD safaris. There's a mill with an aquarium, fishing, and displays on local plants and animals. You can bring a picnic or dine on deer terrine or stew in the restaurant (set menu from €14). There's also a couple of gîtes (4- and 6-person) if you want to stay.

Out & about Morbihan

Big days out

Branféré Park

Ecole Nicolas Hulot, 56190 Le Guerno, T02 97 42 94 66, branfere.com. Feb-Mar daily 1330-1600, Apr-Jun daily 1000-1700 (1000-1730 weekends), Jul and Aug daily 1000-1800, Sep daily 1000-1700, Oct 1000-1600 (check website for changes). €16 adult, €11 child (4-12), under 4s free.

For a day (or more) of educational fun, this stately château and animal park with native and exotic species teaches children how to live in harmony with nature. If you want to stay longer, there are weekend discovery courses involving nature-based sports (canoeing, tree-climbing and hiking), studies into biodiversity and sustainability (how to make your house more eco-friendly) and shadowing the park's animal keepers. There's also a course designed for children (8-12 years) and their grandparents.

Brénature

Bréna, 56120 St-Servant (between Vannes and Josselin: see website for very precise directions), T02 97 75 60 65, brenature.fr. Feb-Oct Mon-Fri 1000-1700, Sat 1000-1200. €3.60 adult, €1.50 child. Child's educational tour of the farm €7.50 for full day, €4.50 half day. Kids aged 6-12 can stay without their parents from Sun evening to Sat morning during the school holidays and learn all about living on a real farm (€36/night with farm activities).

This working pig farm is a great place for children to get into the thick of farm life. As well as the pigs (born every three weeks) there are plenty of other animals to see, including rabbits, chickens, ducks, guineafowl, sheep and goats. If you're visiting for the day, children can take a bucket full of lettuces into the rabbit pens and feed them by hand, along with Machi the donkey and Nestor the dwarf pig, and take an animal (usually the goat) on a lead around the farm. There's also a 3-km footpath where you can gather blackberries in August.

Pigs at Brénature.

Château de Josselin & Musée des Poupées

Place de la Congrégation, 56120 Josselin, T02 97 22 36 45, chateaujosselin.com. Apr-Sep daily 1400-1800, Jul and Aug 1000-1800, Oct Sat and Sun 1400-1730. €7.40. Double ticket: €6.80 adult, €4.70 child.

Kids will get a tingle down their spines just looking at this fairy-tale castle beside the River Oust, which dates back to the beginning of the 11th century. The guided visits to the château (45 mins; some tours in English) are worth it to see the courtyard façade but offer limited access to the interior.

Kids might prefer to head round the back of the château to the former stables at 3 rue des Trente, where there is now a doll museum (Musée des Poupées) with a collection of 600 dolls, in porcelain, wood and leather, dating from the 17th century onwards. There's everything from ancient teddy bears and Chinese dolls to wartime nurse dollies and *High School Musical* dolls. Don't miss the early Barbie air hostess.

Try a bug tart at the Insect Museum, Lizio.

Ecomusée des Vieux Metiers (Museum of Old Trades)

Bobhuet, Lizio 56460, T02 97 74 93 01, ecomuseelizio.com. Feb-Jun, Sep-Oct 1400-1800, Jul and Aug 1000-1200 and 1400-1900. €5.80 adult, €4 child.

Alain Guillard has assembled a vast array of items from Breton life over the last two centuries. There are domestic interiors, clothes, fully equipped shops and workshops for every imaginable trade, a school room and even a 1950s garage complete with petrol pump. For kids it's a fascinating look into a world that is very remote from their iPods and whiteboards.

Insectarium de Lizio (Insect Museum)

5 rue du Stade, Centre Bourg, 56460 Lizio, T02 97 74 94 31, insectariumdelizio.fr. Apr-Jun, Sep-Oct 1400-1800, Jul and Aug 1000-1900. €7 adult, €5 child (4-16), under 4s free.

There's something about kids and insects. It's a love-hate relationship that's just irresistible. This fabulous museum has more than 60 species, including death's head moths, owl butterflies, locusts, cockroaches, snails, Goliath, the largest beetle in the world, and stick insects, the kings of camouflage, exceeding 40 cm in length. A highlight is meeting the actual black widow spider that bit Spiderman. There is an awful lot of "Come and look at THIS!" when you visit with small kids. The shop is also well worth a look (kids will get hours of use out of a bug watcher), and the brave might like to try the pretty tarts in the fridge – look closely and you'll see that the crunchy stuff on top are crickets, mealy worms and other grubs. Yum! If you're still feeling hungry, there's a nice picnic spot out back surrounded by cornfields.

Musée de Préhistoire

10 place de la Chapelle, 56340 Carnac, T02 97 52 22 04, museedecarnac.com. Apr-Jun and Sep Wed-Mon 1000-1230, 1400-1800. Jul and Aug daily 1000-1800, Oct-Mar Wed-Mon 1000-1230, 1400-1700. €5 adult, €2.50 child (6-18). Guided visits €7.50 adult, €4.20 child.
There is such a bewildering number and variety of megaliths in Morbihan that it helps to stop first at the Museum of Prehistory in Carnac. In school holidays there are workshops on daily life in Neolithic times for six- to 12-year-olds, such as making fire, cooking bread, cutting stones to make jewellery, and making a prehistoric boomerang. There is even a small reconstruction of original archaeological digs out back.

Pont Scorff Zoo

Kerruisseau, 56620 Pont-Scorff, T02 97 32 60 86, zoo-pont-scorff.com. Apr, May, Sep daily 0930-1800, Jun-Aug daily 0900-1900, low season daily 0930-1700. €17 adult, €10.50 child (3-11), under 3s free.
If you approve of zoos then this is one of the best in Brittany. All the usual suspects are here including elephants, big cats, zebras and rhinos. Highlights include an area where kids can identify animal dung used to fertilize certain plants and a farm enclosure with tame ducks and sheep. There are entertaining daily shows featuring sealions, *mal-aimés* (unloved) animals

The Scrap Metal Poet.

(snakes and rats) and seabirds. Allow about five hours to see everything. One word of warning, much of the zoo is along steep winding pathways – not ideal for prams or toddlers with little legs.

L'univers du Poète Ferrailleur (The Scrap Metal Poet)

La Ville Stéphant, 56460 Lizio, T02 97 74 97 94, poeteferrailleur.com. Apr-Jun, mid-Sep to Nov, Sun, public holidays 1400-1800, Jul and Aug daily 1030-1900, beginning-mid Sep daily 1400-1800. €6 adult, €5 child (4-14), under 3s free.

Two kilometres outside Lizio, this is one of those unique places that kids and adults are entranced by. The magic comes from the fact that something has been made out of nothing, with just imagination and hard graft. Each of the scrap-metal sculptures, ranging from merry-go-rounds to full-sized flying boats full of crazy people and animals, has a button to press and set in motion an entrancing combination of colour, sound and movement. Once you've finished marvelling at the imaginative concept and effects, you start looking at the bits and pieces Robert Coudray has used to create them: a tap, a fork, a bed-spring, even German helmets that are rung like bells. There's everything here – skill, imagination, humour and a vibrant sense of simply being alive. Don't miss it!

Yves Rocher's La Gacilly

Route de Sixt-sur-Aff, La Gacilly, T02 99 08 35 84, jardinyr.com/sitegb/index.html. Late May to mid-Jun, mid-Sep to mid-Oct Sun, school and public holidays 1400-1800, 2nd half Jun and 1st half Sep daily 1400-1800, Jul and Aug daily 1000-1900. Discovery circuit €6.50 adult, €5.50 child (over 10).

There's lots to see in the botanical garden of Yves Rocher, the beauty products manufacturer. See large nature photographs set within a scented plant maze in the summer photographic exhibition, and learn more about plants in Le Végétarium, a fun museum that begins with a film of flowers opening in fast motion. There's a vivarium full of stick insects, and upstairs there's Réfléchir (Think), with quizzes and hands-on displays, and Voyager (Travel), an exhibition on the uses of plants around the world. In high season there's a free *petit train* between Le Végétarium and the garden.

Girls (and mums) might enjoy the Yves Rocher shop, full of lovely lotions and potions, including little lip-glosses and nail varnishes. When you tire of all things Yves Rocher, there's a nice adventure playground up by La Gacilly's Town Hall.

Carnac-Ville and Carnac-Plage

For a breather between standing stones (see page 152), don't miss a visit to the charming village of Carnac. There's a useful tourist information office (74 av des Druides, 56342 Carnac, T02 97 52 13 52) in the centre of the town and pretty shops that children will love rummaging through, such as Artychaud (21 place de l'Eglise, T02 97 52 07 02) selling toys, jewellery, Breton lighthouse pictures painted on metal, and artisan clothes. There are plenty of family-friendly places to eat, including Pizzéria Héléna (see page 184) and La Marine Brasserie (see page 183) or simply head to the Chevillard Boulangerie & Patisserie (2 rue du Tumulus, T02 97 52 05 56) for sandwiches and cakes to eat in the square.

Carnac-Plage is a popular family resort with a state-of-the-art thalassotherapy centre. Oyster farming is big business too.

More family favourites

Barrage d'Arzal

Arzal, 35 km southeast of Vannes on D139, T02 99 90 88 44. May weekends, Jun to mid-Sep Mon-Fri, late Sep Wed-Fri, all 1400-1800. €3 adults, under 18s free.

This flood dam built at the entrance to the Vilaine Estuary contains a 70 m-long 'fish pass' that lets migrating fish through the dam on their way back up the river. Families can visit an observation room to watch the fish on their way through.

Ecomusée de Saint-Dégan

56400 Brec'h, T02 97 57 66 00, ecomusee-st-degan.fr.

The thatched cottages of this eco-museum in St-Dégan represent three centuries of country life in the Pays d'Auray area. Visit the 17th-century house, where families and animals lived under the same roof, and the 19th-century longhouse and outbuildings. All around the village, the paths and undergrowth tell the same story: sunken lanes, *bocage* (patchwork fields), orchards and crop-threshing. Follow the trail! And if all that walking makes you hungry, you can make your own bread and take it home.

Ile de Groix

Catch the ferry from the Gare Maritime in Lorient and head over to Ile de Groix for a great beach, cool galleries and Parcabout (see page 15). You can orientate yourselves with an island bus tour (Groix Panoramique, T06 33 84 75 38, groix-panoramique.com, €12 adult, €6 child under 12, reductions for reservations), which starts from outside the tourist office in Port Tudy at 1000 and 1400, or hire bikes from one of the places around the port, such as Coconut's Location or Bikini Bikes. There are lots of galleries and quirky shops such as La P'tite Fabric (rue de Général de Gaulle, Le Bourg) selling handmade clothes for kids and women and worth a look just to see the old-fashioned button collection. Don't miss Plage des Sables Blancs, an amazing convex beach (see page 154) and Parcabout.

L'Abeille Vivante et La Cité des Fourmis

Kercadoret, 56320 Le Faouët, T02 97 23 08 05, abeilles-et-fourmis.com. Apr-Sep (call for times), €6 adult, €4 child (4-15), under 4s free.

Kids love this Living Bee and City of Ants Museum in a converted farmhouse in Faouët. Children can observe the hives from close up and watch swarms of bees in glass containers. They can also delve deep into the world of the fungus-farming ants, which carry loads that are far heavier than their own bodyweight, and crawl through a tunnel in a giant anthill full of wood ants. At the end of the visit, the gift shop sells delicious honey-based products.

English Bookshop

36 rue des Trente, 56120 Josselin, T02 97 75 62 55, May-Sep daily (except Mon) 1000-1800, Oct-Apr 1100-1600.

This great bookshop near Josselin Castle is a good source of books about the region and also has a nice children's section. There are sometimes readings for kids on a Saturday morning, in English and French. Call to confirm.

La Maison du Costume Breton.

Hit or miss?

Parc de Préhistoire de Bretagne (Brittany Prehistory Park)
La Croix Neuve, 56220 Malansac, (2 km from Rochefort-en-Terre), T02 97 43 34 17, prehistoire-bretagne.com. Apr to mid-Nov 1030-1900, €10.50 adult, €6.50 child (4-11), under 4s free.

If you're expecting an animated *Jurassic Park*-type experience, this is going to be a miss for you, but if your kids are still in that dinosaur-obsessed stage this will be a massive hit. The park site alone is impressive, covering 10 ha of wild woodland dotted with five lakes and overhung by 40-m cliffs – formerly a slate quarry. A trail is marked out linking 30 scenes with scale models of different dinosaurs, from stegosaurus to brachiosaurus, some in quite impressive battle scenes. There's also a good look at the evolution of man and the first inhabitants of Brittany. Most of the information is in English as well as French. Although the scenes have been reconstructed with help from the Natural History Museum in Paris, they are pretty schlocky and not at all convincing, but overall it's a fun day out and well worth the trip. There's a good picnic space, a bar selling snacks and ice creams and a shop selling fossils and minerals. And don't forget to look out for the doyouthinkhesawus!

La Maison du Costume Breton

Rue du Pavés, 56460 Serent, T06 63 24 96 07, lamaisonducostumebreton.fr. Daily 1400-1830 except Sun and public holidays. €3 adults, under 12s free.

The Breton Costume Museum occupies one of the oldest houses in the quaint town of Serent, the ideal setting for a magnificent collection, shown off on about 100 models. Discover the different traditions of the five departments of historical Brittany (including Loire-Atlantique). From the linen shirt to the ceremonial dress for men, from the minutely detailed feminine embroideries to the starched bonnets, the variety of colours, designs and materials are amazing. The museum also features the *coiffes* (bonnets), symbols of identity and belonging.

La Thalassa

Bd Adolphe Pierre, 56100 Lorient, T02 97 35 13 00, la-thalassa.fr. Apr-Jun and Sep-Oct 0930-1230, 1400-1800 (closed Sat and Sun morning and Mon during May, Jun and Sep), Jul and Aug daily 1000-1900. €6.90 adult, €5.30 child (5-17), under 5s free, €20.30 family.

Climb aboard the *Thalassa*, in the port of Lorient since 1996. There are three decks to explore – visit the ship's dining room, kitchen and cabins – and you can find out about the various jobs of the people who worked on the ship, including the captain, sailor, biologist and oceanographer. Thematic tours are available for children, along with leaflets (in French) detailing treasure hunts.

Le Cartopole

Rue d'Auray, 56150 Baud, T02 97 51 15 14, cartolis.org/cartopol. €5 adult, under 15s free. Call ahead for opening times.

With texts, twitter and email now the norm, it's nice to tell children about the time when we all got excited about sending and receiving postcards – and some of us even had postcard collections! There are around 2000 postcards on display in rooms resembling an early 20th-century village. Kids can have fun identifying sights you may have visited, such as Carnac.

Les Petits Trains de Morbihan

Trains Touristiques F le Bayon, PA Montauban, 56340 Carnac, T02 97 24 06 29, petittrain-morbihan.com. **Trains usually run every half hour in high season. €6 adult, €3 child (under 12).**

These cute Toy Town-like trains offer three circuits: one that gives a tour of Vannes (see page 168), one that explores the Quiberon Peninsula and one that goes from Carnac to Trinité-sur-Mer, taking in the standing stones on the way. All charming and excellent for orientating yourselves with the chosen area. Kids love them.

Musée de la Résistance

56140 St-Marcel, 3 km from Malestroit, T02 97 75 16 90, resistance-bretonne.com. Mid-Jun to mid-Sep daily 1000-1900, mid-Sep to mid-Jun Wed-Mon 1000-1200, 1400-1800. €6.90 adult.

Built on the site of a resistance stronghold in the Second World War, this is one of the most important museums in Brittany. There are vast indoor and outdoor exhibitions (the 6 ha of wooded grounds saw actual fighting) and the national collection relating to the French paratroopers of the time is also held here. Life-sized reconstructions, such as a street during the Occupation and the inside of a German blockhouse, bring history to life. The gardens display cannons, old wartime vehicles and a reconstruction of part of the Atlantic Wall (coastal fortifications built by Nazi Germany), including a 15-tonne rangefinder. Hard stuff for young kids perhaps, but a great history lesson nevertheless.

Parc Animalier Meslan

Pencleaux, 56320 Meslan, T02 97 34 26 72, chezdamenature.com. Apr-Sep daily 1000-1900, Oct Sun 1400-1800. €8 adult, €6 child (4-12), under 4s free.

Milking a cow at Village de Poul-Fetan.

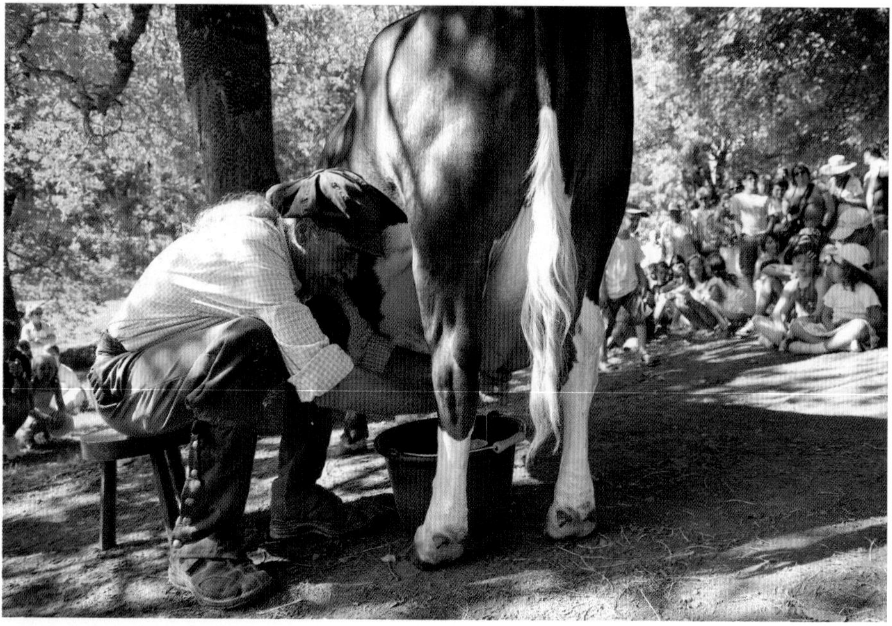

Kids will love this little animal kingdom, which has everything from alpacas to wallabies. There are miniature animals, rare Breton breeds, pony rides, a maze, a kids' playground and a bouncy castle.

Popcorn Labyrinthe

On D768 between Carnac and Auray, T06 60 64 77 52. Jul and Aug daily 1000-1900, Sep Wed and weekends 1400-1900. Maze at night Jul and Aug Thu 2200-midnight. Sep Sat 0930-midnight. €6 adult/child, under 4s free.

Two hectares of adventure paths for children who love mazes. Themed according to the season for kids to run wild.

Village de Poul-Fetan

Quinistinic on D156. T02 97 39 51 74, poul-fetan.com. Daily Apr-May 1400-1830, Jun and Sep 1100-1830, Jul and Aug 1045-1900. €7 adult, €4 child (6-16), under 6s free.

This tiny hamlet dates back to the 16th century but its last inhabitants left in the late 1960s. It's brought back to life every afternoon between April and October, when costumed characters recreate the daily tasks of 19th-century peasants, including milking, wool-dyeing, butter and crêpe-making and buckwheat cultivation. There are also protected breeds of Breton cows, horses, sheep and pigs to discover, plus a tavern selling local produce.

Rain check

Bowling

- **Bowling du Lac**, 13 rue du Lac, 56800 Ploermel, T02 97 72 03 82, bowlingdulac.fr.
- **Bowling Superbowl**, 1 rue Marcel Dassault, BP 90051 Vannes, T02 97 60 62 89, superbowl-vannes.com.
- **Le Master Bowling**, Keriaval, 56340 Carnac, T02 97 52 36 36.
- **Metropolis**, rue Gustave Zédé, ZA de Manébos, 56600 Lanester, T02 97 81 30 18, metropolis-lanester.com.

Cinema

- **Cinélac**, 13 rue du Lac, 56800 Ploermel, T02 97 73 35 24.
- **Cinéma des families**, up the hill from Port Tudy, Ile de Groix, T02 97 86 80 15.
- **Cinéville**, 4 bd Mar Joffre, 56100 Lorient, T02 97 64 66 03.
- **Cinéville Parc Lann**, rue Aristide Boucicaut, 56000 Vannes, T08 92 68 06 66.
- **Le Celtic**, 1 rue de la Libération, 56150 Baud, T02 97 51 00 26.
- **Le Club**, 1 rue Jean-Marie de Lamenais, 56500 Locminé, T02 97 44 22 87.
- **Le Rex**, Zone Saint-Niel, 56300 Pontivy, T08 36 68 69 33.
- **Les Arcades**, 8 rue du Levenant, 56400 Auray, T02 97 24 06 52.

Ice skating

- **Patinoire Patinium**, 6 rue Georges Caldray, 56000 Vannes, T02 97 40 91 23, patinium.com.

Indoor play

- **Le P'tit Delire**, 56400 Ploermel, Auray, T02 97 56 73 51, parc-jeux-petit-delire.com.

Indoor swimming pools

- **Aquatic Club Vannes**, Parc du Golfe, rue Daniel Gillard, 56000 Vannes, T02 97 40 51 51.
- **Carnac Thalasso and Spa Resort**, av de l'Atlantique, 56340 Carnac, T02 97 52 62 44, thalasso-carnac.com.
- **Centre Aquatique du Moustoir**, place de l'Hôtel de Ville, 56100 Lorient, T02 97 02 59 30.
- **Piscine de Kercado**, 28 rue Winston Churchill, 56000 Vannes, T02 97 62 69 00.
- **Piscine de Plein Air Chauffée**, rue de la Plage, 56300 Pontivy, T02 97 25 01 05.
- **Piscine du Bois du Château**, rue de Kerdual, 56100 Lorient, T02 97 83 84 89.
- **Piscine Municipale**, 7 rue du Four Mollet, 56400 Auray, T02 97 24 22 78.
- **Piscine Municipale**, av de l'Etang, 56850 Caudan, T02 97 05 70 60.
- **Piscine Municipale**, Le Faouet, Cours Carré, 56320 Le Faouet, T02 97 23 12 34.
- **Piscine Municipale**, Pont Min, 56110 Gourin, T02 97 23 42 74.
- **Piscine Neptilude**, rue Neptune, 56170 Quiberon, T02 97 50 39 07.
- **Piscine Océanis**, Ploemeur, bd François Mitterand, 56270 Ploemeur, T02 97 86 41 00.
- **Piscine Spot Loisirs du Pays du Redon**, place de Parc Anger, 35600 Redon, T02 99 71 08 49.

Karting & paintball

- **Elite Paintball**, Carrière de Co, 56800 Ploermel, T06 86 51 37 33.
- **Kart Indoor du Pays de Vannes**, rue Kermelin, 56890 Saint-Avé, T02 97 61 83 61.

Don't miss... La Cité de la Voile (Eric Tabarly Sailing Museum)

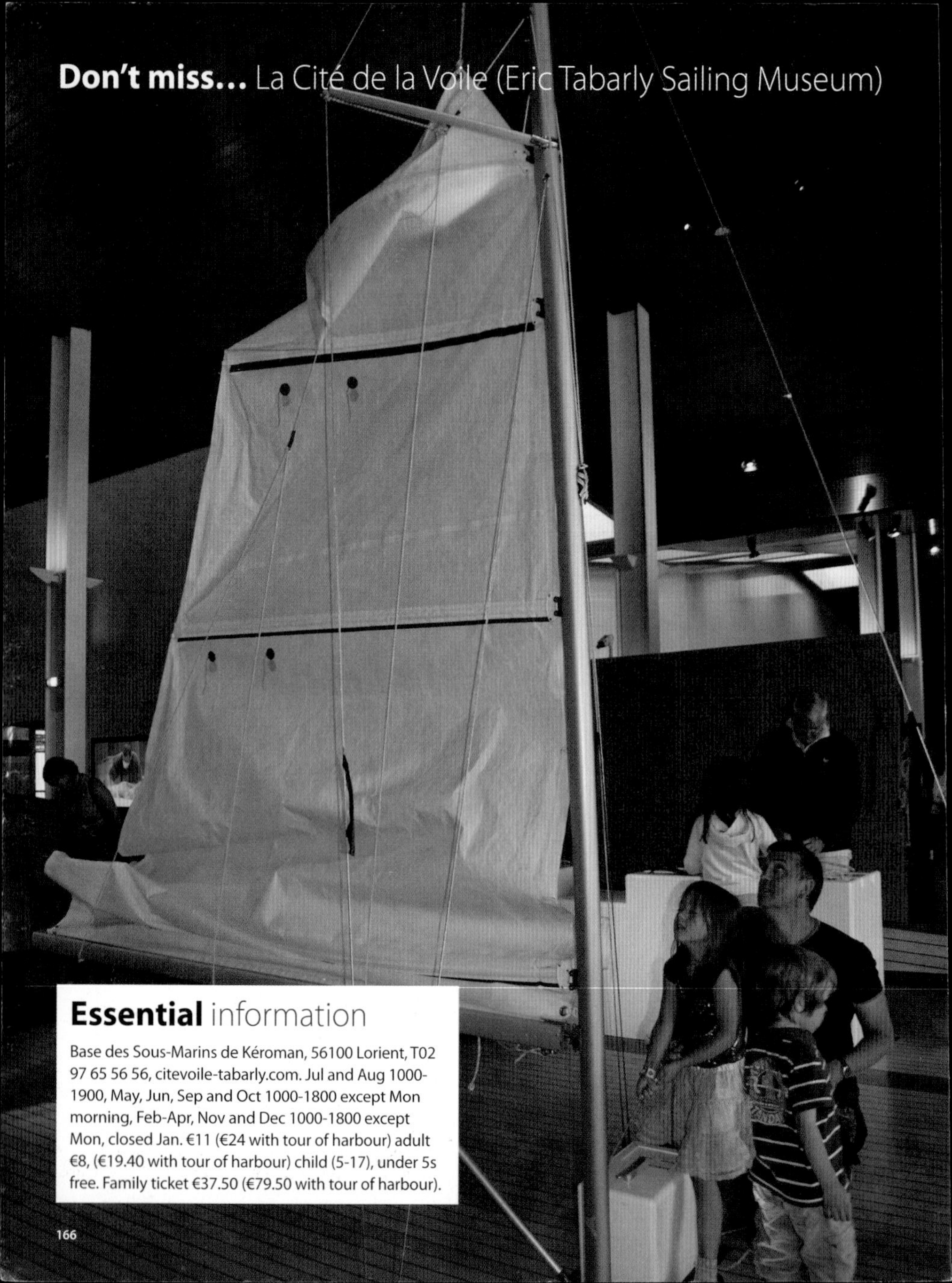

Essential information

Base des Sous-Marins de Kéroman, 56100 Lorient, T02 97 65 56 56, citevoile-tabarly.com. Jul and Aug 1000-1900, May, Jun, Sep and Oct 1000-1800 except Mon morning, Feb-Apr, Nov and Dec 1000-1800 except Mon, closed Jan. €11 (€24 with tour of harbour) adult €8, (€19.40 with tour of harbour) child (5-17), under 5s free. Family ticket €37.50 (€79.50 with tour of harbour).

Inspired by the legendary French yatchsman Eric Tabarly (1931-1998), this cutting-edge museum, which opened in 2010, is the closest you'll ever come to sailing on dry land. Situated near the Lorient submarine base, you can't miss the architecturally striking building designed by Jacques Ferrier.

On the ground floor a vast space is devoted to **temporary exhibitions** on changing themes. During 2010 it was all about Flying Yachts that can reach world record-breaking speeds of over 50 knots, with breathtaking video footage, a flight simulator and a Hydrotère model. The 2011 theme is World Sailing Tours.

The **permanent exhibition** upstairs is where the museum really comes into its own. It begins with an intelligent and graceful look at man's complex relationship with the sea. More like an art installation than a museum exhibit, high-tech screens hang in a darkened space with images of the sea projected onto them – from great ocean swells to mermaids. Evocative sound effects, from wailing sea sirens to sea shanties, add to the experience.

Visitors exit to more conventional exhibits that track the history of sea conquest, from ancient galleys to oceanographic vessels. Questions are posed and answered: What boat for which trip? How is a boat propelled by the wind? You can even design your own sailing boat on an interactive terminal.

Take the helm

Then comes the really fun part, where you can scramble inside the galley of a yacht, take the helm, size yourself up against a great sailor with the help of a simulator, see if you can pull up the rigging, and try out many other sailing skills, all without getting wet. You can also climb into the trimaran simulator and feel what it's like to navigate the Bay of Lorient as day breaks and the sea is getting rough, or take the helm of a model yacht and pit yourselves against one another and other visitors. Lastly, you can walk over the impressive bridge to see the *Pen Duick*, the magnificent boat with which Eric Tabarley claimed his greatest offshore racing victories.

In front of the museum is a real yacht on dry land. Also a simulator, it is situated in front of a large wind machine so that kids (must be between 1.2 m and 1.6 m tall) can 'sail' their own boat. One-on-one instruction on handling the rudder, tacking and so on is provided, and you can even go inside a windsock to measure the wind speed, though this is not recommended for little ones, who are likely to be blown out!

Special activities

Many special family events are held at the museum during the French school holidays at no added cost. These include guided tours of the 'offshore racing station', where you get to see giant multihull boats, trimarans, Figaros and more (every Wed and Sun at 1400).

From April to September, visitors can go on a real sailing boat from the museum's futuristic pontoon. The skipper will explain the basics of handling a sailing boat before you set sail with the Port Louis Citadel and Island of Groix as a backdrop. Kids get to help with the manoeuvres and take the helm alongside the captain. Back on dry land, there are sailor's certificates to be had. If this doesn't get your little ones dreaming of being the next Ellen MacArthur, I don't know what will.

Grab a bite

If you're hungry there's a great little **Café de la Marine** with alfresco tables (ham sandwiches €3) or a posh restaurant called **Quai Quest** (T02 97 65 42 58). There's also a fantastic shop full of well chosen nautical items for adults and kids with no tat whatsoever. I defy any mum not to buy something in there, from Lost Marc'h perfumes (lostmarch.fr) made in Brittany to a child's compass.

A cool activity area for young kids has organized activities like pop-up card making from 1500-1700 daily.

Let's go to...

Vannes

With its stunning medieval centre, small but excellent choice of family attractions and great shops and restaurants, Vannes achieves the impossible – a historic town that's gorgeous to look at, great to wander through, and also fun for kids.

The treaty making Brittany part of France was signed here in 1532, and much of Vannes' impressive fortifications, complete with towers and monumental gates, date from that time. Narrow streets and stone bridges, a cathedral bristling with gargoyles, a fairy-tale tower that used to be a prison and half-timbered houses make an atmospheric setting for fabulous crêperies, *salons de thé* and ice cream parlours, and all kinds of fun shops, from hippy fairy outlets to full-on toy emporiums. All of it is very walkable though there is a pick-up and drop-off bike scheme if you prefer (velocea.fr, 30 mins free, €1/hr).

The Gulf du Morbihan comes right up to the town at place Gambetta. Beautiful tall houses rise on either side of the inlet, which is full of graceful yachts and boats. There's an attractive wood-clad tourist information centre at Quai Tabarly, right next door to an old-fashioned carousel that children adore.

Get your bearings

The best place to start your explorations of Vannes is **place Gambetta**. Orientate yourselves and whet your kids' appetites with a half-hour tour on the cute **Le Petit Train de Vannes** (T02 97 24 06 29, petittrain-vannes.com, €5 adult, €3 child under 12, daily every 30 mins from 1000-1930 in Jul and Aug and until 1830 in Apr-Jun and Sep-Oct, except Wed and Sat morning), with a running commentary in French and English. As it tootles through 17th-century streets such as the picturesque rue St-Vincent, you will spot things you'd like to return to and can set your kids the

Vannes tourist information Quai Tabarly, T08 25 13 56 00, tourisme-vannes.com. Jul and Aug 0900-1900, rest of the year Mon-Sat 0930-1230, 1330-1800.

task of spotting 'Vannes et sa Femme', a famous carving of the man the city was named after and his wife among the half-timbered houses.

Don't miss

Aquarium du Golfe

Parc du Golfe, 21 rue Daniel Gilard, T02 97 40 67 40, aquarium-du-golfe.com. Jan-Mar 1400-1800, Apr-Jun and Sep 1000-1200, 1400-1800, Jul and Aug 0900-1930, Oct-Dec 1400-1800. €8.50 adult, €5.50 child, under 4s free. Joint ticket to Jardin aux Papillons nearby costs €12 adult, €8 child, under 4s free.

The door opens to the warm, wet world of exotic fish, and even to reach the ticket desk you have to cross a pool of sharks and giant turtles. This is a fantastic display of fish from around the world and closer to home with the Breton blue lobster. A recreation of a coral reef is one of the biggest attractions. There's free use of some rather bizarre wheeled high chairs that enable you to push babies and toddlers round at tank height! There are also changing facilities, a crêperie and a bar plus a lawn for picnics. Visit in the morning or when the sun is shining to avoid the crowds.

Capitaine d'un Jour

Parc du Golfe, T02 97 40 40 39. €6 adult, €4.50 child.

A discovery area with games, films and children's naval modelling workshops.

Cathédrale St-Pierre

0900-1800.

Tightly embraced by a network of old streets, the cathedral looms benevolently over the town. Inside, the Spanish missionary St Vincent Ferrier, who died in Vannes in 1419, seems to have elbowed out St Pierre in terms of features dedicated to the saints. His elaborate chapel (under restoration) in an uncommon Renaissance-style tower dominates the north aisle and the

Let's go to... Vannes

north transept window is dedicated to him. Get the kids to spot the 12 niches for the 12 apostles.

Jardin aux Papillons

Parc du Golfe, T02 97 40 67 40, jardinauxpapillons.com. Apr-Jun and Sep 1000-1230, 1400-1830, Jul and Aug 1000-1930. €7 adult, €5 child. Under 4s free. Joint ticket to Aquarium du Golfe nearby costs €12 adult, €8 child, under 4s free.

The Butterfly Garden revels in the beauty of these incredible creatures that children find so fascinating, both for their life cycles and their mesmerizing wings. Here exotic butterflies fly freely around you as you enter tropical forests with banana trees, coffee trees, scarlet hibiscus and many orchids from around the world. It's best to visit the garden when the sun shines in the middle of the day as the butterflies appreciate lots of light.

La Cohue Vannes Museum

9 and 15 place St-Pierre, T02 97 47 35 86. Jun-Sep 1000-1800 except public holidays, Oct-May 1000-1200, 1400-1800 except Tue, Sun mornings and public holidays. €4.10 adult and older child, under 12s free.

La Cohue was the term used for a covered market. In 13th-century Vannes, La Cohue housed the market stalls on its ground floor and the court of justice above. From 1675 onward, the Breton parliament was in exile in Vannes. This fascinating history is all here to discover along with much Breton art.

Musée Château Gaillard

Rue Noé, T02 97 01 63 00. Mid-May to mid-Jun 1330-1800, mid-Jun to Sep 1000-1800. €4.20 (€6 for 2 museums), under 12s free.

It's well worth seeing the interior of the 15th-century Château Gaillard, and the superb quality and rarity of its archaeological exhibits underline the importance of the Gulf of Morbihan area in Neolithic times. The ground floor has changing displays, such as medieval religious objects, with an impressive fireplace in the first room. Up the narrowest of turning stone stairs the huge carved beams of an unpainted ceiling are revealed and the amazing archaeological section begins. It seems incredible that such perfection of polished axes of jadeite were made more than 5000 years ago – that is, until you see the variscite funerary jewellery from the Tumulus de Tumiac (4790-4530 BC), and then delicate shell necklaces from the Mesolithic period (10000-6000 BC). On the third floor, there's a real library and a strange one made of papier mâché, plus a little room of wooden cabinets with painted panels, illustrating religious figures like the Desert Fathers. Up in the attics, with upturned-boat-style roof timbers, are many curiosities brought back from all corners of the world by 19th-century travellers, evidence of the collectors' insatiable thirst for knowledge and wonders.

Shopping

Bilboquet (9 rue St Guenhael, T02 97 47 56 92, bilboquet.com) is just the sort of toyshop parents love as there's absolutely no tat here. Just fabulous toys for all ages, from pretty dollies and dress-up clothes to innovative games, skateboards and juggling gear. Downstairs there's a great selection of kites – a perfect purchase for your Breton holiday. You can't miss this shop as it's the one with a constant stream of bubbles and a multi-coloured spinning toy outside.

Les Saveurs D'Arvor (19 place des Lices, T02 97 42 53 18) is the place to come to stock up on Breton butter biscuits and traditional Breton madeleines in limited edition tins – perfect treats for the car and good presents for friends and family back home – as well as local jam, caramels, cider, liqueurs, fish soup, crêpes and earthenware.

Nature & Découvertes (11 rue St-Vincent, T02 97 69 29 90, natureetdecouvertes.com) is a bit like a French Habitat, with great toys and interesting gadgets for the home and garden. (There are also branches in Brest and Rennes.)

Music & art

Visitors enjoy free street entertainment in summer and at the end of July there's a jazz festival, with concerts, performances and jamming (mairie-vannes.fr).

Photo de Mer is an annual photographic festival celebrating the sea, held in the last three weeks of April (photodemer.fr).

Grab a bite

Café de la Poissonnerie

21 place de la Poissonnerie, T02 97 47 15 58. Lunchtimes until 1500, closed Sun and Mon, except in Jul and Aug.

This café by the fish market is famous for the biggest, finest *croque monsieur* available. You'll never see a toasted sandwich in the same way again. *Croque madame* and other versions too make a more-than-a-snack lunch. In the unlikely event of a carbohydrate vacuum afterwards, try the *riz au lait* (rice pudding).

Dan Ewen Crêperie

3 place Général de Gaulle, T02 97 42 44 34. Mon-Sat 1130-1530, 1900-2200, closed Sun (and Mon out of season).

In an ancient house, this crêperie has a nice atmosphere, with Celtic-style background music, pleasing decor and an interesting range of crêpes for all the family. Seven of the specials are named after the founding saints, the others after Celtic countries. The Ecosse has smoked salmon and potatoes with salad dressed in raspberry vinegar.

La Saladière

36 rue du Port, T02 97 42 52 10, lasaladiere-vannes.com. Daily 1200-1400, 1900-2130.

In the port area, this is a useful place for vegetarians, as the emphasis is on plentiful gourmet salads. Some come with smoked fish or meat, and there's a short list of grills for fresh-vegetable haters. The ambience is bright and cheerful.

Restaurant Le Boudoir

43 rue de la Fontaine, T02 97 42 60 64, restaurantleboudoir.com.

This is a restaurant for real foodies looking for a family treat. Seasonal cooking using only local produce is finished with flowers or seaweed. A three-course discovery menu costs €19.50. There are cookery classes available on Wednesday afternoons for children (in French only).

Bilboquet toyshop.

Let's go to...

Morbihan Gulf

Named 'La plus belle baie du monde' (the most beautiful bay in the world), with one island for every day of the year, so they say, this 100 sq km gulf is a big draw for those who love to mess about on the water.

Whether you want to take a boat tour, walk the coastal path, explore the Ile-aux-Moines or visit the world-famous Neolithic tomb on the island of Gavrinis, the Gulf offers calm waters and constantly changing seascapes. You'll see fishing vessels, oyster boats, yachts and canoes.

Presqu'île de Rhuys

This is the least well-known part of the Gulf of Morbihan, forming an embracing southern arm. It offers many things to see and do whether you seek activity, history or relaxation. Once you are on the D780, the watery nature of the region soon becomes apparent with the tide-mill at Noyalo. Accessible at low tide, the Ile Tascon at St-Armel is a well-known spot for watching winter bird-migrants. In July and August a little passenger ferry runs across to Sené (near Vannes) where there is a nature reserve. Nature-lovers will also appreciate the former salt-working marshes (Réserve du Duer). Sarzeau is the main settlement on the peninsula with shops and services.

Continue on the D780 all the way out to the end at Port Navalo, from where you can take a cruise on the Gulf or walk out to the lighthouse from the little beach. The former *criée* (fish auction) here is now a year-round exhibition centre with artistic and heritage displays.

For an ideal picnic and boat-watching spot, head to the nearby Pointe Bilgroix, the dividing line between open sea and the Gulf. Port Crouesty, by contrast, is a busy marina, with an excellent tourist information office (T02 97 53 69 69).

Most of the 40 islands are private but the two largest, where you can disembark, are the **Ile-aux-Moines** (310 ha) and the Ile d'Arz (324 ha). **Ile d'Arz** is less populated and generally quieter, with a tide-mill and former salt marshes. Its busier neighbour has an attractive welcome with cafés and bicycle hire places lining the quay and fishermen's cottages, winding pathways, old fountains, chapels and ruined windmills to explore. There's a great little beach with a sailing school and yellow and blue beach huts – one even houses a little honesty library (*petit libraire*). Both islands have places to stay and eat, good walking on the coastal paths and cycling inland.

The most famous island is tiny **Gavrinis**, which has a Neolithic cairn with extraordinary carvings (gavrinis.info), and a trip here will pass Er Lannic with its rare stone circle, half in and half out of the water. Boats go from Lamor Baden for the short crossing, which is included in the price of a site visit (Apr, Jun, Sep 0930-1230, 1330-1830, May 1330-1830 – weekends mornings too – Jul and Aug 0930-1230, 1330-1900, Mar, Oct and Nov 1330-1700, closed Wed. €12, family €28).

The Gulf by boat

Compagnie des Iles (T08 25 13 41 00, compagniedesiles.com) also has a range of Gulf options from the Parc du Golfe, plus trips to Belle-Ile and the Ile de Groix (see page 162) further afield.
Golfe Croisières (T02 97 57 15 27, golfecroisieres.com) offers tours from Lamor-Baden with or without a stop on the Ile-aux-Moines. Prices start from €12.
Le Point Marine Evasion (T06 48 13 23 18, lepointmarine.com). Various boat trips. One package offers boat hire (no licence required), lunch at a choice of two restaurants from €54 per person.

Don't miss

Château de Suscinio

Sarzeau, T02 97 41 91 91, suscinio.info. Apr-Sep 1000-1900, Oct, Feb, Mar 1000-1200, 1400-1600, Nov-Jan 1000-1200, 1400-1700, €7 adult, €2 child (8-17), under 8s free.

One of the unusual things about this magnificent château is its coastal situation on low, wet marshland. The elaborate *logis* building from the 15th century reflects its prime purpose as a place of relaxation, with widespread hunting grounds, for the duke and his family. Much of the stone was sold off to builders after the revolution, but restoration has enhanced the site. You can visit rooms with displays about the castle's history and ducal lifestyle. Look out for the colourful decorative medieval tiled floors rescued from the vanished chapel. There are good views over the marsh from the *chemins de ronde* (walkway on the battlements).

Navix (T08 25 13 21 00, navix.fr) is based at the Gare Maritime near the aquarium in southern Vannes. Follow signs to the Parc du Golfe where there is free parking. For a three-hour morning or afternoon trip without disembarking, €20 adult, €13 child (under 17). To add a stop in Ile-aux-Moines €22 adult, €14.50 child and to add on a stop at both Ile-aux-Moines and Ile d'Arz, €29 adult, €19 child. Free for under 4s.

Walking by the Gulf

The tourist office in Vannes has a free folder 'Tour du Golfe' of 16 mostly linear walks around the Gulf of Morbihan.

Fly over the Gulf

30-minute flights are run by the **Aéroclub du Pays de Vannes** (T02 97 60 73 08, €120 for 3 people). **Montgolfière Morbihan** (Lescouedec, St-Avé, 3 km north of Vannes on D126, T02 97 62 76 00, montgolfiere-morbihan.com, daily depending on weather conditions, €230-280 adult, €180-210 child (over 10s only)) offers wonderful tours over the gulf by hot-air balloon.

La Semaine du Golf

Every two years (next 2011) this vintage boat festival in the Gulf of Morbihan attracts vessels of all kinds from bi-planes to traditional pleasure craft, plus concerts, walks and exhibitions (semainedugolfe.asso.fr).

Off the beaten track

Belle-Ile-en-Mer

The islands around Brittany's coast are among its greatest hidden treasures – castaway places with wild and rugged coastlines, stripey lighthouses, pastel-coloured houses, salty seadogs and lots of arty folk in search of their own private idyll. Morbihan's Belle-Ile-en-Mer may be the largest of the Breton islands, but it's still only 17 km by 9 km. Come for the day, and you're sure to want to return for a week or more.

Like the Scilly Isles, Belle-Ile-en-Mer has a rustic charm that belies the fact that it is a highly sought-after destination, beloved of Parisians, who return every year. Even though it's in northern Europe, there's something exotic about catching the ferry with chic Parisians and their miniature dogs, shaggy surfers and excited French teenagers, and heading to what feels like your own private island. For kids, it's paradise. Show them a map, and they'll grasp the lay of the land easily and can pretty much cycle everywhere.

The ferry pulls into the picturesque capital, **Le Palais**, with its twin lighthouses guiding boats into safe harbour. If Noddy's Toy Town has a harbour, this is it. The Belle-Ile-en-Mer tourist office is right on the harbourside, a few steps away from the ferry. It's welcoming and efficient and director Leena Corbion speaks fluent English. Here you can pick up a free island map, leaflets in English and get plenty of advice.

There are three more mini towns neatly spaced out across Belle-Ile: **Sauzon**, **Locmaria** and **Bangor**. Each is a delight to discover just by wandering the pretty streets. Like much of Brittany, they are governed by the sea, and nautical themes are everywhere. Le Palais is dominated by **Le Citadelle Vauban** (T02 97 31 85 54, citadellevauban.com, €5.50 adults, €2.50 child), well worth a visit if your family is into ramparts and history. Dating back to the 11th century, it overlooks the harbour of Le Palais and contains a museum of art and history, a marine room (maps, paintings and nautical objects) and stages temporary exhibitions. It is also a 59-room hotel.

Wander around Le Palais' attractive streets in summer and you'll usually see some street theatre or dancing, and there's the cute Rex Cinema (passage de l'Hotel de Ville, 56360 Le Palais, T02 97 31 33 84) if you fancy a night out at the pictures.

Life here may be on a smaller scale, but it's all the better for it.

Don't miss

Le Grand Phare de Kervilahouen

T02 97 31 83 04. Apr, Jul and Aug daily 1030-1300, 1500-1715. May, Jun and Sep Wed and Sat 1430-1730, summer and autumn half term holidays 1430-1730. €2 adult, under 12s free.

In service since 1836, this majestic lighthouse is 52 m tall. If you're feeling up to it, you can climb the 213 granite steps.

Les Aiguilles de Port Coton

The equivalent of The Needles off the Isle of Wight, Les Aiguilles de Port Coton are an awe-inspiring site off the wild west coast. In stormy weather these rocky shapes look like needles poking out of a ball of cotton wool. They were famously painted by Claude Monet; *Les Aiguilles de Port Coton* are now in the Musée d'Orsay in Paris. Holding little children's hands at the viewpoint is a must as there's a sheer drop.

Other attractions

Just southwest of Le Palais there's an island glass factory (*verrerie*) called **Fluid** (T02 97 31 29 01, ZA Bordilla 56360 Le Palais, fluid-coop-creation-verre.com), and also a cake and chocolate factory (*biscuiterie*) called **La Bien Nommée** (T02 97 31 34 99, labiennommee.com) where families can look around for free and then pick up some souvenirs, gifts and snacks.

The tiny village of **Keroulep**, just north of Locmaria, is home to a lovely goats' cheese farm and farmshop called **Marie Aillet** (T02 97 31 76 28) where you can stock up on goats' cheese

Le Grand Phare de Kervilahouen.

“”

Welcome to Belle-Ile-en-Mer, the island with almost 2200 hours of sunlight per year! The surf school lessons happen on Donnant Beach in the area of Sauzon, among the clifs and the dunes. It is a protected and unique site that belongs to the 'Littoral conservatoire'. It has been chosen for its beauty and its ideal conditions for learning to surf. Due to its full westerly exposure, the site catches all directions of swell, offering waves every day.

Grégory Stephant, director of Ty Surf School (see right-hand column).

and children can watch the goats being milked at 1800 daily, no extra charge.

Little ones will love the **Structures Gonflables** (Parking des Glacis, 56360 Le Palais, T06 42 97 52 63, daily in school holidays, €5 adult, €3 child (2-5)), a collection of colourful bouncy inflatables. Adults must supervise.

Grown-ups might also be interested in taking a peek inside **La Fort des Poulans** (Pointe de Poulains, 56360 Sauzon, T02 97 31 61 29, €3 adults €2 child), Sarah Bernhardt's house. It was built in 1859, bought by the actress in 1894 and sold one year before her death in 1923.

Going to the beach

Hire surfboards and bodyboards in Le Palais before heading to your beach of choice. **Telfisaki Surf & Skate Shop** (5 av Carnot, T02 97 31 29 67) is one of the best.

La Plage du Donnant on the west coast is a great beach for older kids who already like surfing but it can get rough for little ones. It has the **Ty Surf School** (T06 63 86 75 47, Apartment 8, 650 route des Plages, Quartier Acotz, 64500 St-Jean-de-Luz, tyschool.org, daily Jun to mid-Sep), offering surfing, bodyboarding and equipment rental and lessons for all levels, from beginners to advanced. A two-hour session costs €35, three two-hour sessions €90 and five two-hour sessions are €150. There is also a car park overlooking the beach and a life-guard watch.

Plage de Kérel on the south coast is a stunning bay for all the family. There are two parking areas; the one to the west is high up above the beach with a great view over the steep-sided bay and a lovely rugged walk down the valley through heather and pine trees (this approach is definitely not buggy-friendly, but there is a gentler route just further east). There are little boardwalks through the sandy dunes before you get to the golden strand and calm shallow water where a yacht may be moored. It's an uplifting spot with a safe, bohemian vibe, where everyone gets on with the business of relaxing. You may find an enterprising young beach bum selling her home-made cotton bracelets for 50c.

Herlin is a smaller sandy bay with lifeguards, but it's the 2-km long **Plage des Grands Sables**, just south of Le Palais, that dominates beach life here. It is sheltered from the prevailing winds and has lifeguards in the summer months, safe calm seas and the Ecole de Voile Horizon Sailing School (T02 97 31 54 71, belleile-horizon.com), which offers classes for children aged six and up (Optimist, New Cat 12, windsurf and Hobie Cat) and for adults aged 15 and up (Hobie Cat and windsurf).

If it's water sports you're after, try sea kayaking with Vives Eaux (T06 82 05 22 53, vives-eaux.fr). It offers family excursions, on which children can practise sea kayaking with their parents and discover coves and hidden caves, and also child excursions (8-12 years) that teach sea kayaking but also focus on the fauna and flora of the island.

Pitch your tent

There's plenty of choice when it comes to laying your heads down to rest. The island has some fabulous campsites. If you want lots of facilities, including a swimming pool and games rooms, plus chalets and mobile homes as well as pitches, then take a look at L'Océan (Rosboscère, T02 97 31 83 86, camping-ocean-belle-ile.com, year round, pitch from €8.40, adult €5.20, child under 7 €3.05, chalets from €237/week and mobile homes from

Don't miss

Don't miss an ice cream at
the harbour at Sauzon. Try th
coffee or crème brûlée. One sc

€253/week) or Camping Bordeneo (Bordeneo, T02 97 31 88 96, bordeneo.com, Apr-Sep, pitch €7.80, adult €5.50, child under 7 €3.30, mobile home from €280/week, chalet from €350/week).

Though it's far more basic, you couldn't ask for a more picturesque spot than Campsite des Grands Sables (Les Grand Sables, Locmaria, T02 97 31 84 46, belle-ile.com, Apr-Sep, pitch €2.70, adult €4.20, child under 7 €2.20, under 2s free). Set among cornfields, with views of the sea, yachts and the mainland, and just a hop, skip and a jump to the largest beach on the island, when the sun shines this has the feel of a much more southerly campsite. It's one that kids will log in their 'best holiday moments' file.

If you want self-catering, there are over 200 places to choose from on the tourist board website (belle-ile.com), but you must book well in advance to bag the family favourites.

There are also a couple of excellent small, family-friendly hotels here. The two-star Les Tamaris (11 allée des Peupliers, 56360 Sauzon, T02 97 31 65 09, hotel.les.tamaris.free.fr, doubles from €48) is pretty and affordable with a playground. The three-star Hôtel Le Clos Fleuri (route de Sauzon, 56360 Le

Palais, T02 97 31 45 45, hotel-leclosfleuri.com, family rooms from €105 for up to 4), is intimate and easy-going with just 20 rooms. Little girls will probably love the pink exterior and everyone will like the great gardens and proximity to Le Palais.

If you can afford to splash out, **Hôtel La Désirade** (Le Petit Cosquet, 56360 Le Palais, T02 97 31 70 70, hotel-la-desirade.com, doubles from €195 half board, child in room €17, family suites from €350 half board) is a charming hotel with a lovely seaside feel. It has cool yet welcoming nautical decor, a spa for mums and dads, and an outdoor pool for everyone. There are three lovely family suites overlooking the gardens (these are in high demand, so book early). The hotel has a local babysitting service and bikes to hire.

If you're happy taking your kids to a five-star hangout, **Castel Clara Hotel & Thalassothérapie** (Glouphar, 56360 Bangor, T00 800 2000 00 02 toll free, castel-clara.com, doubles from €185, family apartments from €300 with breakfast) is stunning. Overlooking Goulphar Bay on the very spot where Claude Monet loved to paint, this 63-room hotel has upped its child-friendly credentials over the past two years, with interconnecting and family bedrooms, baby menus and a baby-sitting service all on offer. Other facilities include a playroom, tennis courts, and in summer sailing and surfing lessons that can be arranged for older kids. Parents will like the Clara Spa and the fine cuisine.

Grab a bite

Practically anywhere you go on this bijou island has a child-friendly place to eat offering the usual array of burgers, galettes and seafood.

L' Abri Côtier in Sauzon (Quai Guerveur, 56360 Sauzon, T02 97 31 60 50, abri-cotier.fr) overlooks the waterfront and does a luscious hamburger for €9.50, *moules marinières* and frites for €11.70 and a huge seafood salad at €8.50. On the kids' menu, there's ham and chips and a dessert at €9.

Auberge Chouk 'Azé (Chemin du petit houx, 56360 Locmaria, T02 97 31 79 69, Tue-Sun) serves traditional Breton cuisine and has tables outside plus a playground for kids.

Le Caméléon (27 rue Claude Monet, 56360 Bangor, T02 97 31 31 11, mid-Mar to early Nov) is one of the best spots on the island for pizza, or you can try **Crêperie Chez Renée** (21 rue Sarah Bernhart, 56360 Bangor, T02 97 31 52 87). President Mitterrand used to fly over by helicopter for a buckwheat pancake at Chez Renée. It also has excellent home-made ice cream.

Local goodies

Belle-Ile-en-Mer, Spécialités Régionales (3 rue Jules Simon, 56360 Le Palais, T02 97 31 34 82). Stock up on sardines, butter biscuits and tasteful nautical knick-knacks to take home.

Island essentials

Belle-Ile-en-Mer Tourist Office, quai Bonnelle, 56360 Le Palais, T02 97 31 81 93, belle-ile.com. There is an excellent English version of the website: just click on the Union Jack.

Getting there
Catch the **Compagnie Océane** (T02 97 35 02 00, compagnie-oceane.fr) from the Gare Maritime/Port Maria in Quiberon to Le Palais, a 45-minute journey (return adult fare Apr-May €27.65, Jun-Sep €28.15, return under 25s Apr-May €16.45, Jun-Sep €17, under 4s free. The rates for cars depend on the size of the vehicles, with return rates starting from €134.30 (less than 4 m); €158.40 (4-4.39 m); €256.10 (4.40-4.79 m) and so on.

If you are leaving your car on the mainland, drive to Quiberon and park in the Parking le Sémaphore as you drive into Quiberon and then take the shuttle to the Gare Maritime/Port Maria. The shuttle takes five to 10 minutes and leaves every 15 minutes or so.

You can also get to Belle-Ile-en-Mer in a taxi-boat or take a sea fishing trip, both run by **Atmos' Air Marine** (02 97 31 55 55, belle-ile-marine.com).

Getting around
Island car hire
As this is such a tiny island there's no need for a big motor. Cute little jeeps or a 2CV are ideal, and children will love them. There are many hire companies on the island, but try **Belle-Ile Auto** in Le Palais (T02 97 31 30 93, belle-ile-auto.fr) or take a look on belle-ile.com for more choice.

Island bike hire
Designated cycle routes are shown in green on island maps. Do not attempt to cycle on the coastal walking paths (they are not suitable for prams or toddlers either). There are several places to hire bikes in Le Palais. **A Loca Scoot & Vélos** (T06 16 48 63 26, velo-scooter-belle-ile.fr) is a good one to try. You'll find more listed on belle-ile.com.

Horse power
Trotting around the island on horseback is a holiday treat that kids will treasure. Head to **Domaine des Chevaliers de Bangor** (T02 97 31 52 28, equitation-belle-ile.com). It has 12 ha of purpose-built riding trails and specializes in rides for beginners (children and adults), though there are also horses for experienced riders. Neigh, a great place to begin your family's equestrian pursuits.

Markets

Au Coin des Producteurs is a twice-weekly farmers' market (summer only). Twenty local farmers gather their produce in a house-shop in Mérézelle every Friday (1800-2000) and Saturday (0900-1300).

A lively market is open every day of the year at **Place de la République** in **Le Palais**. You'll find locally caught fish and shellfish and vegetables from the island's market gardens. In summer, other travelling stall-keepers join the market, selling delicatessen meats, biscuits and pastries from Brittany, cheeses from Belle-Ile and locally made arts and crafts. It's perfect if you're self-catering or looking for picnic goodies.

! Book your ferry crossing well in advance for peak season (Jul and Aug), especially if you intend to take your car across. Similarly, if you intend to hire bikes or a car on the island, book these by in January or February for the following summer.

Pick of the pitches

Camping des Menhirs

Allée St-Michel, BP167, 56343 Carnac, T02 97 52 94 67, lesmenhirs.com. May to mid-Sep. Pitch with car €29.80-40.50, €8 adult, €5.90 child (2-7), under 2s free; mobile homes €280-718/week.

The fabulous location of Les Menhirs, just a short stroll from the seaside resort of Carnac Plage, makes this holiday park an economical and action-packed choice for a beach holiday. There's a swimming pool complex with giant waterslide, covered pool and kids' pool as well as pony rides, bike hire, football, basketball and boules. A children's club (ages 5-8) offers arts and crafts.

Domaine du Roc

Rue Beaurivage, 56460 Le Roc-St-André, T02 97 74 91 07, domaine-du-roc.com. Apr to mid-Sep. Pitch €6-13, child (2-6) €2.50, under 2s free; mobile home (4-person) €320-650/week; family treehouse €95/night.

This campsite near Lizio is alongside the Nantes–Brest canal, making it a good base for walking or cycling on the towpath. Riding and canoeing can also be arranged, and there's a heated pool on site. As well as tent pitches and the rental of mobile homes, you can also stay in a wood cabin in the treetops.

Campsite des Grands Sables

Belle-Ile-en-Mer

See page 177.

Camping des Sables Rouges

Port Coustic, 56590 Ile de Groix, T02 97 86 81 32, campingdessablesrouges.com. May to mid-Sep. Pitch €5-5.60, adult and child (over 7) €4.70-5.10, under 7s €3.30-3.40. Dog €1.30-1.50; bungalow or mobile home for family of 4 €260-420/week.

This is a leafy campsite, and the only three-star site on the Ile de Groix. As well as pitches, it has mobile homes and bungalows. There are open-air fitness areas, board games, football, and table tennis. The setting next to the beach is stunning, and great for bathing. Boats can be moored at the campsite's beach.

Municipal Campsite

Near Port Mélite, Ile-de-Groix, T02 97 86 81 13. May-Sep. Pitch (2-3 person tent) €3.40 adult, car €3.40, caravan €3.40 adult, child under 7 €2.20.

More basic than Des Sables Rouges, but set in a beautiful valley leading down to the sea. There's a small playground, but it's also good for teenagers. The island is safe and sleepy but also charming, with discos in the summer and a film festival in August at the fab old cinema in Le Bourg.

Farm favourites

Brénature

See page 158.

Ferme de la Cavalerie

La Cavalerie, 56920 St-Gonnery, T06 33 69 27 81, gite-cavalerie-morbihan.com. Gîtes €219-409/week; chambres d'hôtes €80/family of 4/night with breakfast.

This is a lovely place to come if you want to stay on a farm but you don't want to be overwhelmed by farm life. There's a pretty three-bedroom gîte that sleeps up to five plus baby, or you can stay in the *chambres d'hôtes*. You won't find any designer touches, just good honest, value-for-money family accommodation.

Best of the rest

Cours des Artisans

Cours des Artisans, 56460 Lizio, T06 25 51 19 32, coursdesartisans.com. Doubles from €52 with breakfast.

This tiny find in the heart of the pretty town of Lizio is one of the most stylish B&Bs in Brittany, and the owners welcome kids with open arms. It has three rustic-chic bedrooms. There's also a little pottery opposite which offers kids lessons.

La Maison Magique

Allee du Vieux Blavet, St-Nicolas-des-Eaux, 56930 Plumeliau, T02 97 51 86 02, lamaisonmagique.com. La Maison Magique (sleeps 10) €830-1470/week,

Cockatoo Court (sleeps 6) €485-810/week, Swift Court (sleeps 6) €460-730, Heron Court (sleeps 5 + cot) €460-730/week and Garden apartments (sleep 2 + cot) €360-610/week.

The Magic House is a self-catering farmhouse with three gîtes on the banks of the River Blavet. The traditional French interiors are comfortable though not flash; it's more about what's outside – an outdoor pool, a bar, crazy golf, boules, a playground and bikes to hire. There's also a games room, hammocks, picnic tables, fishing rods and a boat for hire. Families are close to towpath walks, bars, crêperies, and canoe and pedalo hire.

Le Clos du Tay

Le Tay, 56200 La Gacilly, T06 65 55 36 58, closdutay.com. €96/night with breakfast for 4; €250-470/week gîtes sleeping 2-6.

This is a lovely place in rural surroundings. Didier and Caroline are committed to ecological principles and they hold a 'Clef Verte' award. The B&B rooms (one suitable for disabled use) are spacious and comfortable, with tea-making facilities. Kids will love the Ouessant sheep, goats and poultry plus the donkey treks.

Le Moulin du Bois

La Ville au Vent, 56230 Berric, T02 97 67 04 44, moulindebois.com. Family room for 4 €110-150 with breakfast.

This former water mill just southwest of Questembert is now an enchanting and family-friendly *chambre d'hôte* with a genuine Breton feel. A one-off gem, it has three family-sized rooms, an outdoor pool, and gardens with slides, swings and toys as well as boules, croquet and darts for the adults. There's a nearby pond and river for fishing and boating, and a couple of donkeys called Pipo and Oslo.

Les Buntings

Les Tregouets near Serent, book via Holiday Lettings, holidaylettings.co.uk/rentals/malestroit/77584. Sleeps up to 8. £350-750/week.

Surrounded by cornfields, this house and barn conversion is a great base for a family of up to eight. Kids will love the rope swing on the oak tree and the huge games room. The house is English-owned and the feel is of a well-loved, family holiday home. There are three double bedrooms and a cute twin bedroom. The SuperMarche is 3 km away in Servent and the coast and many attractions are just a drive away. Great if you want a remote countryside retreat up the end of a track, yet you feel totally in touch with English TV channels and efficient Wi-Fi.

Hôtel Albatros

24 quai de Belle Ile, 56170 Quiberon, T02 97 50 15 05, hotel-albatros-quiberon.com. Closed mid-Nov to mid-Dec. €135 family rooms.

Of the many two-star hotels along the front, the Albatros is near the Gare Maritime, the springboard for boat trips. It's a friendly place, with a bar and restaurant on the ground floor and decent rooms above. Rooms at the front have balconies with sea views, and a scenic breakfast buffet is served on the first floor. Family rooms sleep up to five. Request one with a seaview and a balcony.

Manoir de Montgrenier
Coet Bugat, 56120 Guégon, near Josselin, T02 97 73 02 54, manoir-de-mongrenier.com. B&B €70 per room plus €16 for an extra bed; gîte €359-825/week; cottage €175-300/week.
This 13th-century manor house near Josselin has been lovingly restored. The accommodation, in the adjoining farmhouse, comprises two B&B rooms, a gîte (complete with Godin stove) sleeping six plus baby, with a separate cottage for two. There's badminton, volleyball, pétanque, outdoor chess, a games room and barbecue.

Pierre & Vacances
Port de Crouesty, 56640 Arzon, T02 97 53 85 35, pierreetvacances.com. Apartments for up to 5 people €184-500/week.
A large complex of well-equipped apartments on the Presqu'île, with good facilities and organized activities. There's a kids' club catering for all ages, from three months to teenagers.

Splashing out

Château de Locguénolé
Locguénolé, 56700 Kervignac, T02 97 76 76 76, chateau-de-locguenole.com. €330 for an apartment for 4.
This Relais & Châteaux grand pile is set in parklands with lawns rolling down to the Rade de Lorient. There's a Michelin-starred restaurant, heated outdoor pool, Turkish bath, tennis, four golf courses nearby and babysitting services. You can even take the dog.

Hôtel des deux Mers
8 av Surcouf, Penthièvre Plage, 56510 St-Pierre Quiberon, T02 97 52 33 75, hotel-des-deux-mers.com. €75-105 doubles, €140-165 interconnecting rooms for 4.
Beautiful family hotel with oodles of character between two dramatic coastlines. Bedrooms have sea views and interconnecting rooms for families. Penthièvre beach is on your doorstep, with surfing, sand-yachting, kitesurfing, diving and fishing.

Le Lodge Kerisper
4 rue du Latz, 56470 La Trinite-sur-Mer, T02 97 52 88 56, lodge-kerisper.com. €140-270 junior suites for 2 (extra bed €35 or free baby cot), €230-380 apartment suite for 4 people.
This beautiful hotel is a real treat for the whole family. It has a lot of neat homely touches for kids, from teddy bears to little cubbyholes, and a heated outdoor pool. Facilities include a wellness centre, mountain bike hire, games and DVDs, babysitting, and baby cots on request. Close by are three golf courses, water sports and riding.

Cool & quirky

Ranch de Calamity Jane
Kerhouriette, 56440 Languidic, T02 97 65 81 13, leranchdecalamityjane.com. 4-person tipi €85.
If you'd like to play cowboys and Indians in tepees, Ranch Calamity Jane is for you. Wild West and horse enthusiasts Nadine and Fred Audo run a *tipi d'hôte* like no other. Instead of buffalo, you'll be surrounded by Highland cattle, sheep, donkeys, horses and Australian Shepherds on the small farm. Yee-ha!

Vallée de Pratmeur
Le Rohuic, 56310 Quistinic, T02 97 51 72 02, valleedepratmeur.com. Treehouse €115/night; gypsy caravan €79-110/night; thatched cottage €450-550/week; B&B €60-75/night; yurt €80/night.
This is a magical place where families can stay in treehouses. The delightful Minochen treehouse, built into a beech tree 5 m above ground, is accessible by a suspension bridge. It sleeps two adults and one child (over six). There are also gypsy caravans, a thatched cottage, a former miller's house, yurts and a B&B. Attractions include a playground, donkeys horses, and bike trails.

Eating Morbihan

Quick & simple

Bistrot du Port

St-Goustan, 7 place St-Sauveur, 56400 Auray, T02 97 29 15 38. Daily.

The old port St-Goustan in Auray has a whole string of bars and restaurants, with something to please everyone. This is a no-nonsense catch-all with crêpes, pizzas, steaks and *moules*, all good value for money. Kids' menu from €6.50-7.50, adult menu from €9.50-18.50.

Crêperie le Mael Trech

13 place du Bouffay, 56140 Malestroit, T02 97 75 17 72. Year round 1200-1400, 1900-2130, closed Tue and Wed out of season

Sit outside in the main square and enjoy people-watching as you eat. This is more than just another crêperie, as the menu features plenty of main course salads and a few meat dishes such as *boudin noir* (a sort of black pudding sausage) with apples cooked in salted butter. Friday is *moules frites* night. In high season this place is packed, so go early. Kids' menu (€7.20) includes ham and egg galette or sausages/ham with chips, a sweet crêpe and juice.

La Casa Varadero

19 bd Francheet d'Esperey, 56100 Lorient, T02 97 64 20 77, casavaradero.com. Daily except Sun lunch.

The best pizzas in Lorient. There's a 'menu bambino' for under 10s for €8.40, with mini pizzas or ham and chips followed by ice cream or chocolate mousse and a drink.

Les Enfants Gât'thés

24 rue Lafayette, 56200 La Gacilly, T02 99 08 23 01, lesenfantsgatthes.com. Open 1215-1430, closed Wed, salon du thé 1530-1830.

The name of the restaurant/café is a play on words (spoilt children and tea). The chef here, Caroline Douaron, is from Le Clos du Tay (see page 181). The food is organic, with salads memorable for their dressings and the edible flower content, and there's a lovely outdoor seating area. A €15 set menu includes a delicious nettle tart starter and *clafoutis* dessert, but plenty of child-friendly dishes too.

La Liziotaise Crêperie and Grill

Rue de la Fontenelle, 56460 Lizio, T02 97 74 93 68.

This welcoming crêperie and grill is made for families. It has plenty of room inside and tables out. Sugar crêpes from €2.10, menu of the day €9.50 with a starter, main course and cheese or dessert. Kids' menu €7 for steak or ham with chips followed by a chocolate crêpe or ice cream.

La Marine Brasserie (Hotel de la Marine)

4 place de la Chapelle, 56340 Carnac, T02 97 52 07 33, la-marine-carnac.com.

Nice tables outside and little plastic playhouse with slide for young kids. Ham baguette €3.40, *moules frites* €10, Breton salad €8.50.

La Sarrazine

51 bis rue Glatinier, 56120 Josselin, T02 97 22 37 80, creperie-sarrazine.com.

This is a great local find with a terrace overlooking the Nantes–Brest canal. You'll find just about every kind of galette on the menu here from ham, egg and cheese to more fancy cheese, smoked salmon, crème fraiche, dill and lemon. From €2 upwards.

Le Café Breton

8 rue du Porche, 56220 Rochefort-en-Terre, T02 97 43 32 60. Mid-Jun to mid-Sep daily; Apr, May, late Sep closed Wed morning, Thu; Oct-Mar Mon-Wed lunch only, Fri-Sun all day.

The interior of this fine old house is the main attraction. Feast your eyes on the local frescoes by Alfred Klots before tucking in to excellent crêpes. The dessert ones are especially good here.

Le Chalet

3 bis Promenade des Estivants, 56930 St-Nicolas-des-Eaux, T02 97 51 88 87. Year round, closed Mon out of high season.

You expect to emerge from this wooden cabin onto snowy slopes rather than the delightful Blavet riverside. Apart from the attractive setting, there are excellent crêpes, with a wide choice of combinations. It's a family-friendly establishment, with a lovely children's play corner, and even a clown crêpe with bananas and Smarties.

Le Passage des Carmes

8 rue de la Gare, 56800 Ploermel, T02 97 72 36 76.

This modern restaurant decorated in very bright colours is made for easy meals out with the kids. An extensive menu has pizzas, pasta, salads, fish and meat dishes. Pizzas start from €7.20. Kids receive a little pack of goodies including crayons and a puzzle pad. Takeaway also available.

Le Safran Crêperie/Pizzéria

25 place de l'Eglise, 56590 Le Bourg, Ile de Groix, T02 97 86 58 72. Daily 1100-1500, 1800-2300.

If you make it over to Ile de Groix, head up to the pretty little town of Le Bourg. Right by the old-fashioned carousel is Le Safran, a great little crêperie and pizza restaurant with red-and-white gingham tablecloths and tables inside and out. A hearty margarita pizza costs €7.50, a classic galette with ham, egg and Emmental €3 and a sugar crêpe €2.

Les Ateliers Gourmands

7 rue Beaumanoir, 56800 Ploërmel, T02 97 72 10 76. Tue-Sun lunch and dinner (from 1830).

In one of the oldest houses in the town, La Maison des Marmousets,

you can eat in the upstairs dining room or walled courtyard at the back. The menu revolves around savoury tarts, gratins (salmon, potato, creamed leeks and cheese is very tasty), salads and crêpes. Nice people, good value for money and kids very welcome.

L'Olivier

5 rue Général de Gaulle, 56120 Guegon, Josselin, T02 97 75 64 99. Daily.

Five minutes' drive from Josselin, this wonderful family restaurant is a real find. The set lunch menu is ridiculously cheap at under €12, with a buffet of imaginative home-made starters and a 'chariot de desserts' where you can help yourself to chocolate or fruit confections and unusual treats like pears in mint-flavoured juice. Highly recommended.

Pizzéria Héléna

1 av de la Poste, 56340 Carnac, T02 97 52 21 57. Daily high season, Fri-Sun low season.

This jolly pizzeria in Carnac village has a lovely courtyard. Children are made welcome and there's plenty on the menu to entice them from pizzas to good old chicken and chips. Breton pizza €10.80.

Posh nosh

Hôtel Le Cobh, Restaurant

10 rue des Forges, 56800 Ploërmel, T02 97 74 00 49, hotel-lecobh.com. See website for opening times.

It's hard to believe that the chef here is only in his mid-twenties – Cedric Riviere is certainly a name to watch for in future in the world of gastronomy. The whole dining experience here is memorable, with the pretty decor creating an intimate, relaxed atmosphere, and impeccable service. The great-value *menu du midi* might include fillet of sea-bass, lentils and chorizo. The desserts are to die for. Highly recommended.

La Côte

Lieu-dit Kermario, 56340 Carnac, T02 97 52 02 80, restaurant-la-cote.com. Jul-Aug 1215-1415, 1915-2115, closed Mon, Tue lunch; Sep-Jun also closed Sat lunch and Sun eve.

Easily the best place to eat around Carnac, opposite the alignments of Kermario. Pierre Michaud has made quite a name for himself as a culinary star, and this is a place where the food is both serious and fun. Just reading the menus makes your mouth water: opt for the light selection at €24 or a more expensive feast (various menus up to €80) – all is creative and exciting. There's a children's menu for under 13s from around €9, with hearty dishes such as oven-roast chicken breast with potato forked mash and veal jus followed by home-made apple tart with creamy caramel sauce.

La Criée Maison Lucas
11 quai de l'Océan, 56170 Quiberon, T02 97 30 53 09, maisonlucas.com. Open 1215-1400, 1915-2200, closed Mon (and Tue out of season).
Right by the port, this is the restaurant of the Maison Lucas, a company famed for its smoked fish. In a nautical-style dining room you can enjoy a mighty *assiette de fruits de mer* or a range of super-fresh fish dishes, such as salmon and camembert, or curried prawns in layered pastry. Booking advisable.

Thon Bleu Restaurant
52 rue du Général de Gaulle, 56590 Ile de Groix, T02 97 86 58 86, othonbleu.com. Daily until 2300.
This is just the sort of restaurant that makes children realize why it might be a fun idea to sit at a table for more than two seconds and eat a meal. With its bright white-and-blue clapboard interiors and vast decked terrace, the nautical theme is strong and upbeat. There's a vast choice on the menu, from Roquefort salad (€16) to *moules marinières* (€12.50). There's a *menu des Moussaillons* for under 12s, which includes a main such as burger and chips or pizza, a dessert and a drink for €8.

Local goodies

Brasserie de Lancelot
La Mine d'Or, 56460 Roc St-André, T02 97 74 74 74, brasserie-lancelot.com. Tue-Sat 0930-1230, 1330-1800 (Fri 1700).
A well-known brand of beer is made here, with seven different types in constant production and five specials from time to time, including one just for Halloween. This company also created Breizh Cola – get kids to compare it to the real thing. The shop is open every afternoon. Guided visits are also on offer.

Chantier Ostreicole Tibidy
171 route du Pô, 56340 Carnac, T02 97 52 08 15, tibidy-huitres.com. Year round.
Excellent oysters and all kinds of shellfish on sale straight from the producer. A great chance for kids to get up close and see what they fancy.

Chevillard Boulangerie Patisserie
2 rue du Tumulus, 56340 Carnac, T02 97 52 05 56. Daily.
If you just want a snack, the *salon du thé* attached to this excellent bakery has good sandwiches or pizza/quiche with salad, followed by a quality cake for less than €7. Stock up for picnics too.

Côté Sauvage
Z.A. de Kergroix, 56510 St-Pierre Quiberon, T02 97 30 73 38, saumonsauvage.com. Tue-Sat 0930-1230, 1430-1800.
Smoked wild salmon to taste and buy, plus factory visits on offer.

Groix & Nature
Port Tudy Harbour, Ile de Groix, groix-et-nature.com.
This fabulous shop overlooking Port Tudy harbour on Ile de Groix is packed full of local delicacies. Fish pastes, sardines, Breizh Cola, fish soup, onion confit from Roscoff, galettes fines de Belle-Ile-en-Mer – they're all here.

La Quiberonnaise
5 quai de Houat, 56170 Quiberon, T02 97 50 12 54, laquiberonnaise.fr. Apr-Oct daily 1000-1215, 1530-1900.
All manner of conserved fish products, such as soup, sardines and much more. Good for souvenirs and presents.

Malestroit Market
Visit the market in Malestroit on a Thursday morning and stock up on picnic food for a picnic along the Nantes–Brest canal.

Inroads

Getting there

By air Two budget airlines connect the UK to Brittany. You can fly to Dinard airport from the East Midlands or Stansted with **Ryanair** (see ryanair.com). Prices from €20 one-way. Dinard airport (dinardairport.net) is at Pleurtuit, and does not have a shuttle service, so taxis will be necessary to get to the nearest big centre at St-Malo (9 km/ allow €20). **Flybe** (flybe.com) has budget flights into Rennes airport from Southampton (from €40 one way), Manchester, Leeds, Edinburgh, Glasgow and Belfast. The airport is 20 minutes by bus (No 57) from the centre. Both Ryanair and Flybe have flights to Brest (airport.cci-brest.fr) at Guipavas. From here a bus shuttle service (€4.60) goes to the city centre and station. (These flights are not year round, so check websites for details.) **AerLingus** (aerlingus.com) flies from Dublin to Rennes and Aer Arann (aerarann.com) from Ireland to Lorient (lorient-aeroport.fr) and Brest. **Air France** (airfrance.fr) flies from Paris (Charles de Gaulle airport) to the regional airports of Rennes, Brest, Lorient, Lannion and Quimper.

Car hire facilities are available at all the airports. The companies with offices in major towns are Hertz (hertz.com.fr), Avis (avis.fr), Europcar (europcar.fr) and Sixt (sixt.fr).

By sea Direct ferries to Brittany are run by **Brittany Ferries** (T0871 244 1400, brittanyferries.com), with sailings to St-Malo from Portsmouth (9-10 hrs, usually overnight from England), or from Plymouth to Roscoff (6-8 hrs). There is also a service from Cork in Ireland to Roscoff. The website has a timetable and prices, but these vary according to how far in advance you buy a ticket. Off-season schedules are published only briefly in advance. An alternative route is to cross into a Normandy port such as Cherbourg and then drive, but there will be the added cost of motorways tolls and petrol. Other cross-channel ferries companies are **P&O** (poferries.com), **Condor** (condorferries.com), **Speed Ferries** (speedferries.com) and **LD Lines** (transmancheferries.co.uk). As well as Brittany Ferries from Cork, Irish Ferries (irishferries.com) sail from Rosslare to Roscoff and Cherbourg.

Ferrysavers.co.uk is worth a look for getting the best deal, as there are many permutations according to season and choice of crossing ports.

By rail You can travel by **Eurostar** (eurostar.com) from London St Pancras to Paris, Gare du Nord (2 hrs 30 mins), and then continue by high-speed TGV from Gare Montparnasse to all the major towns in Brittany (Rennes 2 hrs, Brest and Quimper 4 hrs). Changing from the Eurostar at Lille and proceeding direct to Rennes is easier, avoiding the station change in Paris.

European Rail (europeanrail.com) and **Rail Europe** (raileurope.co.uk) have details of timetables, fares and ticket booking. Discount passes for young people and senior citizens are available. For timetabling information within France, see the rail network SNCF website voyages-sncf.fr.

By road Driving from the Channel ports will take up to seven hours from Calais, about three hours from Caen and Cherbourg. Allow three hours from Paris to Rennes (348 km) and five to go to Brest (593 km). There are no motorway tolls once you get into Brittany.

Michelin, the standard road maps have a route-planning service (viamichelin.com).

You must have a valid driving licence, car registration documents and insurance (check with your car insurance company whether an international insurance certificate is required). A red warning triangle and at least one reflective safety jacket are also obligatory. Don't forget that your headlight beam must be adjusted to the right, or buy stickers to achieve the same effect. If travelling by **coach**, **Eurolines** (eurolines.co.uk) provides services to Rennes, St-Brieuc and Brest.

Getting around

By bicycle The main towns have cycle lanes. Rennes and Vannes have bike (*vélo*) schemes whereby you can pick up a bicycle from one of the special ranks and drop it off at another elsewhere in the town. The bikes have baskets and some have child-seats. Rental times vary from an hour to a day or week, but advanced registration and a large deposit are needed. The relevant tourist offices have details, or see levelostar.fr (Rennes) and velocea.fr (Vannes).

Bike hire is readily available from cycle shops or camping sites; tourist offices will have details or, for a useful list of providers near Green Ways, go to randobreizh.com. The largely car-free islands have bike hire near the arrival ports. There is no cycling on coastal paths.

By bus/coach Each district has its own transport network, with urban and rural routes. The system is reliable and efficient, although the countryside is not especially well served. More buses cover coastal routes in summer when demand is high. The local bus station (Gare routière) is the place for information, and there are special offices to provide help in big towns. General information is available on T08-36 35 35 35. **Ille-et-Vilaine**: illenoo-services.fr and star.fr; **Côtes d'Armor**: tibus.fr; **Finistère**: viaoo29fr and bibus.fr; **Morbihan**: morbihan.fr.

By car Driving in Brittany is a pleasure, with generally good roads, no expressway tolls and comparatively little traffic. Petrol is also cheaper than in the UK. You must give way to traffic from the right at junctions, unless otherwise indicated.

From Roscoff or St-Malo, the rest of Brittany is easily accessible via express routes: N12 in the north (Brest, Morlaix, St-Brieuc), N164 in the centre (Carhaix-Plouger to Rennes, still with some single-lane sections) and N165 in the south (Quimper, Lorient, Vannes). Rennes is at the hub of major routes.

Parking is usually paying in central areas in towns, and you must get a ticket from the machine (*horodateur*). Be carefully not to park overnight in squares where markets are held early the following morning. Blue-lined parking bays mean you must buy a limited time disc from a *tabac*. These are useful if you're spending several days in one place. If you are staying a while in Rennes or Brest it makes sense to use the huge central underground paying car parks.

Police can impose on-the-spot fines for offences like not stopping properly at a Stop sign or running a red light. Pay strict attention to drinking and driving regulations (0.5g/L) and speed limits: patrols and testing are common.

The best **maps** are Michelin (michelin.com). IGN (ign.fr) blue topographical Cartes de Randonnée with walking routes marked are useful for driving on smaller roads and worth buying if you are based in one particular area.

By train The state rail network **SNCF** (sncf.fr) has a good TGV (high-speed) service within Brittany connecting the main towns. From Paris direct to Rennes is about two hours. The northern route goes through Dinan, St-Brieuc, Guingamp and Morlaix to Brest. Rennes has a link with Quimper, or there's a southern route via Nantes to Vannes and Quimper.

Within the region, the **TER network** (ter-sncf.com/Bretagne) connects coastal spots like St-Malo, Roscoff and Quiberon and important towns like Pontivy and Carhaix-Plouger, but in general rural central Brittany is not well-served by public transport. Their website has details of the Korrigo card, which can be used on regional trains, and other public transport networks.

You can check routes, timetables and price options or book tickets on voyages-sncf.fr. When travelling around, you must validate (*composter*) your train ticket (orange machine on platform) before getting on board.

Various discount schemes are available from SNCF, including the **Carte 15-25 ans** for young people, and the over-60s **Tarif Découverte**. Some restrictions of travel may apply on using these. The **Decouverte à deux** gives 25% off for two people travelling together.

For details of facilities for disabled passengers, see the Mobilité Réduite information on voyages-sncf.fr.

Tots to teens

Discounts are usually offered at attractions for children up to 16 years old, and those under four are often given free entrance. Tickets for a *famille nombreuse* gives a price for three or more children accompanied by two parents.

Babies (0-18 months)

Renting a gîte or holiday caravan gives you the flexibility and independence to maintain baby-care routines. Look for properties that provide baby gear to save you having to pack cots, sterilizers, etc. It's not unusual to take babies to hotels in France, and you'll usually be welcomed with open arms. Most bike hire places have trailers for small ones.

Toddlers/pre-school (18 months to four years)

Make sure your gîte or holiday park is as toddler-proof as possible with enclosed gardens and fenced-off pools. Days on the beach demand vigilance with this age group, but Brittany is fantastic bucket-and-spade territory, so there's always plenty to entertain them. Brittany also is packed with great attractions for this age group, such as farm visits, aquariums with touch pools, and even treetop adventures for children as young as two.

Kids (four-12 years)

These are probably the best years to take kids on a camping holiday. It's still an adventure for them and they can help out with basic chores, like fetching water. They also get the chance to hang out with French kids and perhaps learn a bit of French. Brittany is a great place for kids to learn to sail.

Teenagers

Brittany is gradually undergoing a cool sea change and you'll find surf schools and sand-yachting activities along the coast. Alongside all the traditional music and Fest Noz, there are several world-renowned rock musical festivals that might catch the eye of teens. If you want some quirky accommodation to keep them amused, try a treehouse or even a pod in a tree.

Single parents

Check whether attractions offer single-parent family admissions. With their organized activities and onsite entertainment, holiday parks are a good way to meet up with other families. The Single Parent Travel Club (sptc.org.uk) is a good support network.

Special needs

Brittany is gradually updating to provide better access and facilities for disabled visitors. The regional Tourist Board has a download of accommodation adapted for reduced mobility (see tourismebretagne.com). For wide-ranging information on equipment, activities including sporting options, transport possibilities and accommodation, have a look at the site bretagne-accessible.com. This also provides useful localized details.

The French Tourism & Disability seal is awarded to tourist accommodation, sites and visitor areas that provide a warm welcome and a high level of accessibility. For a list of accessible, officially listed Tourism & Disability establishments and leisure facilities, consult FRPAT (regional federation of Brittany's tourist areas) at frpatb.net or visit the website of the departmental tourist boards, which publish regular updated lists. Information can also be found at tourist information centres.

On Grand Sables Beach at Belle-Ile-en-Mer, AIPS (Association, Information, Prevention, Santé) offers beach attendants and hikers free use of two 'tiralos' (wheelchairs for mobility-impaired people for use in the sea and on the sand) during July and August if the sea is calm. Contact Lifesavers on T02 97 31 89 79.

Index

Index